Complaint

Complaint

GRIEVANCE AMONG FRIENDS

AVITAL RONELL

UNIVERSITY OF ILLINOIS PRESS
Urbana, Chicago, and Springfield

Publication of this book was made possible in
part by the generous support of Georgina Dopico,
Dean for the Humanities, New York University.

© 2018 by Avital Ronell
All rights reserved
1 2 3 4 5 C P 5 4 3 2 1
♾ This book is printed on acid-free paper.
Printed and bound in Great Britain by
Marston Book Services Ltd, Oxfordshire

Cataloging data available from the Library of Congress
ISBN 978-0-252-04157-0 (cloth : alk.)
ISBN 978-0-252-08322-8 (paper : alk.)
ISBN 978-0-252-05023-7 (ebook)

University of Illinois Press
1325 South Oak Street
Champaign, IL 61820-6903
www.press.uillinois.edu

For some reason, this work took a lot out of me. Even so, there were one or two illusory moments when the convocation of language seemed curiously effortless: who knows complaint better than I? As destination and accelerator of its many launch forms, I have intimate knowledge of the codes by which this particular type of utterance logs in. Grievance has hit me in many ways.

Given such breaks, I had every reason to assume that I could handle a work of this magnitude—or diminishment, where suffering meets its unintelligible limit and annoying recurrence.

Trying to find an end to the work proved to be precarious. I was cratered by a number of endings, often unbearably hard-hitting. When the time came to close out this account, I lost two beloved friends. Anne Dufourmantelle and Werner Hamacher were two—or many, for they were many—interlocutors whose disappearance knocked me out, making me despair of moving forward with this or any work, including the work of mourning. Hölderlin has pointed out the insufficiencies of mourning and Derrida explored how mourning falters: the work of mourning does not work. In a certain sense it must not work if we are to remain true to the searing woundedness of removal, different levels of deportation and cruel expulsion, whether visited upon individuals or entire communities. Mirroring the distortions of finite being, the withdrawal of loved ones leaves us staggered with grief, bereft of address. Sometimes when they go missing, the friend becomes a strangely stabilized area code of complaint. I complain to the departed all day long.

On another register entirely, I recognize that everyone must go down. Sometimes, I think, finitude metes out the only justice we shall ever know. This recognition does not serve to make existence bearable.

Both Anne and Werner discussed with me the regions of complaint that I explore in this book. Werner wrote a response to the section involving his texts on lament, the way grievance binds us. Seeing my nurturance withdrawn, facing political distress without them, felled me and for a long time I was down for the count. I am not sure that I will rock out of my hellhole anytime soon.

I could not have finished this work without the strength and light of Willis G. Regier. (One needs an uncommon measure of support when wrapping up an assignment; every book carts an environment that needs tending to: the ability to summon lucidity and resources for social activism in dark times—not to dwell on the work of getting up in the morning, training one's energies on reading or teaching or firming the resolve to shelter as one can younger generations of scholars and artists, straining to live up to the task of coaching world-class troublemakers, finding language when it goes on strike.)

When Bill first approached me at the beginning of my bumpy career, when it seemed that nothing could be secured, my fate turned and I could start writing with a sense of protection and freedom—a condition that has become increasingly rare among those who think and write in the fractured world we inhabit together, making a home in the deracinating grid to which we have been subjected: our *undwelling*. How can we practice and live with our divergent forms of writing under the circumstances of mutating distress? In ways that still need to be understood, Bill Regier was able to sustain so many diverse creative runs and theoretical commitments in the United States, constructing a wildlife sanctuary around writers, including me, some of whose fragility is well accounted for.

It may seem off point that a Book of Complaint would be dedicated to this stellar colleague and friend, a great and courageous editor. What can I say but that he has been an enduring address, a crucial interlocutor of my plaintive despair and jubilant comebacks, however ironized and subject to mournful concession.

Contents

Introduction: Taking a Knee   1

1   Raising the Visor:
    The Complaint of Modernity   15

2   *Ach!* The History of a Complaint   28

3   The Trouble with Deconstruction   84

4   A Pass of Friendship   118

5   Hannah Arendt Swallows the Lessing Prize   175

6   The Right Not to Complain:
    On Johnson's Reparative Process   199

Notes   225

Index   239

Complaint

Introduction

Taking a Knee

As chief symptomatologist and head of the Existential Complaint Bureau, I learned the hard way that we are trapped in a grid of grievance, the noble part of which is losing steam. For my part, it seems to be the case that I am often steamed up, prepared to launch a complaint against this or that egregious injury and social injustice, but—get this!—I am also allergic to snivelers and complainers who come up against my psychic shield, traumatically disbanding my relation to world (such as it is, or was, this constitution of "world"—one of the themes of this book). Intrusively cutting in with their chronic sense of disturbed privilege, the complaint traffickers are dead set on riling me up. How I despise the incessant whiners and moaners! How much more I scorn those who, unperturbed by all manner of injustice, find *nothing* to complain about—even nowadays—and are all smiles, grotesquely content, blocking the gateways to protest and righteous indignation. *I am a mess.*

This vexed situation is not my fault, because I am merely a reflector, made to absorb destructive habits of my contemporaries and neighboring social encroachers. Charged with fielding different morphs of civic grief, I find myself redirecting oversized libidinal aggressions that attack our shared zones of encounter. The present work tries to determine whether the registry of complaints by which we are seized constitutes a bug or an essential feature of the conditions of our being-with, our *Mitsein*.

Despite the disturbance of which I am capable, I am all about pain relief. When facing down obsolesced strongholds of power or pushing back on the killjoys among us, I sometimes dispense emergency supplies of meaning, as Nietzsche would say. But mostly I stay with the fractures in being, scaling the limits of intelligibility, tapping into nearly inaudible shrieks of stifled despair. Whether tracking the way things are recorded, remembered, incorporated or disavowed, falsely accepted or gradually integrated, or sizing the climate of resistance in any given situation that thickens with ethical anxiety; whether

I am intent on exposing the stagnations that still affect the way we think and live—I try to find and offer some relief (despite the odds—and a native charge of skepticism). Such a goal-positing for one's writing is at once necessary and seems improbably aspiring, even to me, as I suit up and woman up to rescue something or someone susceptible to unconscious aggression or material slight, object of consistent battering. I have been enrolled in Kant's squad of theorists who fire away at tropes and behaviors of injustice, shooting blanks into the night of egregious bursts of social immaturity. I have to set my sights on what I can handle, which does not mean I have mastered coping skills with a view to calming a fragile nervous system or that I have more than a frazzled sense of how to improve the minor, and increasingly minoritized, sector of a world for which I feel responsible, in a surrender of perpetual shortfall.

Unlike outraged protagonists of Greek tragedy, we no longer have a chorus to bounce hair-raising grievances against, but instead we spin our wheels in solitary chambers of dropped calls. Once in a while, someone shows up to sub as receptor for the emitted complaint, or a container evolves, in the form maybe of an analyst's office. Unlike Antigone, we no longer *glow* in the issuing of a world-clashing repudiation of law. Still, one seeks relief—without a proper address, without a god to help us now.

Ever in a state of epistemic alert, the work looks at what accommodates or expels from philosophical premises considerations that greatly ail us, if covertly or simply left corrosively unattended. It may not seem that the topos of complaint belongs to the historical instaurators or can be situated in the major leagues of becoming—even though the most dangerous leaders of our time belong to the guild that I study of chronic, narcissistically troubled complainers. An increasing portion of history is made up of misfired complaints and resentful pouts of grievance. On the whole, any cause for indignation lands on my desk, and the worry over the demise of certain forms of protest dominates my files. The capacity of protest to hold and defend the incapacitated still stirs my imagination, and supports the wish, however unfulfillable, to approach those who stand in desolated infirmity. Agitated *Sorge*—worry, worry, worry— keeps me awake. I understand that the complainant's disaffection rates as the most dismissible of language carriers, showing up as that which is not to be taken seriously. That is why they put me on the case, so that I can backslide, record missteps, check infrastructural concerns while investigating a slighted utterance that nonetheless tops the charts of historical language usage. Even those who chafe against it ride out the complaint. They may say "Don't complain, don't explain," but the suppression of complaint also acknowledges its immobilizing heft.

Introduction

Though low on the totem pole of articulated stances and positing poses, the complaint haunts our era of desperate justice. Libidinally charged, addictive, yet uncathectable, it appears to command a wide range of mainly stalled action. At the same time, a core vitality still stirs in the complaint, here and there prompting political arousal and different types of care or articulated dissidence and rights advocacy that involve institutions of medical and legal complaints, available to those who can formulate their lives according to the formats supplied by plaintive protocols.

The book deals with the complaint through different modalities of convocation, exploring protective sites marked by language and ethical proneness, feeling-tones. In an effort to scan disturbed representations of our being-with—our forms of relatedness within a dearth of relatable affirmation—we have turned our attention to an unrelenting buzz of distress, leaning into the encounter with linguistic and ethical impotence. Unlike the lament that carries and succumbs to the weight of its own authority, complaint folds as it sounds off, irritates as it rouses, tuning one out of its static-filled calling system. If it should manage to function as a GPS, it has lost its signal, leaving us on our own within the range of a directionless pronouncement. Short on authority, it nonetheless contaminates and occupies stronger forms of language usage and political utterance, creating a standstill where breakthrough or new types of address and innovative breakdowns might have been hoped for. Not quite fired up like indignation, the complaint is on the way to protest, only to be abducted at the moment of critical takedown.

Still, complaint carries with it a launcher, a starting capacity for doubling down on the riot of injustice strapped to the very fact of existence. "I didn't ask to be born" stacks up against other starter-utterances that revile the world as it now stands, deflating its portion of promise. The complaint is a way of making failed bids for the authority of that which cannot come to pass, a face-off with stated insufficiencies of being. Always on the brink of self-collapse, roaming incongruently on frequencies of refused assertion, too often bringing off no more than a cannonade of inconsequential nagging, the complaint is parasitized by ghostly calls for just reset and retribution, dimly radioed in to our spheres of worldly receptivity. It still pushes for change where lament bangs hard against the unalterable.

It is true that complaint only rarely comes from a good place, but that's the frugal boomerang effect I am going after—seeking out the rare and promising, where possible and legitimate, making lemonade out of its stuckness. At times the complaint springs as an offshoot of Nietzschean *ressentiment*. A gnawing, bellyaching, grumbling, and mean-spirited missive of revulsion, it heads nowhere on fast triggers, squeezing out drops of stifled rage. In some ways it is at once world bound and that which abominates world, bent on expanding its vocabulary in secular tonalities. Despite having racked a number of downgrades, complaint is where repair is still deemed possible. Lament, to allow for a momentary flicker of antinomy, abandons alteration or the push for anything but its own annulment.

It is in the nature of the complaint to hammer a point home, without establishing residency in the House of Being. It insists and harps; it increases its velocities, becomes a shrill sonic signature traveling behind its possible meaning fields. It goes to work on nothing but spares no one. An abrasive counterexample to philosophical demonstration, and responsible for the disruption of normative types of rhetorical and political dispute, the complaint pulls down the aspiration of the language bearer to change the world and become, despite it all, an enduring host for the occasional outburst of meaningfulness, even purposiveness, if without purpose—a structure that Kant has taught us to welcome and integrate. The complaint brings every transcendental signified down to earth.

Still, the Bible books many complaints and teaches at times the virtue of the carper's plight. Or, it stokes the anger of the Almighty, who increasingly raised His expectations with the demand for praise while showing some willingness to abide with lamentation. Jeremiah and Job count as two exemplars of human and prophetic complaint bearers. When Jeremiah complains, trying to shake his persecution, the Lord says, setting the tone of responsive putdown: "it will get worse." Jeremiah was one who was sorry he was ever born. Nor was he lightly borne, this prototype of the early impotent rant, the premier biblical malcontent. From its parade of petulance onward, the name of Jeremiah was recruited to designate both the tipping point of lamentation, a mournful complaint, and a cautionary or angry harangue: the jeremiad. The Bible teaches us that you can stomp your feet all you want: it will get worse.

A problem that undergirds any serious study of the complaint involves its tendency to prolong the span of an injurious misdeed. Lining up as a species of mourning disorder, it just won't let go but repeals any petition for reprieve. Tenacious and often enough exhausting, drearily unrelenting, the complaint can bring movement—one of Hannah Arendt's definitions of freedom: *freedom of movement*—to a standstill, shuttering a world closing in on itself, drained of vitality. At the same time, it makes an unceasing production of annoyance stand out with a kind of whistle-blowing poise, as an emblem of strength, almost as if complaining emanated from a position of pure and laudable conviction.

In a way, the complaint's rumble through the neighborhood of being represents one way of saying "No justice, no peace," influencing a shakedown of that which should not be tolerated. The complaint, in its clumsy, diminished

Introduction

yet partially befitting manner, takes aim at the unbearable. It almost makes the unbearable bearable to the extent that it arranges a reduced rate, a place for its charge within the bargained spectrum of mere annoyance—the bickering firing range that makes life's hardships manageable, maybe containable, if hopped-up on repetition compulsion. Under favorable conditions, the complaint eventually can bring a defective structure down though, mostly, let's face it, disturbed minds are left impervious to the nattering insect-like bites of language. The target often enough stays intact. Regardless of its effective range of motion, it can never be cleared of suspicion when it comes to determining what side of the complaint lands with justice or promotes further evildoing. For the complaint looks like it is in collusion with the very iniquity it criticizes, if only to the extent that the picked-off problem extends its shelf life when becoming the object of the reviler's fixation.

In the German language, one form of complaint or lament, the *Klage*, flips easily into the juridical semantics of *Anklage*, accusation. The undecidable limit between complaint and accusatory claim—a rollover prompted by Walter Benjamin's study of Karl Kraus—will provide a basis for some of the analyses I present in this work. Pursuing the underworld of "phrase," I try to consider, in the shuttle between philosophical and literary points of urgency, the unsystematizable contingency, an environment of failed performatives that motor micro-events unleashed by complaints and their lethal counterparts—for instance, I explore what it means to throw a curse at someone, to nag the target toward and to death.

At certain points the effort to understand the nature of the complaint may seem like menial labor in the fields of language theory and political advocacy. Squelched in advance, the complaint does not appear to have the measure of its object. In defiance of its slim returns and lack of authority to make things happen, the drone of inoperable complaining presses on. Distressed and unstable, the complaint offers a glimmer of hope that something might snap into action, awakening a dormant sector in the rhetoric of justice. It shows the capacity to shake the body awake, offering a somatic-phenomenological scan of wronged being, marking those persecuted and subjected consistently to creature discomfort. Gregor Samsa's body convulses into a condition of metamorphosis due to the quirks of vague complaints that have lodged in his unpinnable build. The complaint of injustice drops in on our most intimate quarrels with existence.

Caught in the crosswinds of vanishing protest and the newly visible stoppage of social movement—as threat, phantasm, or historical-material deflation—it seemed relevant to return to the drawing boards of language that slogans, pleads, accuses, demands, and despairs, calling out with no assured address or

Introduction

hope for a beseeched rejoinder. Besides, I am a partisan of noncanonized tropes of moaning and bitching, a language stash of which I fear I haven't produced enough myself, even though, as a born troublemaker, I tend to veer toward mined zones and difficult access routes to marginalized objects or themes of thought with noisy trespass. Few would want to claim the degraded realm of language's castoffs and get into the down-and-dirty grit of language usage, the gutter of *Gerede* or gossip, with me and my girl squad of alpha bitches.

In some ways, the complaint serves up the antidote to the *parole du maître*, staving off, in terms of tonality and rhythm, any master discourse. Yet, running a low profile, unmanly and coarse, angling, in terms of cultural codifications, with the intent mostly to rope women and children, it is also behind and ahead of the scenes of its deployment, serving as the ground of language, the place from which any act of phrasing takes off. Language begins and expires in protest of its own dispossession and broken ability to ensure the solidity of world. Nearly every baby, at least in the West, shrieks her complaint at first sight of her earthly guardians. I won't go there now, but I do find it curious that the theme of maternal complaint, whether lethally heeded or abjectly borne, recurs throughout the texts under study. Besides being a structuring form, part of the teaching corps of grievance, the complaint, wielded by something like a maternal superego, comes equipped with frightening outreach programs. The mother of Alexander the Great famously besieged her warrior son with all kinds of demands, unsolicited strategic advice; she regularly fired off complaints against which the great soldier could not adequately defend. The conqueror griped that rent for nine months in the womb really was a bit steep.

In the pages that follow, I trace the contours of plaintive aggression that felled a thinker-warrior, Philippe Lacoue-Labarthe, as he considers the constitution of any phrasing, be it poetic, philosophical, uncategorizable burbling. As it turns out, Alain Badiou complains about the way Lacoue handled the lethal discharge of complaint that his mother had aimed at him. Both philosophers have known the need to fend off the destructive plaint of reproving mothers. In fact, their work and common political passion emerge as a defensive strategy built around the damage caused by the "immaternalist" incursion. Whether maternally cast or recircuited through socially untrackable broadcast systems, the complaint, numbing and dumbing down, also threatens to prevent the arrival of change or make way for new forms of sociality, part of a shrinking inventory of political supply and ethical grammar.

Then there are those who can't complain. They squeak by with the rejoinder of meek desistence, "I can't complain." A blockbuster, nearly congenial utterance, a staple of amiable denial that I examine closely, it runs like a street translation of a Paul Celan poem: they know that there is no address in the era of the becoming-anonymous of Gd. Who would pick up your call? Those who live in stubborn destitution cannot complain. Nor do sovereigns, those who rule in Shakespeare or in scattered world posts. All the same, by stating that they "can't complain," the abstainers, those who resolutely desist, raise the issue of the complaint, its necessity and futility, insinuating a store of complaints at the ready, but withheld: I could complain, but I renounce the temptation to do so. Anyway, who, in a Rilkean syntax of being, would hear me? On some level of ethical responsiveness, I am mandated to refrain from unloading the complaint.

The office of friendship, however, allows for complaint and even generates a plaintive structure. Without brandishing a certificate of therapeutic legitimacy, the friend, whether ghostly, futural, or closely bound in time, receives the brunt of the complaint, attends to injuries and consents to tallying the damages together with the allied plaintiff. Not all friends engage this way but, structurally at least, the friend remains open for business during psychic droughts, listening in for the pings and pangs of disillusionment, the advent of compounded pain, the spread of disturbance on existential and mortal lines of disappointed expectation. The friend, in some districts, accompanies traversals through the desert, horse-whisperer to the deflated companion, capable of containing the diffuse splurge of despair, modeling the remoter regions of reparative justice. *OK, a girl can dream.* Sometimes, when the chips are down, the friend relinquishes you, receding into careless spaces of nonrequital, for a moment, for a lifetime in dog time, booking out.

Aristotle charts the way friendship easily overturns its stated stakes, switching into enmity when the time of nonresponse grows, leaving you stranded and suddenly ahistorical, stripped of shareable narration.[1] The neglect of friendship, the depleting derangements and signed-off nonrenewal forms, whether explicitly rendered or eventually comprehended, easily become the premier object of complaint. Lost love may score lamentation, but the treachery of friendship—a close cousin that courts a different apportionment of love, sometimes in excess of the loving protocol—calls home the complaint.

Productive of another experience of mourning, the closed account of friendship awakens to a lexicon of disappointed worldliness. Arendt runs across this issue when she refuses to refuse the ambiguous bestowal of a prize, trying to make friends with her tentative German hosts and Jewish ghosts. Ethically bound yet effectively compromised, Arendt reluctantly defers to the Lessing-Preis by organizing her acceptance speech around the theme of complaint. Feeling the pressure of world-binding expectations building up around her name, she strains to repair a historical breach. She tries to befriend the unforgivable. Friendship, a start-up engine for the encounter of politics and justice, rallies to causes that tend to collapse as they approximate their lofty goals; nonetheless, friendship spiritedly gives us a glimpse of the what-should-have-been of the what-is: it bears the responsibility of an ethical prod and supports the disciplined follow-through. In the middle of his poem of mourning, "Andenken" (Remembrance, thinking-of), Hölderlin's meditation jolts, asking "Wo aber sind die Freunde" (But where are my friends?). This question constitutes the axis around which the great hymn of the mourned and lost figures of friendship turns. Where are friends when called upon?—a central complaint of ethical proportions and political consequence, outlining the fillet of affinity, alliance, kinship, group identity, affiliation, the links of confidant, partnership, colleague, companion, teammate, as well as the weld of all the fixer-uppers of recalcitrant acquaintance, ongoing familialisms, the intimate flips of queer recombination, the strange abundance and fabulously unreadable calling cards of relatedness.

Derrida has pointed out that the politics of friendship is motored principally by masculinist prompts. Historically, women are not considered to be friendship material. Philosophy backs up that premise. Friendship, it's a man thing. This in part goads me to weave friendship—for which I have obtained only a fake ID, and little if any metaphysical authority—into the narrative of the complaint. The irony of a girl making friends goes against so much inherited inhibition. In so-called popular culture, a feminine foray into the friendship zone may be designated, by irony lite, as "Besties," BFFs, and other abbreviated markdowns. If anything, a woman is, since at least Hegel exposed the fine print of the metaphysical contract, the enemy of the community. She can be enemy, but not friend. I see no trace of a dialectical turnover in the Hegelian demonstration. My effort to be a friend, to make friends and create pretend families in conditions of documented hostility, is calculated to go up against such durable walls; the whole plight of my contrapuntal history of friendship must be read allegorically-ironically, pinched with a stinging grain of salt.

So much militated against such an extravagance: *the hypothesis that women were meant to be friends.* Language, philosophical habits and markers, existentially pitched checkpoints were stacked against us. On what basis could I possibly befriend another? According to what ledger of determinations, approved contingencies, contractual loopholes, or transferential coordinates? The blocked passage to friendship remains a dilemma for those constituted, if only in passing, as women. The restrictive covenant is a rigorous part of the order of things. When you're a girl, friendship doesn't just happen; you have to be willing to go against all sorts of grains and traditionally set restrictions, the blowback of cynical postulations. Still, no flex of muscled lucidity will help you make the grade as Friend, for the situation is not a matter of some accidental lockout. Our metaphysical heritage has rigorously demanded the embargo on the female clasp of friendship.

Despite revolutionary breakthrough stances or carefully attended displacements, one still remains tethered to a grating heritage that defines, oppresses, structures, feeds, regulates, or plumps any attempt at reconfigured personhood, setting up the rules and regs, metaphysically speaking, that make politically tinged aspects of relatedness an affair of men. Metaphysics, our homeroom language and shared existential springboard, puts a ban on friendship among women. The stakes are undoubtedly high, for the motif of friendship insures the modeling of all sorts of vital ethical and political dispositions, grounding our sense of justice. As Derrida has argued, friendship serves as the blueprint for political discernment and for amorous cleaves. On this stagnation and related tropologies, women, for the most part, have been assigned to the historical sidelines, even though they prove adept at traumatically intrusive break-ins and manage to achieve a modicum of social rewrites. One thinks of Antigone, of Heinrich von Kleist's feminine figurines that shoot out counter-memory to block historical narratives of entitlement; one continues to be struck by the howls of one-woman-lone-warrior types like Valerie Solanas; one continues to stress over the seething deflations of Ingeborg Bachmann and the ongoing peel-down of Sylvia Plath. (I have more names in mind; I love enumeration and memorializing remembrance—I can go overboard with my lists, but this is not the place.) *I am on repetition compulsion; but this consternation bears repeating, calling out, obsessing with, lamenting.* There's simply no call for friendship among women in the metaphysical dialup—at most, girls were accorded some provisional and retaliatory alliances, identificatory contrivances, or other busts in the consolidation of *Mitsein. Ach!* I don't think that Hegel, who was in it to win it, was dialectically angling for the capture of powerful affect, for raising the stakes of friendship by turning women into standout enemies, though. When you scroll down the philosophical corridor of determinations, *becoming friends*—the interlocution or supplement of narcissistic annexation that this assumption may imply—is always and strictly a man's affair. We inherited this relentless state of things, remain inscribed by its persistence, no matter how far removed from the injurious logic of metaphysical say-so one might hope by now to be.

Under the circumstances, what was I to do? How could I not be swallowed up in the recurring loop of complaining?

I have a fertile imagination and can make all sorts of improbables happen. Like the emotionally fragile beings that one occasionally comes across, I can embrace across the distance any number of *best* and *only* and *absolutely singular* friends. I am always in earnest and elfishly intense. Still, I try not to be a psy-

Introduction

cho about it—about the making and keeping and responsibly tending to the custodianship of friendship, whether real or make-believe. As a Nietzschean, I do not scare away easily from the virtues of fiction, from masks, and play, and the dance of *Dis-tanz*—the separations and parting of ways that make nearness at all possible. One does not bag a friend; rather, one approaches from a distance: maintaining position, one tries not to violate the air space of the other. In the cases before us, though, to invoke a Shakespearean way of squatting in language's felicities, I am very likely sharing the *heir* space where one tries very hard not to collide or puncture the flight plan of the other. In Shakespeare, "air" and "heir" keep each other going, or knock each other out. The responsibility of finding temporary residency in another's work and highly cathected air/heir space is enormous, nearly unnegotiable—especially if you are coded as a girl and must take into account all the problems of legitimacy and the history of catfights that this tangle traditionally implies. Not that men aren't parricidal, fratricidal, genocidal—don't get me started.

So. How to get around this embarrassment and still make some sort of legitimate program primed on the protocols of friendship stick? My share of *Penis-neid*, my part in penis envy, is wrapped up in withheld friendship, an attachment or disposition, an inclination of being-in-the-world declared off-limits to women. Of course male designees yammer staggeringly, from Aristotle to our day, about the nearly impossible attainment of friendship, but that plaint operates on an entirely other level and register of constraint and taboo.

Ach! Maybe I was called up by a different politics of friendship, a different grid or writing practice that pulls one close to another's distress. *Do you by the way know what it's like to be a girl?* To take corrosive insults all day long—to have to wrestle down insolence all the time, to wear yourself down proving and outdoing yourself, overcompensating, pushing hard, becoming exhausted to the point of blanking, so much so that you can't even complain?

Don't get me started. And so I enter in this work the strained ground rules that got me started, or that allowed for so many false starts: the off-the-charts chronicle of my career. My engagement with the university began prior to the time that a vocabulary existed to designate, approximate, or contain the winds of harassment, the false grievances and aggravating dismissals that women and minorities routinely endure. I have tried to turn my experience into a wind farm. You'll judge if I have pulled off my project without the drag of resentment. Do not hesitate to read the scars that crater the textual body!

Impotent yet threatening, the complaint shows up in all sorts of corners of existence that pull you in, giving you a listen. It kind of butt-dials you. It's a call that you didn't ask for, and no one wanted to initiate. Perhaps I would

Introduction

ask that this is how I'd like the book to be considered, though I well understand that it is not up to me to tell you how to read. What I can say is that the work frequently lapses into exclamations, off which meaning slips: *Ach! Oy! Aaaiieee!* The complaint butts up against its own stock of unsayables, in accord with the most sublime poetry of stuttering precision. These linguistic sighs, or moans, these signs of surrendered meaning and exacerbated strain, punctuate a place where one can say no more, only expire, say and write while saying and writing, like Kafka in "My Neighbor," "I'm not complaining, I'm not complaining" (*Ich klage nicht, ich klage nicht*). The doubling of the phrase indicates that a complaint is being registered, entering the repetitive injunction to which all complaints subscribe. As indicated, I give ample room to the determined utterance "I can't complain," so I will not drag out the hermeneutic residue of the quasi-denial and its stumbling recuperative swing at this time: I can't, I must complain. The structure of "I can't/I must" informs many of the textual instances under scrutiny in this work. They all teeter on the edge of "I can't anymore." In some regards, refusing to complain—a gesture of "what's the use?"—also tells us that one doesn't complain enough: things are far *more* calamitous than we allow. But let me pull back from this precipice—not where we want to end.

Portnoy's Complaint can be hard for a girl to connect with; yet, the nature of this study and a trustworthy reader's report prescribed it for this work. I do not scare easily and can take the provocations of defiant pornology with relative ease. In fact, outrageous texts sugarcoat my existence. Off-ramps to racisms and sexism make me *writhe*, that is, write, however. They make me write or scratch a text, if in protest, understanding that obscenity very often needs to take socially repugnant byways to sustain its punch. I get that, but my bodies can't always cope. For example, I cannot hold it down when vulnerable forms of Dasein are insulted: belittling injury would be my heart-thudding grievance, my staple complaint, and I have made myself clear on this point of obsession a good many times in and off the writing machine. Nonetheless, a number of poignant threads converge in Philip Roth's novel, which are certainly worth noting. In the first place, which is to say, the last place, the work screeches to a halt on three full lines of aaaaaaaaaaaaaaaaaaaaaaaaaaaaaaaaa aaahhhhh!!!!! A reinscription of "oy," an arrow pointing at "aie" and "ach!" the final asignificatory heave expires, listing the fate of all complaints, returning to the origin of writing's scream, heaving an initiatory sigh: ooo-aaa, *the petit a*, or the beginning of our alphabetico-logical cultures. In any case, the final ejaculation of aaahhh!!!, etc., marks the place of extreme renunciation, the place where the text says, with a heavy Jewish German/Austrian accent: "Now vee may perhaps to begin. Yes?" Allowing for a re-beginning and affirmation,

Introduction

"ahhhhh" etc., launches the supplementary "Punch Line," a microgram and playlet following the ending, aaaaaaaaaaaaaaaaaaaaaaaaaaaaaaaaaaaahhhhh!!!!! "So [*said the doctor*]. Now vee may perhaps to begin. Yes?"

I would be tempted to let my own analysis begin here, and maybe indeed it does. For Roth's protagonist, *kvetching* may be the only form of truth to which access is given. It is as if truth has had to take cover in the ambiguous light of dismissible speech. It may also be the case that unspeakable damage must be packaged in a type of phrasing that undermines its portentous holdings, self-annuls and passes for something anodyne, laughably insufficient to its task. Regardless of how grating, the complaint tranquilizes the brunt of an insufferable history, bringing it down a notch to a level of repetitive deployment. Overexposure of phrasing serves as erasure, allowing for the repression of the very thing evoked. Any phrasing tends to weaken or stupefy under the pressure of its nagging iteration. Still, in Portnoy's case (the novel presents itself as a case study), as in others that dwell on the complaint, there is a matter of displacement that the text points to. Suggesting that it cannot permit itself, in our day and age, to raise itself to the level of elegiac disclaimer, unpretentious about its incapacity poetically to touch the base of pain, *Portnoy's Complaint* opens a window on its disturbed tragic milieu by means of a dialogue with sister. The complaint, according to the record left behind by the novel, marks the voided space of Nazi terror.

> Can you give me a tentative date, please? When will I be cured of what I've got?
> Do you know, she asks me, where you would be now if you had been born in Europe instead of America?
> *That isn't the issue, Hannah.*
> Dead, she says.
> *That isn't the issue!*
> Dead. Gassed, or shot, or incinerated, or butchered, or buried alive. Do you know that? And you could have screamed all you wanted that you were not a Jew, that you were a human being and had nothing whatever to do with their stupid suffering heritage, and still you would have been taken away to be disposed of. You would be dead and I would be dead and
> *But that isn't what I'm talking about!*
> And your mother and father would be dead
> *But why are you taking their side! (. . .) I suppose the Nazis make everything she says and does smart and brilliant too! I suppose the Nazis are an excuse for everything that happens in this house!*
> Oh, I don't know, says my sister, maybe, maybe they are, and now she begins to cry too, and how monstrous I feel, for she sheds her tears for six million, or so I think, while I shed mine only for myself. Or so I think.[2]

About this work: It should have been an elegy. It should have closed a mourning period, shuttling the stubborn schedules of unsepulchered pain. Instead, the work grabbed onto defeated outlets, letting the complaint, obdurate by nature, turn over its hoarse engine.

Whew! Have I got grievances! Do I harbor hatreds I didn't even know were there! Is this the process, Doctor, or is it what we call "the material?" All I do is complain, the repugnance seems bottomless . . .[3]

Raising the Visor

The Complaint of Modernity

Hamlet Stalked. Philosophy has a bid on complaint structures, and literature keeps itself riled up, fed by the alternate motivators of rage and constraint. The complaint has swarmed all sorts of discursive fields and referential sectors of vital encounter, depleting or, in some instances, accommodating the way things fall in place, line up, to facilitate or block existential pathways and psychic runs.

Our social networks are saturated with complaint, increasingly dependent on its reach and ability to sustain a semblance of relatedness. Instructed by Derridean indicators, let us keep tuned to the culture of litigation, grievance, and complaint in legal and medical tracking systems and triggers. Derrida did not teach us a "method" as such but sensitized his students to Nietzschean transvaluating machines in order to tag the programs, often contradictory and aporetic, that control our appropriations—the way they stick, like the spirit of Christianity, or falter, like the spirit of Christianity. Or, to put it somewhat differently, he keyed us into *la disjointure*, the out-of-jointedness instructed by Hamlet as he sets his complaining machine in gear.

Disjointure opens the relation to what has been concealed. It may resemble what Heidegger says in the context of technological dominion about breakdown: the essence of technology, he observes, is disclosed in its breakdown. About to teach that very passage, one day on the Bay Bridge en route to Berkeley, I caught a glimpse of the essence of my car when it broke down. I tended to the stalled vehicle with disclosive anxiety when, precisely, it stopped working, leaving me stranded on a bridge to nowhere. I was deep in ontology, staring down the unfairness of it all, checking my watch. I called upon my father's spirit, as I do in times of trouble, to pull me out of the existential-mechanical ditch. My attention turned to a litany of woes, the sheer stuckness of being: my stupid life. Alone on the bridge. It's really not fair, none of it. Hamlet, equally stalled by whatever drives him, possibly even to a more ontological-legal effect, famously pauses to rue a tightening relation to time; addressing his complaint to spite, he deplores the way that time, out of joint, commands him to set things right. His predicament has him squarely facing off with the question of rights and the pursuit of justice within the jurisdiction of the complaining subject. How will he handle his father's grievance? To what extent does every grievance wake up a ghostly origin and command post that calls you to action? Time's disjointed character proffers a sword that cuts both ways: it functions both as a call for justice and as the announcement of evil, pinpointing an evildoer or an awaiting cluster of disavowed wrongs. These two possibilities—of justice, of the advent of evil—remain indissociable; they exhibit the two sides, each concealing the other, of the same danger and urgency, "d'une même désarticulation due à la violence de toute loi dans son irruption auto-fondatrice " (pertaining to the same disarticulation due to the self-instituting violence of law), splitting its origin by means of a general alterity.[1]

In *Specters of Marx*, Derrida raises the visor, asking, "How to distinguish between two disadjustments, between the disjuncture of the unjust and the one that opens the infinite dissymetry of the relation to the other, that is to say, the place of justice?"[2] As Heidegger reminds us regarding a passage in the Anaximander fragment, the Greek *adikia* means not only injustice, but also being-out-of-joint (*aus den Fugen sein*). Heidegger's commentary of the *Fragment* drives a conciliatory movement of accord, the assumption of a rejoining and regathering, a communitary suture that Derrida's positions confront. The complaint of Hamlet, the fragmenting disturbance of Anaximander, cannot resolve into an erasure of différance accomplished by summoning tropes of plenitude. Heidegger's report on the derailment over which Anaximander grieves and Hamlet complains tries to take the edge off and envisage a way for being to get back on track. The complaint doubles down on the riot of injustice strapped to the very fact of being—that our days are borrowed, that language lashes out arbitrarily, grievously misfires intention, dowses meaning, outsources feeling to remote and approximate fields of saying, sideswiping the aims of lament, downsizing the house of praise—hinging the advent of evil on the demand for justice.

Hamlet, attached to language—"It speaks!"[3]—swung by its over-the-top lapse into the madness of saying and reciting and recycling phantom-directed horror, toppled by the Opheliac demise, drives his complaint home to the essence of man, to the way the *anthropos* works, is worked and chronically disjuncts: "What a piece of work is man!" The enigma of man, whether or not it is worked out, riveted by destructive impulse, continually readjusted by considerations of warlike tactical forces, theoretical adherences and the clutch of reason, focuses the complaint. What is man? How does this thing, human all too inhuman, *work*? Often latched on to the work of mourning, the functioning of man, like the work of mourning, according to Derrida, does not work. Nowadays we continue to say, when downscaling, "She's a piece of work!," indicating trouble and a coded history of difficult behaviors.

The Plaint of Flouted Sovereignty.

The Plaint of Flouted Sovereignty. A designated passageway to modernity, *Hamlet* has been viewed as fashioning the first full-fleshed modern man. The range of his world-class anxiety discloses depths and a hint of interiority that Hamlet's predecessors could not know. Yet the metaphor of depth puts tragic language on furlough, no matter how substantial and rhetorically wrought each expression of doubt, unmanageability, and outrage can be. Hamlet staggers and stalls over the demeaned form of language usage with which he, ever a loser son, is saddled. The many times that he lets his sentinels or even the great friend, Horatio, step ahead of him or walk with him, stage a level of hierarchical breakdown unheard of, giving way to a stunning if silent strike out of royal protocols of convened *écriture* and gestural syntax. When everything is relegated to Horatio's notational skills, we learn that the bestie may not be the best of memorializers, may not be the best man for the job. Hamlet addresses the testamentary task to a so-so writer.[4]

How does the tragic adherence to the complaint implicate man, and what does it tell us about the stalls and neutralizing tendencies of acts (or passivities) of complaining? How does the complaint struggle for legitimacy in the rhetorical bid for power? Or are the thrusts of complaining just the necessary cohort to powerlessness, capable only of showcasing the illegitimate lunges made at referential authority and what it means consistently to fall flat on the face of linguistic positing feints? The complaint bickers constantly with its stated insufficiencies, the limits it hits with regard to reach and intention. Proffering only the spectacle of a failed bid for its own authority, the complaint incorporates its flailing dumb show as it tries to subdue its recalcitrant auditor.

It's touch and go in *Hamlet*, for the plaint that triggers the dumb show hits home, suffices to "catch the conscience of the King," sending Uncle Claudius reeling and kneeling like no other language form of attack. To the extent that charging with language can be at all gendered—a contestable but inescapable temptation of comprehension and argument—thus failing the test of maintaining even a hint of manliness in the making of claims and executing turnarounds, the plaintive bout is not only the destitute cousin to all language, coming from the wrong side of the referential tracks, but says something about the plight of those beings that take recourse to language and lose ground, fight it out time and again with only paltry results and powered-down amplifiers.

Raising the Visor

Hamlet puts into gear a drama of flouted sovereignty, for the throne of Denmark has been seized illegitimately, by intimate usurpation. That the power grab extends inextricably to Gertrude tightens the knot of sovereign assumption and desire. Dethroned, the ghost can only rattle his son, who in turn can only rattle his chains, locked into a signifying chain that allows for little latitude. Fogged in and frozen in place, Hamlet constructs the precarious edifice of his complaints. There are moments when he breaks loose from his peculiar confinement, when he lunges at Polonius and arranges for the execution of his friends as part of a demonstration of rage misfiring, going after a secondary tangent.

The complaint as premier attribute—as zero stage of linguistic throwdown—offers up a sense of man in relation to the decline of sovereignty. No sovereign, no pose of subjective mastery, would be caught dead complaining! Or, more to the ghostly point, the sovereign must be dead in order to complain. The supreme complainer, Hamlet's ghost attracts doubt to the veracity of his claims, inspires his interlocutor to pull in, to suspend action if not belief. Both Hamlets strain the terms of their suspension, in air and as heir. All possibility for dramatically conceived action famously hangs fire. Hamlet cannot target a first responder, someone who would be roused to vengeance by a readably convincing war cry. What gets transmitted is not so much an order, a perlocutionary speech act, but the suspensive stance, occupied by the phantom utterance, of the supreme complainer—the dead paternal trope. Fathers are not supposed to complain; mothers, well, this is another story, currently under investigation, for mothers can go at it: they do not commonly risk in terms of language games the threat of castration and no one really cares about their gripe, the on-switch of an inconsequential cannonade of nagging. Sometimes, however, they are pushed to murderous extremes in order to lodge a complaint, make it take hold in view of an entire, horror-stricken community of onlookers, the so-called innocent bystanders who have, to some degree or another, let it come to this.

The royal Father asks that his son "remember" him, bring him back his member, recall and strengthen his pose of commanding power. Yet both figures of father and son catch the contagion of memberlessness, and so Hamlet, too, libidinally crashes, must give up the girl. Thematically, this hypothesis runs like a near tautology. The Hamlets lose their sovereign premise because, having been deposed, displaced, they have effectively lost their sovereignty. One could formulate the downturn in terms of the hits their language has taken, sinking to a level of usage that grinds down on the prestige of rule and efficacy. Their language shifts or loses ground, loses its performative edge and the punch of sovereign resolve it enjoyed before the drama opens, shrouded in the linguistic fog hanging over Elsinore, leaving them to the plight of trading complaints—a way both of staying on the scene and losing all footing.

CHAPTER 1

By the time he appears on the ramparts, the father spirit is short on authority, low on credibility. Hamlet, the son and receiver of ghostly broadcasts, famously cannot for the most part act. He remains stuck in the rut of complaining and diffuses the shrieking cognates of his thoughtful pauses—ranting, railing, screaming, shadow-boxing, ghost stalking, scrambling, power-plummeting verbiage. Is this not the fate of the subject of modernity, to fall into the crevices of a speech that cannot stick but only stymies and freezes all kick-start myths leading to action? It is almost because of the experience of the downgrade of speech that war breaks out everywhere to prove a sticking point, almost arbitrarily, as Fortinbras says and storms, if fatally and with horrific aim. In the meanwhile, mankind lurks. Reflecting on a ghostlike partnership, man stalks aimlessly, traversing phantomal fields peeping with chatter, barely attaining to the velocities and depth of lament, the ability to trace loss to its outlying retreat arc. Capacious in its effort to explore the disjointure of things and world, the *Unfug*, or spray of nonsense, *Hamlet* maintains a channel emitting chatter, clutter, patter—language's descent into the mad patterning conventionally associated with the muted feminine stutter, whose lead singer, on Hamlet's off days, is Ophelia.

On Automatic Repeat—"The Time Is Out of Joint." Time is not only off, off its hinges—if we remain within the approximate metaphorical field granted us—but out of joint. What it means to be "out " as concerns time merits consideration, for the complex that links "air" and "heir" depends also on where the locator can settle on the outness of time, which regulates the successiveness of time held by jointure with the rights of succession, the technicity of which Claudius rigs and abuses. But disadjusted time also indicates an out-thereness where all nonmasterable aspects of time are at a remove, extratemporal, if not extraterrestrial. For Derrida, the relation to what is not there invites us to heed the ghostly, non-present other, to turn toward those who are voiceless, in some senses silenced and inhibited. Whether relegated to a past or a spread of unknowable future, their dimmed grumble calls for ethical responsiveness.

We advocate for those whose presencing is compromised. This kind of advocacy, bequeathed from beyond (or the past, or the jurisdictions of beckoning futures) may well extend in one form or another, to everybody and nobody or to every nonbody, for a ghostly apparition claims body without material grounding—but what do I know, I am merely a scholar who tracks the dimension of unknowables, at the edge of falsifiable evidence. Hamlet's father, a semi-fiction, aligned with the fiction of paternity, is plated in armor, packaging only a vague insinuation of body. Forcing an address to that which eludes presence, the ghostly apparition, not presently living out his life, but walking the afterlife, returns to Elsinore in the name of justice. For Derrida, the scene, which throws into question all "scenes," all modalities of seeing or possible sightings, calls up "the principle of some responsibility, beyond all living present, within that which disjoins the living present, before the ghosts of those who are not yet born or who are already dead, be they victims of wars, political or other kinds of violence, nationalist, racist, colonialist, sexist, or other kinds of exterminations, victims of the oppressions of capitalist imperialism or any of the forms of totalitarianism . . . without this *non-contemporaneity with itself of the living present*, without that which secretly unhinges it, without this responsibility and this respect for justice concerning those who *are not there*, of those who are no longer or who are not yet present and living."[5]

The disadjustment that Derrida reviews along the lines of Hamlet's grievance—slashes of untimeliness posed and exposed by the ghostly interlocutor—says that justice is still outstanding in the sense that it is still due, undelivered. Any call for justice approaches us with the delivery systems of the phantom, latent but persistent, part of a patrimonial logic that shakes us awake, usually at midnight, when daytime is de-occupied, and the non-contemporaneity of what is serves an ethical subpoena. Derrida speaks of the visor-effect of the specter that summons Hamlet, the way the ghost sees without being seen in terms of the face that he conceals, and, we can add, in tune with the drastic superegoical broadcast system that the setup entails.

The question that leaves us hanging is one that bears down on our political bodies, their inscriptions and orientations, still baffling—and as untraceable as the origin of a categorical imperative: from whom (or what) do we take our orders, whether these are marching orders or the ordering sense of world; under the sway of what or whom does one feel prodded, become answerable, motivated or immobilized, deprogrammed, set for action, ideologically retrofitted, and so on? In other words, which plaintive transmitters acquire legitimacy in the lineup of calls taken, flooding the sonic atmosphere with purposeful alarms racing at us from elsewhere? Even our most mundane political callouts and deliberations, our temptation fed continually by the thought of action, crucially involves a spectropolitics. Just consult Marx or any revolutionary transmitting system that deals out canny political analyses and listens to the unsaid, often accompanied by tremendous static.

Complaints launched against Claudius come to a standstill due only in part to a neurotic relation to time—who does not have a neurotic relation to time, a hysterical sense of speedup or melancholic slowdown, and so forth, or not, precisely, no forth; well maybe Heidegger does not have a discernibly hysterical relation to time, but who writes two or more volumes on time, crosses

CHAPTER 1

one of them out, resumes differently, returns to lost premises, casts them off again only catastrophically to misread the historical times disdaining all sorts of temporal tip-offs and archaic regressions, crossing back into time and being, and so forth? One would need to consider rigorously the differing flow charts of time in Heidegger—waves of granting, types of favoring, the beat of poetic donation, denials and instabilities of and in time set between moments, undecidably given as trace, as well as figuring the modalities of time given as indeterminacy (archē, lapse, moment, eschaton, duration, present, suspension, telos, hurried instances, diachrony, the rush of ec-static temporality, etc., etc.).[6]

In all this expanse and depth of reflection, does Heidegger also give consideration to temporal drain-offs, to the depletion calibrated by time's destructive recoveries and irretrievable losses—does his work showcase the Complaint of Time, recalling the way Erasmus produced *The Complaint of Peace*, which, in that case, elucidates how she has been forgotten, maligned by misbegotten theorems, turned the wrong way? The answer is by no means simple and, in some ways, yes, he does, for time has needed to be rethought and reset. Clearly, the larger cast of these questions must be engaged elsewhere. On the one hand, in shorthand, there is in his work little room for complaint, or even for the too-Jewishly flavored lament. Perhaps some vital aspects of these questions can be handled with the password "Hamlet." (Admittedly, my own/disowned, ex-appropriated hysterical relation to time and being makes me precipitate, fall out of the succession of scholarly pacing and theoretical measure: I apologize for the quasi-rant, a modality of complaint, held back by the complacencies of insinuation and lost ground. *Ach, ach!*)

I apologize for being in such a hurry—and anyway, I am clearly mistaken, one could say that all of Heidegger is one big complaint about the oblivion of Being even though, as Emmanuel Levinas has observed, Dasein, never seen eating, can also be said never, ever, never to complain, isn't it the case that Heidegger has no viable admissions policy for the thought of *Klage*, complaint—oh, maybe I am entangled in the aporetic trap of *complaining* about Heidegger, as if one could take recourse in any hope of avenging oneself on his work, or put up a fight against his call to Being, a preposterous theoretical stance and index of false intellectual heroism. End of quasi-rant.

The complaint that Claudius has abused power cannot entirely fly, either. The exercise of power is always haunted by its susceptibility to abuse, rendering the trope that handles the abuse of power a mark of sovereignty. There are at least two ascensions to contend with, illicitly if intimately wrought: that of Hamlet, King of Denmark, to the ghostly realm, that of Claudius to the material, worldly realm of sovereign decision. The complaint against the abuse of power can never fly to the extent that it guarantees the sovereign hold, which

Raising the Visor

in some respects bounces charges of abuse off its shiny armor. It may be that Hamlet's father, laying the complaint on his son of his predicament, commits abusive language acts as deposed sovereign. In this arena, the complaint keeps one in the throes of an irretrievably losing streak. One is out there, voided, ghosted, twisting in the air.

Among so many time-released questions and effects of language, Hamlet raises the question of what it means *to make things right*, or to presume that one was called upon to do so. How one encounters the grievance coming from above depends on any number of strategic considerations and incalculable pulls in the direction of reparative justice. Is the death of one's father something that can be repaired? Can one go up against maternal *jouissance*? How to count down the days of regulated mourning when the reigning king asks that you get with the program, integrate back into social connectedness and viability?

I will limit my stab at an answer to the subject at hand, with the understanding that the text continues to pound out a number of pertinent angles on its failure to commit to the dictation of conventional forms of vengeance, some more compelling than others when it comes to understanding the way justice is meted out or utterly sideswiped, returned to sender. The double plaintiffs, Hamlet and Hamlet, are barred from taking action following coded protocols of revenge-seeking engagement. We get a clue of this when Prince Hamlet pulls out a pen rather than a sword, moving to the arena of writing, erasure, and deferral, under ghostly dictation, noting the paternal grievance, penciling in a schedule for recovering the damages. The quickened pulse of law understood as revenge based halts for a moment of rigorous indecision, purposefully miscarried. The complaint is entered as part of a writing machine rigged only to interrupt the call of immediacy, the demand for equivalency (on which justice, according to Nietzsche, is based) and closure. Hamlet will obtain his end, we could say, but this sense of finality does not coincide with closure. Such a structure that resists closure runs analogue with the mourning disorder that wears him down until the suicidal ending in excess of closure, leaving Horatio to write it up and Fortinbras to marshal the new influx of troops, effecting a flex of law enforcement that abandons the endless reflection on justice off the revenge clock and in the generality of time. Time is up; a new army of tropes takes over the scene without justice rendered or evil-doing accommodated. The complaint has run its course without a final checkpoint or wrap of meaningful conclusion. Perhaps the "without" indents the fateful moment, a formulation of "out" that still hinges on a remnant of "with," the dependency that Derrida elsewhere has marked as the privation of "without," ever dependent in English on "with," an enduring indication of being-with struck out but still precariously retained. I am without you, hanging onto the memory of a "with" taken away.

As he lays dying, Hamlet's split second of sovereignty, with Claudius counted out, is without historical duration yet nonetheless constitutes an event, a political fracture. The quiver of ascension to a vacant throne drives him to make a decision that was neither called for nor secured under law: the tremulous ascension coupled with imminent decline allows for Hamlet illegitimately to "elect" Fortinbras as his rightful successor.[7] It is hard to time Hamlet's dying or resolve on the merits of a death certificate, for he announces his demise according to different clocks of deferred finality: I am dead, Horatio, I die, I am dying, I die, I must, it speaks—winding down according to a staccato, a lurching sense of timing, an intemporal spasm of expiration. The drama leaves it unclear where the complaint eventually falls—on the side of justice or evil. To the extent that it has drawn out its time and outrun the limits of clocked action, the complaint as disposition and defiant halt, initiated by Hamlet the Dane, appears to be in cahoots with the very wrong it criticizes: it has known only to prolong the span of an injurious misdeed.

In *Specters of Marx*, when auditing the economy of vengeance and punishment, Derrida discusses disjuncture as the very possibility of the other. Without hitting the pause button, he names Hamlet in the context of the complaint: "If right or law stems from vengeance, as Hamlet seems to complain that it does—before Nietzsche, before Heidegger, before Benjamin—can one not yearn for a justice that one day, a day belonging no longer to history, a quasi-messianic day, would finally be removed from the fatality of vengeance? Better than removed: infinitely foreign, heterogeneous at its source? And is this day before us, to come, or more ancient than memory itself?"[8] Derrida puts out a call for justice that would roll out of Hamlet's plight, redescribing the struggle with a complaint paternally conceived.

Give Me Another Round. There is something that has obsessed me, a kind of recurrent motif, a plaintive cry, put out in my prequel work, and that seems to be calling for attention now, again. Embedded in the book on "loser sons" as provisional site of ending it all, source and motor of devastation—the book, I mean, and historical misfortune it documents—one will find a sustained reflection on late puberty and the phantasm of maturity. Let me ask you this: have you ever met a truly mature being (in the sense that exceeds mere checkpoints of aging and the disposition that allows for stepping back, lucidly cooling one's engines)? There may be some human states of exception here and there, but they, too, show the tendency to lapse into immaturity. Goethe, one of the historically maturest beings according to the tabulations turned in by Nietzsche, fell hard for a teenager when hitting his seventies. But even Goethe, who transcended first chakra nationalisms, regressive familialisms, and all manner of tribal bonding needs, credited his growth to "wiederholter Pubertät," recurring puberty. The oversized writer counted on the returns of puberty to move on with creative and libidinal abundance, inviting the double edge of abandon and sovereign trespass. He abandoned himself to the returns of adolescent exuberance. At the same time, he was the poet who pressed claims about the correlative intensities of joy and suffering—puberty consigns the upsurging child to pits of pain smoothed over only by the tranquilizing boons of so-called adulthood. Speaking of the *East-Westerly Divan*, I have seen streams of immaturity strike even the wisest gurus and sensible teachers who suddenly go infantile, giggle, play, shriek with laughter. It is not clear where to situate laughter on the developmental scale or when evaluating psychic and somatic outburst, how to account for the spiritual or purifying capacities of laughter and its openness to gender reassignment—or even the way it functions as a gift in Freud and, in terms of disrupting vital registers of significance, has left an explosive hole in the writings of Georges Bataille and Jean-Luc Nancy.

Puberty, perhaps not philosophically mature enough to have become a fully developed concept, sets up a breach, flagging a destructive passage on the road to majority. The minor hits a snag that may never entirely resolve but is bound to return and deliver an unexpected knockout punch. Sparing only a few, puberty comes around the bend for the second and umpteenth time, to offer faux replenishment or the bumbled bad news of your finitude, foretelling an imminent crash. Driven perhaps on the ontic level by metonymies of the newly flaunted sports car, the unaccountable affair, a new store of aggression and ensnaring spree of *Selbstbehauptung*, the body bump of untimely self-assertion, *ach!*, the return of puberty undermines the flattering growth chart that humanity assigns to itself. As shock and disruption introduced to the concept of developmentality, puberty is linked, via Jean-François Lyotard's political essays, to Kant's remarkable statements about immaturity.

Kant sets out from the insight that one *wants to remain* immature, tethered to authority, kept on a short leash, in an existential and political comfort zone that stalls growth and prevents seasoned decision. In the chapter "*Was war Aufklärung?* / What Was Enlightenment ? The Turn of the Screwed," I interrogate such a moment of faltering self-assumption as the passage through puberty.[9] I return to this passage—through puberty, in *Loser Sons*—in order to seize on an issue that has not received sufficient air play, or heir play, and can help us move forward, if that is conceivable, with the Hamlet dilemma, looping a hysterical knot that to this day tightens the noose around what we continue to incorporate and attach to, often unconsciously, as the political body. As weighty as Hamlet has been in terms of inheritance and gateway to the staple of infra-structuring themes of modernity, the play's remarkable resilience is also due to the flaws it exposes, the way it flatlines and plays dumb, trying to prompt a traumatic truth to speak. A dumb show haunts the dramaturgy as it explores the limits of saying and showing, wondering aloud if it is capable of instigating confession and aligning with justice. One is throttled and voiceless, dependent on a ghost's directives and plaintive insistence for motive and intelligibility.

Hamlet, who no doubt has slimmed down or was considerably photo-shopped for the portrait we may carry of him, wallet- or poster-size, started out as a pudgy adolescent. Bulked with body excess, he faces off with the bodyless inflation of paternal overdrive. How does Hamlet carry the weight of his heritage? When Lyotard moves on troubled adolescent awakening, he knowingly dwells at the limits of philosophical statement and determination, rehearsing that which may well lie beyond the scope of philosophical reach and investigation. Maybe the overweight waddle of Prince Hamlet is not a matter for speculation or the corporeal zoom, part of sizing his portion of indecisive agony. Or, maybe he needed the carriage of young portliness, a way of taking up space in the kingdom that at once counted him out and reluctantly counted on him. What about the body of the prince? How does it reflect the political body, bloated with gluttony, morally emaciated according to the transcripts the prince handles, in contrast to the vanished body of the king?

This line of questioning, its imprudent check on a figure cut by the prince, seems no doubt out of bounds for philosophical inquiry as we know it. Phi-losophy nowadays won't be starved out, however, and goes after the most minute triggers of obsession. Adolescence, the cusp of immaturity, fits only with difficulty into its bodies, protesting all manner of unjust burdening, and philosophy itself has to be prodded and poked if it is to start reasoning with the unreasonable.[10] This is where Hamlet pushes Horatio on the point of what can happen in excess of philosophical dream schemes: like a girl, a philosophy can dream . . .

I return to this arena in order to lift a latent strand of thought that may provide us with access to the *jouissance* of the complainer, who may be held back by the line of Kantian immaturity. Hamlet can be seen to join the ranks of Lyotard's Emma and Abraham to the degree that he, too, is staggered by a mode of address that can be integrated only minimally, if at all. They have not reached the level of maturity that could reasonably field a call of the magnitude that befalls them. They are traumatically called up by a force or voice or prod that cannot properly be deciphered yet produces "a strong alteration"—Freud's designation for the episode of puberty—that occurs when the turnover from childhood to majority is marked.[11] Off target yet on the way to them, the call fatefully diverts them and something drastic happens, an uncontrollable spill of being that jostles the kids, relating them to the unrelatable. The jolt that they receive when picking up the untranslatable call or the call that only ever relays its own untranslatability, evokes the shock of puberty—"the rebellious blur bleeding out of the dilemma of impaired comprehension: 'what is happening (to me)?'"[12] I did not want to miss out on focusing a piece of Hamlet's commando reactivity—the specific way he remains enraged yet stalled, rebellious yet unable to execute a plan or hit an assigned target, girlfriend-bound yet mother-fixated, cute but yet to lose the baby fat—as part of the unaccountable upheaval, the social out-of-jointedness pertaining to a condition at once common (everyone, more or less, goes through this self-estrangement) and alien (what kind of freakish monstrosity just got released on the community of family, friendship, and political observers?).

According to Lyotard, the shock of puberty, the rattling call, shapes our political narratives, even as it apparently recedes to raise havoc on more unconscious channels of social behavior. If I am getting this right, the brand of hysteria ascribable to puberty cuts into spheres of political performance and agonized concern for justice in a number of ways. My own assessment, reading psychoanalysis, including K. R. Eissler, Lyotard, and the victims of recurring puberty, is that the excited teen, running high on self-inflationary fuel, and disrupted by an untranslatable address, sparks the scene of action. Puberty's claims announce themselves each time uniquely, in full revolt of what is.[13] The runaway teen spirit, going nowhere fast, riveted by a sudden arousal, an awakening, enters a stretch of being that remains enigmatic and active, infiltrating all manner of social practice. Occupied to a considerable degree by adolescent tropes of giddiness, overabundance, sarcasm, and ruin—the despondencies and grammars of excitability—the stoppers and starters of social responsiveness still need to be accounted for, even if we lack a grid to tabulate the saturation of the political according to adolescent excitability.[14] Aligned with Abraham and Emma, in terms of the disturbing jolts visited upon these hapless receptors and written up by Lyotard, Hamlet proves to be terror riven as he tries to field a deracinating call that spurs him to stand up in submissive readiness. On one level they share the predicament of receiving an instruction, an intrusive charge and convocation. They are commanded to respond to a call: ready or not, adolescents are made to assume that a call is meant for them. Hamlet understands that "readiness is all." But was he ready for what was coming at him? The call rips through them before they are prepared to become who they are, marking an experience of shattering decision that, paradoxically, makes them who they are, skipping the beat and reassuring timing of becoming.[15] They are riveted and invaded by a ghostly call under whose authority they are bound to freeze up.

The numbed reluctance to assume responsibility for what continues to arrive unannounced, the coercive pull to take the call sustains the affective haze of political torpor and childish recoil. Still, there are calls, as I have tried to track elsewhere, that should not be taken and are really not meant for those overactive teenagers who presume to be born to set things right.[16] *Ach!* This is all very difficult to sort out, yet a plan at least has been outlined, emerging from these primal and pulsating jolts that exhort us to adjust a practice to the endangered stance of rigorous hesitation—a concept developed by Lacoue-Labarthe in the thought of cautious ethicity. The child, hesitant and ever incredulous on the one hand, prematurely triggered, tight and ready to spring to action on the other, must lean into the emptiness of the voiding call, another name for puberty's shakedown. According to Lyotard, Kant paved the way of a steep slope on the downside of nothingness, "the Id-side to which I am singularly host and hostage." Drawing puberty onto the political platform of deed and reflection, Lyotard attempts to maintain something of a philosophical claim: "to speak in an intelligible fashion on the subject of the Id-side of the articulable, that is to say of the Nihil."[17] Turning away from an interpretation of drives, Lyotard scrolls down to the Kantian Id-side of things—even though Kant has remained too strongly attached, Lyotard observes, to subjectivist thought, that is, to a philosophy of consciousness. Adolescent hysteria undergirds political performance in considerable ways, requiring us to revisit time and again some circumscribed zones of unmarked intensity.[18]

It would be wrongheaded, I believe, to think that one could simply skip over the motif and developmental-historical stopover of puberty when modern politics have depended so emphatically on teenaged mythologies and fast-tracking disasters.[19]

Perhaps the time-out still observed by *Hamlet* requires a renewed reflection on political action (in the sense of Arendt) and the complaint of puberty (in the sense of compromised sense). Hamlet, excessive and ineffective, modeling the shocked incomprehension of a social body, has only himself to complain to. Hence the famous soliloquy, a filter of the unanswered call of anguish. In the end, Hamlet doesn't provide us with a philosophy of complaint: it *is* a complaint, identifying what makes an utterance a complaint for our historical receptors. An enduring haunt, it tells us that all beings are somehow bound by the spectral reverberations of an idiomatic complaint, often cryptically relayed and laid out in terms of a nation's anxiety, preparing the ground for adolescent overkill.

Raising the Visor

Ach!
The History of a Complaint

On the way to l'anguish. Among scholars, hanging onto a friend is laughably difficult, nearly impossible. It is not easy to *make* friends in the first place, not when one is tethered to the book, bound by its exigencies, overwritten by dead zones, held in existential lockdown day in and day out—don't get me started. The question of whether a friend is even *wanted*, and if so, whether a friend is wanted dead or alive remains an open one, especially in our age of undead socialization. Nowadays you are haunted even if the other proves to be more or less alive!

Scholars notoriously spin on a solitary axis, despite the steadiness of their gathering rituals when they book flights and attend conferences, sit on panels, evaluate incoming manuscripts, and offer the occasional keynote—all of which implies, in the end, a passion for relatedness. Friendship is a hard nut to crack when everyone is sitting in solitary, conferring with Nietzschean shadows in the aftermath of what Derrida has said that everyone else has said about the constitutive glitches in having or being a friend. How much dependency gets uploaded into the zones of friendship?

If you want to keep a friend, assuming such things are possible, you have to make a number of concessions, besides scheduling the narcissistic time-share. When you get up close and personal, decide not to run away and manage to hang in there, really liking them despite glaring flaws and savage inconsideration—*ach!* don't get me started—the resolve to stave off the cannibalistic libido can indicate one such concession, which for some Daseins is a tall order. All of this becomes decidedly complicated when one measures the difficulties, tracked by Montaigne, Emerson, Blanchot, and others, of presuming to know the friend.

Emerson levers the friend as a figure for the unknown, a kind of dead brother, making the visitation with the dead a crucial component of your claims on friendship.[1] Aristotle said that, in terms of non-reciprocity, it's like staying tight with your ancestors. One honors, commemorates, bows before the majestic escalade of a cherished absence, not expecting much in return, not even in terms of some dreamed-up favor from beyond or protective spiriting while slumming through our earthly existence (my off-the-rails-but-viable translation of Aristotle's stated intent).—Oh, but the withholding pattern of the non-reciprocating remote ones runs us into a thicket of anxiety. Let me drive *philia* in another direction, in an effort to get the inclinations right.

For the most part on good behavior, I tread lightly. My rap sheet shows that I haven't gobbled up the friend the way I imagine doing with (or *to*) libidinally invested objects. Still, I have more than just one of them firmly introjected. The process of introjection indicates some violence, but I think they can handle it; from the looks of it, they have successfully staved off many sorts of transferential addresses and currents coming at them from all sides, with their strong sense of *Dis-tanz*.

Ach! I know, I know. Pluralizing the singular friend brings trouble, for how many friends is one allotted? Multiplying friendship into a near-horde quotient is gross, according to Aristotle. If you are overpopulated with friends, you have no legitimate claim on friendship. But how many is too much?, asks Derrida.

Friendship opens up timelines, putting you within earshot of finitude's atomic clock. Capable of shifting intensities and barometric pressure, friendship refines skills associated with the organization of limits and stopwatches. For Nietzsche, the friend was the future, non-contemporaneous, a promissory note. For others, the friend offers different modalities, thwarts and comforts, of non-presence. Even if, as Derrida has taught, quoting a long lineage of friendly agitators, there is no friend.[2]

But wait. In order for the friendless announcement to stick, I have turned toward friends to scope the vacated space of friendship: "O my friends!" Turning *away* and turning *toward* make up part of the same movement of friendship's address to which one inescapably bears a relation, not excluding such times as when the friend is quietly dismissed or rigorously unavailable, ever cutting away from a given callout. Even the littlest of people make friends, move in and out of early stages of intimacy and play, know the staggering experience of breakup. Some of us, shy and reticent, are still frozen in time, quietly playing with dolls, our pretend-friends. *Am I able to have a friend, I wonder?* I get attached and put together a make-believe family. At least I appear to stick to the tropologies of husbands and wives, brothers and sisters. Regressively hanging in there, I cling to discarded familialisms that I have earnestly contested, endlessly written off only to return to their greedy ambushes. What the hell is wrong with me, I wonder, as I ponder my entrapment in the paleonymic temptation, taking a bite out of its legs and legacy. How could I not submit

Ach! The History of a Complaint

my records as a complainant? It used to be *Avital v. Wagner*, but now, let's face it, the time has come for the obsessional neurotic showdown: *Avital v. Avital* or, better yet, drawing on a built-in paranoid disposition, let us add the introjected (if collapsed) *State v. Avital*, sending even more of a whack from the precincts of familialism, whether falsely minted or weirdly posited, made to stick as deadly merger of family and intrusive governance, chaotic yet recognizable predatory regulation.

I have matured since the days of miniature tea parties with my dolls, when I could coddle a selected stand-in for all proximate beings, a stuffed animal. (I never really *played* with dolls, but that's another matter. They were real, even then, and in some ways still are so.) At one point, I must have set out to find more fleshy friendships, though I can see Nietzsche's point about the non-contemporaneity of the kindred spirit, the way he alerts us to the inescapable disappearance, the dropped call, of friendship: one should expect a locator malfunction when it comes to fixing the *Gesprächspartner*, the species of friend built up around the interlocutor as inner dream team, the friend as fantasy, as fiction of address and tireless reader of one's exploits, inner recesses, persistent disarticulations.

Let's face it. On the outskirts of academic endeavor one is commonly on one's own. I am provisionally counting out the specular colloquy and private horde of cowriters, well-established dictators who populate one's solitude, the offshore friendship account, the secret store of cheerleaders, those who show up when you can't go on, you must go on. Closer to the core of university life, friendship scores some points here and there, but tends quickly to snag and fold, perhaps as is to be expected in any theater of work or in the shadow of competitive exertion. Still, one needs allies, craves a kinship network—whether disruptive and improbable or reliably bolstering, familiar—and wants to think of oneself as capable of making friends. *At least let me be able to make friends.* For Bataille, reading constitutes the sovereign act of friendship. Emerson follows other but similarly run protocols that requite friendship with reading.

The legendary performativity of *making* friends, or the injunction to fake-it-until-you-make-it friendship, leaves one insecure and feeling basically alone, unprotected—the affective *Grundstruktur* of any workstation in the university or at the writing desk. I can speak only for myself. Pause. It took me forever to secure every term and turn of that last sentence, what a whopper: "I can speak only for myself." How long did it take me to lease out a "myself," or even to squeak and speak, *to presume to speak?*—I won't even go into the inaugural "I" that continues to wobble when propped up as if one could start a sentence, any

CHAPTER 2

life sentence, in such a counterfeit manner. I must go on. So. I can do this. In the fledgling stages of becoming-intellectual (I use shorthand; "intellectual" does not cut it, keeps you in the rut of modernist paleonymy, stuck with obsolesced concepts and habits, but what's a grrl to do?)—when priming the intellectual program, I start off out of tune, a bit of an outcast, a somewhat defiant but mostly vulnerable misfit. Defiance was not meant to style my original stance; I was a painfully earnest baby scholar, dedicated, conditioned for every sort of servitude, understanding that doing time, whether in graduate school or as part of a teaching body, amounted to acts—or, rather, passivities—of cultish subjection. Returning to some sense or fiction of self, bootstrapping up, I let myself be inspired by Asian figures of warrior apprenticeship, by Muhammad Ali and his rope-a-dope techniques, by activists in the civil rights movements whose morphs and urgency to this day recruit my sensibility, by Bettina von Arnim and cohort Emma Bovary, who, bereft of address, had no one to write to but kept it flowing until, in the end, for Emma, the ink flowed out of her mouth, body-crashing out of the writing pad.

The solitude was not icily absolute. One formed aggregates and quasi-gangs in graduate school. One could be menacing to others—that's a relationship in itself. One certainly could not afford to practice extreme forms of social isolation. *Are you kidding?* One needed to move in and out of sectors of the group psychology dialup. We could regroup, fall apart, regroup, change the menu, shift ground, switch it up, regroup. I was a primal horde with Laurence Rickels, but that's about it, and this spare social diet, with only some add-ons, seemed to suffice for us in our salad days as stand-alone graduate students, delighting in the discovery of each other's abysses and near misses. In graduate school I was known as Miss Prision, a name initiated by me, meant to prophesize the stances I wanted to hold as a strong reader, capable of all sorts of duplicities and deviations while running with a text of any caliber. Reading your friends, what is this? Yes, for Bataille it involves a "sovereign operation." Reading your friends, in friendship, in the emphatic overhaul of the "philo" that heads up philology, may take you into the perils of a close-up, scaling regions of the close call, or getting up close and personal in a way that would seem inescapably menacing if this particular exertion didn't also have you practicing the Nietzschean calibrations of *Dis-tanz*, the dance of distance and dis-identification, keeping one remote, unhinged. One doesn't often survive such operations because there is the matter of incorporation, and the three *V*'s that regularly beckon at the door to friendly appropriations: *Verneinung, Verfwerfung, Verdrängung*—negation, rejection, repression—modalities of denial, foreclosure, and shutdown that come into play and aporetically make you even friendlier in the zones of reading—or eating—the other. Yum! There is something about the encoun-

Ach! The History of a Complaint

ter with friendly fire, when allied to the friendly signifier, that can leave you debilitated. I am willing to take that chance and will not be intimidated—not even by my most monstrous of friends, and their indigestible parts!

Speaking of Bataille, let us take as our model his interpretation of Manet's crucial slippages, where he swarms instances of Manet's "unique cheek."[3] Bataille shows how Manet's manipulation of his predecessors incessantly "overshoots and transgresses," but he manages nonetheless to succeed in *elongating* the works from which he springs. Not that one would presume—or want—to *elongate* some of my peeps, *um Gottes willen*, but let me hitch a ride that is programmed in a certain way by Bataille to overshoot its mark—despite all good intentions and the installation of nearly orthodox reading protocols, evened by a sensibility for the brushstrokes of inscriptive verve. On the best of days, the reader-friend transgresses and overshoots her mark. In this instance, she dances with worry around the task of assigning herself a write-up of the stellar friend.

So, I was known in those days as Miss Prision, meaning that you should expect of me the highest incidents of misreading and failed reappropriations of textual histories, including no doubt my own. Princeton was not exactly a nurturing haven for the sassy yet anxious, horribly serious young scholar, already set for sleeplessness and off-the-chart intensities. Brimming with Kantian enthusiasm and our sick/healthy humor, my cohort and I were not entirely appreciated and, for my part, I was consistently depreciated even though I wore tight dresses and sparkly rhinestones, always trying to look my best as I delivered papers and listened to my teachers without once retouching my lipstick during seminar.

When I was revving up my engines, with no sense of insurance coverage for what I was going to do and missing out on the institutional warranty, I must have thought that I needed some allies. The point was to make some friends, set up some networks, fall in intellectual love, quick. Even if one was inflamed in those days with the narcissistic sure-fire sense that one could and must do it all on one's own, with no pat on the ass (when they did come, they were impudent and all sorts of tensions ensued), you needed an address and number, a way of connecting to other solitudes and creating world. I pause as I write this: *did we really need friends in those days?* I ask myself. We were such hermits, sealed into our workspaces, in touch with eighteenth-century philosophers and a galaxy of poets. *Did we even come up for air in those days?* The occasional social protest brought us out, after which we were returned to our primary confinement, if one or two of us was not first arrested and fingerprinted for future reference.

When I was a child I used to have best friends on steady rotation, though I was the loyal one. Part of the soil on which I was set to take off was American.

The childishly cheerful tone of North American culture does not conceal the dark side of childhood drama. Children are easily inserted into the protagonist slot of narratives of horror. Or, with a bit of a dialectical tilt, practices held over from childhood hold sway in American forms of sociality where the culture reverts, if ironically, for instance, to the code of "besties" or BFFs of yore. In a Nietzschean way of questioning, one must wonder: when did the *need* for friendship arise, and what ends did such a need serve? I can't count out the hypothesis that, actually, I must have needed friends, the fictional props of friendship's aliases, desperately. (*Or not at all*. I still can't tell. I try not to be a psycho, and so grab on to somewhat acceptable forms of sociality.) Family was a bust; school—*ach*, school! a penitentiary culture and scene of blunting, unremitting cruelty. My love for this or that teacher remained, for the most part, unrequited. Among the spectacularly messianic teaching corps, I was nearly nobody's pet. Once in a while, yes, counter-transferential zeal came my way, locked and loaded, but how long could that last before I was buried in teacher's pet sematary? Friends could turn around the undeflectable losing streak, I told myself.

Some of my friendships, I admit, were hitchhikers on the death drive. They frazzled my nerves and wore me down, hitting me in the sensitive parts of my *Geworfenheit*. Others were vital to my growth. Still others remain to this day mired in opacity, inenarrable; yet, I am convinced they have saved my life, such as it is or was. Even so, the *need* for friendship, whether intellectually called up or close to the vest, unruly or stealth, rich and cheerful, feels like it may require some genealogical purging, for this need may signal some part of a steady weakening, a long-term or mere bout of existential fatigue, unsovereignty. When King Richard II gives in to his takedown, he laments:

> I live with bread like you, feel want,
> Taste grief, need friends. Subjected thus,
> How can you say to me I am a king?
> (*Richard II*, 3.2.180–82)

Lodged between grief and subjection, coming on the heels of hunger and want, the king, unhinged, admits to being in need of friends, thus twice-over losing his title, of which the play's title has already shorn him: Shakespeare has declined to name the play *King* Richard II, and the failure to use this title is addressed within the dramatic unfolding as a grave fault, a mark of sovereign faltering. Finding oneself in need of friends is often delineated in Shakespeare as the default position of something like psychic stability, and the needy are

Ach! The History of a Complaint

ever on the way to meeting the same destiny as Hamlet's BFFs, Rosencrantz and Guildenstern, sent to their death— notwithstanding, as Freud reminds us, Hamlet's supposed paralysis. Despite his legendary indecisiveness and world-historical stall, Prince Hamlet still sends his friends to hell. Blowing off friendship, he powers up and goes into action, on a killing spree. Horatio, another cut of friendship, is preserved in order to write up Hamlet, assuring his epitaph, ensepulchering him in narrative tribute.

Whether poised to write your obituary or set to accompany you on part of the dharmic voyage, each friend is responsible as well for surges in writing—or, more discreetly offered, for flagging the relation to writing that threatens to undermine us all. Friendship witnesses and sanctuarizes the squeeze of writing-being, standing by, in my idealizations, at least, like Max Brod or Leonard Woolf, eyeing the threatening loom of language, when not embodying it. If it weren't for this threat, and we were not faced continually with an unstoppable fear of freak-out, the store of complaints that writing announces, who would bother to undergo the submissive extremism of writing—I mean who would bother *to write*? How does writing, despite unavoidable slippages and off-the-mark assertion, with its tendency toward world-positing hazard, account for itself or the spectral friend, score the luminous point or two, make breakthrough runs for something that resembles our ideation of justice? Maybe it holds to unjust commitments in order to break the mold of their complacent destructions? In many ways writing gives us a close-up of the unbearable brunt of existence. Is it in the end part of the Heideggerian *Schreiben/Shrei*, the *cri/écrit* or a Nietzschean slice of a relentless series of complaints launched like so many smart missiles at our metaphysical tradition? Or does thinking—for Heidegger no longer *philosophizes*—unfold only in the neighborhood where a plaintiff's cry has been restlessly subdued?

Thinking is seamed with thanking: *denken* und *danken* involve a turning toward something other than a self, or any kind of proximity, in the surrendering pose of gratitude. Of course Nietzsche ran with this long-distance thought of thankfulness according to an untimely clock-in, and kept on saying to his close ones "fuck you very much" (more or less), even to his rehab leader, Heidegger, who tried very hard to clean up his act and put Friedrich Nietzsche back in commission after the Nazi hijacking. Heidegger sets out to rehabilitate Nietzsche in *Was heißt Denken?* He lashes out at those who have demeaned the Nietzschean *Schrei* by turning it into so many forms of idle chatter, a large-scale ideological raid. Heidegger's reprimand, set on *pianissimo* (even though some thinkers have to **SCREAM** to get their points across: thus Nietzsche), tries hard to stay the course and avoid becoming a complaint. At this point in his disturbing career path, Heidegger explicitly resists high decibels, what Freud calls in the end of *Civilization and Its Discontents* the *überlaut* (mega-decibel) clamor of certain claims. This from the guy who put the death drive on mute. If one turned up the volume in *What Is Called Thinking?*, it would be difficult to ascertain whether Heidegger's work involved a series of epistemological draws, issuing a complaint, grousing, even given to downplayed *rants*—but this description could amount to a distortion, possibly part of a theoretical projection that wants desperately to hear the querulous grumble, a breakup of his troubled silence in the meeting with Paul Celan. Sometimes the thinking woman's complaint is nothing but a matter of tone, notoriously difficult to fix or stabilize for the purpose of conceptual runs and determinations, even when she rules the concept. Derrida came up against the limit-case of tone in philosophy when tapping different registers of meaning in Kant's work, establishing a set of concerns relayed forward to Peter Fenves in our neighborhood.[4]

The way we were: German Studies, A Cold Case. Let me roll back the clock and open some memory banks, go back to the days when a number of deals had to be cut and choices made. For French-accented Americans who plunged into the unsure depths of German studies, there were only two possible, if incompatible, ways to go. It's the early eighties. I was—characteristically—split. One option that I saw before me (if it *was* at all an option: for my part I had *no choice*, but that's another issue for this pro-choice sister-scholar) was to follow and learn from Werner Hamacher's theoretical acuity and handling of texts; the other was to take the off-ramp of German literary studies and pursue the media technological and poetic byways owned and innovated by Friedrich Kittler. One had to size their operations, particularly if one wanted to clear some critical abysses, develop a viable repertory. At times it seemed as though these two proper names were responsible for the gang wars of and around *Germanistik* and its satellite empires. Here we hit a logical snag or two. For no one would dispute the fact that, for all intents and purposes, the discipline of *Germanistik* was left in the dust by Kittler and Hamacher, who mutated and reconfigured the very program by which we understand the study of German letters, the fraught relations that bind the discipline. Their membership in the field remains tense and, in some sectors, unforgiven, even disavowed. From where we sit they were, and remain, titans of a field that did not hesitate to issue penalties that had them thrown off the very premises they evermore defined.[5] To be sure, there must be some stragglers or old-timers who do not subscribe to my description of these top-of-the-line border disputes, and by now there may be some hybridization to account for. But I am not aware of

Ach! The History of a Complaint

such crossovers. Some exceptions, nearby, come to mind and include the strides of Martin Schäfer, Nikolaus Moeller-Schoell and Gerhard Richter, the work of Cornelia Visman and flares sent up by Thomas Pepper, Nicola Behrmann, Jeffrey Champlin, Peter Banki, the bi-hospitality of Laurence Rickels, whose direction shows awareness of clashing turf wars, a host of younger professors and graduate students, and my own Nietzsche-friendly contradictory stances. Samuel Weber, lucid, prolific, top-notch, had his own travel plan, a type of itinerancy that sometimes coincided with particular aspects of this near polarity I am describing by means of the proper names, Kittler and Hamacher. Sam started his run with more or less American identity papers, which may have complicated the specific caste we are trying to identify in the evolving character of German studies. Close to Theodor Adorno, Peter Szondi, and Paul de Man in the breakaway days of his career, he was, before and also after he closed ranks with Derrida, resetting all sorts of registers of critical thought spanning France and Germany, relayed to and from the United States. I insinuated myself with a sense of urgency into the cartography I am trying to establish here. In any case, I have in my possession updated travel passes to these destinations—they were a destiny and in typical Avi fashion, I had to negotiate two or more singular sets of brawler's markings on my writing body.

Some of the runs I made were provisional, or not particularly "authentic," maybe tryouts or auditions that Superego may have signed me up for. Only, no matter how cautiously tentative I tried to keep it, every step or misstep eventually stuck. Sometimes I walked into a situation, more like a stumble, landing me in an undecidably wrong or right way. Still other considerations and memory traces come to mind. It is not uncommon for me to find myself faking my identity at some junctures in order eventually to settle into the ways and idioms that bounce off each singularity that legitimately claims me. In my head I am a Derridienne, a Hamacherian, a Kittlerian—a mutant French theorist and a relentless Germanist, an uprooted Anglo-Americanist, keeping company with Weber and his own kinship network of German comparativists and psychoanalysts. I also like to think of myself closely in line with scholarly insistence as *Wissenchaft* that meshes Hamacher and Lacoue-Labarthe within the reflective-poetic zones and stirring discretion of Ann Smock, close to the probing inventories of Christopher Fynsk, Kevin McLaughlin, a number of French thinkers and writers, and essential crossovers of Jean-Luc Nancy. Susan Bernstein points us to the way philology implies the forgetting of original friendship, love, attraction, inclination; yet, philology, she reminds us, is grounded in friendship, in philia, as "philo-philologische Beziehung"(philo-philological relation).[6] I am trying to remainder this relation to the interruption of philosophy that philology marks for Hamacher and Bernstein.[7] But I have not finished with my lineup. In the interest of full, if somewhat warped disclosure, I should state that I interned in some significant ways with Professors Hans-Georg Gadamer and Jacob Taubes, among quite a few other mentors and teachers. These lists, which fail to account for the touching and teaching spirit of so many, are by some indecent necessity incomplete; my apprenticeship was long and hard. I was tossed about, shared and divided, often enough nearly snuffed out. Some friends took me in other directions. Once in a while I jumped ship. Bill Regier was always there to save, read and publish me. The position of a persevering editor cannot be overestimated, requiring its own historical signature. Frédéric Boyer in France, Anne Dufourmantelle, Suzanne Doppelt, and François Noudelmann in France have kept me in fine and French print. (I have so many more to sign up in this regard, including the elegant German publishing houses maintained by Brinkmann und Bose, Fink Verlag, not to mention the far-out Indiana University Press, the presses that have hosted works in Israel, Argentina, Mexico, Italy, and Korea, each of which in a distinct way struggle against the prevailing time's threat of erasure. I halt the list prematurely.) *Ach!* We know from Barbara Johnson's reading of Paul de Man's reading of Baudelaire's reading of himself that enumerations notoriously derail you: they spin the wrong document and crush complicated textures. So many players in my own feebly crunched numbers are MIA—the teachers, even the bad ones against whom one sharpened; the ambivalent ones who showed some responsiveness but nevertheless signed the pink slips; tender and epiphanic ones; the flashback lineups of hiring and firing squads, each essential and structuring, traumatically upturning the dirt on which I was raised. Certain names come up, and I make a grab for them. Hélène Cixous once asked that we reflect on what it means to use proper names in this way, tagging our belonging or our way with language when we add names to our work field. If you're close to Celan, much of the relay remains anonymous. *Ach!* It looks like I am a hysterical spiller.

I come from a blended family, a no-man's-land flagged by shared custody of lost and forgotten causes. As a cub Germanist I was utterly forlorn, mostly on my so-called own, before I discovered my "we are family" stride. But this was not easy, nor credible. I developed outposts in Virginia, California, Berlin, and Paris, and was very much involved in creating a line of French-styled German studies as well as German-based French and American readings. I am relocating to Latin America, but that's another story. When I met Judith Butler, together with Donna Haraway and Elizabeth Weed, another corridor lit up, another curve of the kinship throw.

In the area of German studies one had to struggle to get beyond the many stalled checkpoints, and being a crypto–de Manian did not help matters either.

Ach! The History of a Complaint

German was closed off to anything that could break away from hermeneutic or phenomenological explorations—the field at its best. Usually the folks were tied down to thematic types of textual interpretation or Brechtian flavors of Marxism, pitching in some underserved authors as well. So, usually, in the neighborhoods of theoretical work, when one was not caught in the crosshairs/ heirs of Walter Benjamin and Adorno, the Frankfurt School and Marxism, and so forth, one had to choose or lose, in the next generations, among Werner Hamacher and Friedrich Kittler and Samuel Weber. Am I right, or what?

I said theoretical work, so do not come at me with other names, with Niklas Luhmann, for instance, or the other one or two of them. In philosophical and publishing Länder I remember Jürgen Habermas as having blocked entry for many among us, a forbidding Türhüter or Kafkan doorkeeper.

Even though I made them signposts along the way of my critical training, I do not doubt that they would scoff at the idea that "Hamacher" and "Kittler" bore meaning for the fate of *Germanistik*. For his part, Hamacher was trained in comparative literature and philosophy and had in the early days, like Sam Weber, worked under the fabled professor Peter Szondi and, later, Paul de Man. Kittler, nurtured by Heidegger's work at Freiburg, split from the scene of *Germanistik* as soon as he passed intellectual majority. Apart from this yield of more or less empirical-institutional data, they could not have been integrated into what passes for German studies at any point along their trajectories, except by way of a distinctly American view, and even here I am giving only a partial shot. The good part of German studies, I would think, is what stirs in the uncomfortable chill that hounds its adherents.

Sure, there are those who blithely go about their *Germanistik* business, who don't carry around the burden of shame and distress, and simply continue to address the letters of "Goethe und Chiller" without blip or obstacle in their course or courses. The unhappy few approach this area of study with apprehension, a permanent case of the jitters, or at least with latex gloves. Here is not a hint of specular narcissism, the boom of self-discovery except, occasionally, for the remote blossom of negative transference or the identificatory pathos of those who are called to the splintered terrain of German studies for some sort of impossible retrieval, meeting the limit of a reparative economy, indulging a fantasy of psychic restitution and historical rebalancing—proved and widely impugned delusions. Then there are those who clamor too loudly in catastrophic districts and draw *benefits* from interested and shameless identifications. In French departments people can still walk around beaming cultural pride, wearing a beret and scarfing a baguette, keeping it down. OK, this is a fantasy-formation. When is the last time I saw a colleague walking—no, swaggering—in the hallway supplemented by the iconic props of baguette and beret? The hyperbolic projection aims to underscore a dissymmetry. Namely, that there exists no excuse for such a cultural identification on the Germanic side of things, though things appear to be changing now.

Well, I think I've made my point, and, to be sure, in some departments the embeddedness of shame goes underground or remains latent. They are not sleepless, anxious, aporetically straight-jacketed by their object of study, I tell myself. It could even be the case that nobody gives a shit, except for me and a few nightwalkers. *Recently, a German scholar of considerable note said to me that he could not believe that I spent one minute on German texts after everything that has happened—namely, after what should never have happened. "Why would any injured party cast their thought in this direction?," I was asked by Anselm.*

For some of us the work of Lacoue-Labarthe was the only secure bridge to get us to return to German letters, and Derrida as well as Lyotard seemed to stand for the most direct conduits to get one near scathing German texts or dormant philosophemes of the German Idealist tradition and their bold inheritors. Together, yet according to very different entry codes, Lacoue-Labarthe, Nancy, Kofman, Blanchot, Lyotard, Lacan, and Derrida made it possible to close in on unbeatable texts such as those of Schlegel, Nietzsche, Hegel, Husserl, Heidegger, Schmitt, Kafka, Celan, Bachmann, E. T. A. Hofmann, Freud, and Benjamin. Anyone who thinks she has had an E-ZPass to the study of works that sail under these names is blocking off the spray of toxicity directed at this area of study, making critical approach hazardous. For the most part, the field has failed to distinguish or renew itself, though there are signs of growth in restricted sectors of the academic world. One could hazard the hypothesis that, until fairly recently, the relative mediocrity of the field functions as a defense mechanism, a response to the disastrous historical undertow that cannot reasonably be contended with. This is understandable, that an entire field would be more or less on numbing meds in order to avoid itself. Exceptions are luminous, and beginning to pulse. I see new growth areas among graduate students—with the paradoxically unbearable outcome that they have only diminished institutional safety zones in which to shine. On the whole, though, the field record does not dispense bragging rights.

The underachievement of German studies is not new on the horizon. For somewhat different reasons but propelled by the same evaluation, Benjamin himself was put off by German studies. Ironically, allegorically, and allegorico-ironically, Benjamin must say his piece on German by switching languages to French, when writing to Gershom Scholem from Paris on January 20, 1930. Calling out to the friend (reverting to the German original, calling Scholem

Ach! The History of a Complaint

"Gerhard"), and announcing that the great interlocutor will think him out of his mind ("tu vas me trouver fou sans doute"), Benjamin explains that he can only write "sur mes projets" (on my projects) if he allows himself to skip over to another language—not any language in the Babelian inventory, but only if he can do so by means "d'alibi qu'est pour moi le français" (with the alibi that for me is French).[8] Concerning German literary criticism, Benjamin intends to take it to the next level, since the work with and in literary studies in Germany has been uniformly mediocre:

> C'est d'être considéré comme le premier critique de la littérature allemande. La difficulté c'est que, depuis plus de cinquante ans, la critique littéraire en Allemagne n'est plus considérée comme un genre sérieux. Se faire une situation dans la critique, cela, au fond, veut dire : la créer comme genre. Mais sur cette voie des progrès sérieux ont été réalisés—par d'autres, mais surtout par moi. Voilà pour ma situation. (101–2)

> The goal is that I be considered the foremost critic of German literature. The problem is that literary criticism is no longer considered a serious genre in Germany and has not been for more than fifty years. If you want to carve out a reputation in the area of criticism, this ultimately means that you must recreate criticism as a genre. Others have made serious progress in doing this, but especially I. This is the situation.[9]

In order to tell his best interlocutor about his German project Benjamin has had to break his silence, crossing over to French letters for the purpose of signing a promissory note in which the intent to take over German letters is announced. If we indulged a luxurious sidebar here, we would interrogate the "Task of the Translator" at this juncture, summoning Derrida and de Man's work regarding that task, the expropriations that it implies and spin-offs that it mandates. "I will be the Number One critic of German lit," Benjamin avows—in French. How does the language trade-off leverage Benjamin's strategic takeover? Does the French OK a guarantee, offering a sort of transcendental seal-the-deal contract; or, on the contrary, does it ironize the determination with which Benjamin makes this Germanic claim for himself? Or, is it the case that, already at the time, on his watch, in order to get at the core value of German letters, find an approach, critical or even psychological ("You will find that I am out of my mind"), one had to shuttle in on the French language? Benjamin may be updating earlier practices of borrowing on French letters, but his plan remains unique in a reverse Mme de Stael sort of way. He announces to Gerhard his plan to put in place "un échafaudage ferme à tout ce travail" (a solid scaffolding around this work, 102), for the purpose of securing "la théorie de la connaissance de l'histoire" (an epistemological theory of history). Traveling this route, he prepares an encounter of another kind with Heidegger—an encounter that follows a collision course, undecidably set between a meeting and a clash, maybe a clasp: "C'est là que je trouverai sur mon chemin Heidegger et j'attends quelque scintillement de l'entre-choc de nos deux manières, très différentes, d'envisager l'histoire. / Quant à mon séjour actuel à Paris il est d'assez courte durée" (102; "This is where I will find Heidegger, and I expect sparks will fly from the shock of the confrontation between our two very different ways of looking at history. / My current stay in Paris will be rather brief.").[10]

The trip to Paris, of short duration, proves just long enough to set up the historical rendezvous with Heidegger—a knockout bump on Benjamin's path consisting of very different historical stances. The run-up against Heidegger is anticipated ("j'attends') by Benjamin as part of the species of "Choc-Erlebnis" ("l'entre-choc"), what Benjamin famously designates as the numbed experience, the difficulty in experiencing experience, that characterizes modernity. The "scintillement" indicates that their clash will dazzle—perhaps as *sparkle*, perhaps as the *glint* of traumatic residue. Heidegger and Benjamin will meet, finally, according to the French original, in the spark *between* shocks, in the *entre*-shock of contending manners of vision, the glare of historical vision. Writing in French, inching toward German letters, widening the scope to involve history and host Heidegger, Benjamin nominates himself as contender. He tells Gerhard that he wants to occupy this place. The glint: a dazzle of encounter marks the spot where Benjamin plans to meet Heidegger, on doubly foreign ground. He writes about the fate of his work, his projects and sense of place in the disturbed scene of German letters. Yet he has in his sights Heidegger and History.

German literature, driven from its home language, given over to the task of the translator, becomes atopical. Nonetheless, Benjamin is on his way to creating a new genre borne of strife and encounter, buoyed by philological audacity and a fighting spirit. He turns to his friend with the shield of foreign subtitles, making his way back to German literature by means of clashing viewpoints, through the mediated hospitality of the French language. In the split screen of translation's divide, Benjamin will encounter Heidegger according to terms no less grave than those of historical knowledge, at the edge of his own end of history. When Benjamin fell, there was no off switch that could erase the traumatic flashback of his elimination from the material and critical scene of writing. Henceforth, the grounds of Germanicity were to become, for many, off-limits. It was as if the German language had gone into shutdown.

The new unintelligibilities. That Benjamin chose to write to Scholem in French says so much about friendship's intimacy and its refusal of transparency, the way it holds to an idiom of correspondence, but also marks

Ach! The History of a Complaint

a recoding of purported transparency between friends. One could see the relocation to French as part of a Schlegelian friendship pact, issuing permits for posting new unintelligibilities, forsaking myths rooted in sheer understanding upon which some friendships are scantily built. Not that homing in on a so-called native language guarantees transparency. Redirecting the exchange to foreign captions may render more scruple and transparency to those who tap for language near abyssal limits. Benjamin tells his friend that he cannot in any case meet him in the shared part of a German background on this path and passion. *Some were never able to return to the German language.* For Benjamin, ahead of the curve, yet ever falling behind, as for many others, after the war—from Peter Szondi to Reiner Schürmann (in different ways and different outs for Hannah Arendt, Erwin Panofsky, Theodor Adorno, and scores of others)—German, no longer a host for futurity, became a condemned site, either strictly verboten or a matter of securing a complicated pass. In these instances French was the go-to language where one sought refuge, or at least the semblance of safe harbor. France offered its own thicket of historical hurts and problems, but at no specific instance did the language associated with that cast of linguistic and political entities turn into a phobic site, sponsoring the language of the unspeakable. Levinas refused to go to Germany. He was not the only one to avert his gaze, to experience—or decide upon—blocked passage. Szondi, at the invitation of Scholem, turned away from the German language, choosing to teach in French at the Hebrew University in Jerusalem.

German itself became the language of *Klage* and the *Anklage*—complaint and accusation—a poison-language of non-address, faced evermore by the historical plaintiff. (It squeezes the sensibility to write even somewhat "poetically" about the destitution of a language, the reciprocal abandonments and solitude into which nearly all contenders were shoved, the historical lockdown. Can one even say "evermore," or is it too pretty, a protective backslide to Shakespearean ground? Do the bumps of paratactic syntax suffice to convey the way we were all thrown off on a permanent basis and *parabasis*? The initiating sentence of this very paragraph breaks up over the story it tries to tell, collapsing into a Germanic underswell of disarticulating remarks, the pile-up of names, hard to hold together under the circumstances of a flight from language that one is hard-pressed to describe. In a sense, though, German always knew this about itself and tried to push away from the complaint of harshness that it lodged against itself. Some speculate that German became proficient in *music* in order to cope with and fend off its inherent harshness.)

Ach!

CHAPTER 2

The complaint of the tragic scholar begins faintly. For Friedrich Kittler, the encounter with German letters, softened by a *Seufzer*, commences in a sigh. Even though he turned out in long stretches of his legacy to be a man's man—he fires up the technological libido and shows a ballistic drivenness, delving into forbidden war cathexes, sleuthing in the cut-off narratives of our time, revisiting shrouded theaters of battle and the persistent glare of computer terminals—Kittler started up his own engines with feminine accents, as if to match his long flowing hair and sweet-toned accent. He brought to the podium the spritely, forgotten, but crucial Bettina von Arnim with his unforgettable paper, "Writing into the Wind, Bettina," a now-legendary intervention first offered at the colloquium where Derrida presented a typescript bearing the title "Law of Genre/Gender."[11] Hamacher, too was on-site, as were Weber, Christopher Fynsk, Paul de Man, and so many other A-listers in this Woodstock-at-Strasbourg of German philosophy and literature. Kittler's voice, though commanding, was quietly supported by his lilting inflection and tender intonations. A soft-spoken advocate for any number of lost causes and genders in those days, he was capable of summoning up women's reading habits in the eighteenth century, Nietzsche's new stock of girl students, the flooding of the secretarial pool that changed the fate of letters and love stories in the nineteenth and twentieth centuries (men started writing up the collective transference onto the secretary and Gal Friday figures, the sudden population boom of Della Streets and Lois Lanes), the first time "Ladies" was added in the form of a public address: "*Ladies* and Gentlemen! Meine *Damen* und Herren!" And Kittler famously zoomed in on the *ach!* of Sprache—the ache of whatever thus spake, the indwelling "alas!" that he drew from language (*Sprache*). He observed in fact that German literature commenced in the *sigh*: "Die deutsche Literatur hebt an mit einem Seufzer."[12]

Somewhere between moan and lament, *Seufzer* rings out at the starting gate of the literary adventure, tilting toward the eternal feminine of language utterance—one is tempted to say *mutterance*, in a trans-linguistic sweep that involves a maternal marker, *Mutter*, and the English drone of muttering, something that gets said under the breath, just below the sonic level of sense-making. Perhaps the mutter is a way of revving up the complaint, as well as the inventory of German literature: is one addressing oneself, a split-off part, or simply falling chronically short of a proper address when muttering to oneself following the covert boomerang trajectory of the whimpered shortfall? Yet, this is how Goethe has Faust start off when he opens the scene of the modern German language, the start-up fund of German literature: "Habe nun ach! Philosophie" (Have, oh my, philosophy: I have philosophy, medicine, etc., and unfortunately also theology under my belt, alas!), and so forth, mutters Faust. The scene

Ach! The History of a Complaint

opens on a complaint, just as Werther enfolded the right to complain as one of the principal themes of the Sturm-und-Drang suicide novel. Faust groans that he's at a dead end: he has done all the work, knows everything, yet knows not enough of what really counts, that is, the incalculable, and cannot be satisfied by mere knowledge—the cognitive controls available to him. Nor can he be expected to keep himself in a restricted Kantian zone of knowability. This is a loose translation of a steadfast canon, but on point and battle ready. (I'll defend it against any philological busybody.) *Faust*, breakthrough work of German modernity, comes on line with a hysteric's wish for *more*. Many of us remember the Freudian joke that asks, "What's the difference between a hysteric and an obsessional neurotic?" The hysteric says, "Is that all there is?" The neurotic, stalling, stopped short by the overwhelmed sense of encroaching things, says, "This is too much." Faust opens up the hysteric's *demande* for more and better, but with *"ach!"* interceding there is the matter of an initiating surrender, a ready resignation—the place where the complaint strikes out *demande*. I will unpack this shortly, to show how, on another register, the complaint serves notice to the analyst, functions as the psychoanalyst's defeat, erasing the *demande*—an intrigue for which analysis must pay back all sorts of psychic loans: *"Ach!"*

Kittler could have chosen, I suppose, to render *"Ach!"* as a groan, following the schema of sexual difference proposed by Shakespeare in *Richard II*, when a sigh is apportioned to the feminine, the groan to—well, to the deposed king, which makes its way toward the feminine but still retains more of a masculinist majesty as the "unKinged" mans up. (Let us note that the recently served injunction to "man up!" indicates that one has yet to retrieve or attain to manhood, for one is clearly not man enough if one still has to man up, lasso the transcendental ideal of manliness.) As the king takes leave of his queen, each repairing to a different type of banishment, he coaxes the separation: "Go, count thy way with sighs, I mine with groans" (5.1.91). The shaky difference between sigh and groan leaves the only remnant of sovereign decision, a sonic signature anterior to language, landing somewhere in the vicinity of Shakespeare's famous "The rest is silence." Yet the shivering distance between sigh and groan is not quite silenced, continues to insinuate itself without respite. There is no rest, no quiet time, for sexual difference.

The sigh that initiates German literature grew up in the neighborhood of the swoon, the eclipse of meaning that populated so many texts of the eighteenth century, where the experience of *Ohnmacht* has said something about textuality and its diminishing capture, its suspension of consciousness at moments of decision. In Heinrich von Kleist's *Marquise von O. . .* the protagonist faints and the text follows her down by instituting a dash at the non-rendered core of events. The narrative ceases to be; it simply cannot say what has happened. The story disappears into a syncope. We are given to understand, by the insertion of a diacritical mark and her bloating "figure," that the text was unable to control or tell a rape scene. For Kleist, the origin of inscriptive saying, here and elsewhere, is smeared by an initial violation. Everything subsequently grows around the textual gash, a traumatic seizure that marks the dilemma of all texts: tenacious silencing and embedded disturbance, an origin that cannot testify for itself, knowing no witness or advocate to haul in a lost causality, some generative principle to call up hospitable ground. The text, left to fend for itself, ducks into corners, substituting for storytelling with a stock of trip ups, descents, and blushes. The blush, in particular, serves to carry an entire phrasal regime in Kleist that vies with muted language. The red splotch, or *read* splotch, registers a level of affect or meaning that remains at a loss for words, uncontrolled, unreadably lodged between shame and excitement, confession and disavowal—it indicates the bleeding qualities of a text that swarms its boundaries, spilling into shock areas that cannot be subdued by so much as a glint of understanding or even, for that matter, perceived by any subject. In the case of the Marquise, one wonders if the blush speaks for her, at moments when she cannot stand up for herself, or does it rather betray her with a sudden spread of skinned mapping, releasing a secret or indexing a moral blemish, a pigmentation in concourse with the scarlet letter and birthmark of Hawthorne's brandishing. In some instances, the blush manages to register a complaint for the reticent Marquise, and it signs off on an unspoken accusation. As blossoming of sense, blushing betokens involuntary emergence, though it has been layered with cultural significance: who is capable of blushing, of evincing moral indignation or decency's outrage? The ability to blush, to show a purported inner life of morality, has delivered some troubling racialist output that no one wants to overlook.

The history of the blush wavers between feminized forms of reticence and confiscated indexes of the white man's moral privilege. It raises a red flag over disavowed areas pinpointing a muted complaint—unreadably imprinted in the best of cases, forced into the dilemma of excess readability in the worst of historical cases.

One never complains to the right person. *"On ne se plaint jamais à la bonne personne,"* said my friend Jérôme one day during a conversation in Paris. We were considering different cultures and valuations of complaint. There is a distinct, if *political* appropriation of the complainer's stance in the French tradition, even if no one is so foolish as to expect a complaint or movement of protest to land squarely in the right place. Carrying to the limit of political praxis the aporetic tensions of righteous denunciation, a flex of indignation's outcry, is a matter of civic pride.

Let me continue to drive them together—a scandal in its own right, an inescapable wrongdoing but not entirely unjust. Behind their remarkable oeuvres, neither Hamacher nor Kittler sign, properly speaking, a German critique. I would say that each, according to scales of very unique deliberation and consequence, with distinct backdrop and sound system, *registers a complaint*. I'll constellate the grievance that they filed separately, imagining a hearing for the persuasive plaintiffs, accommodating where I can the relevant schemes of noncontemporaneous simultaneity. Let us not pretend to deal out results or final assessments and dialectical summations of the way they tuned their work to what Hamacher calls an "advokatorischen Ethik" (an advocatory ethics)—for who (or what) has the right to complain?[13] Who represents those who cannot even complain? And what gives one a free pass as concerns a rich diversity of plaintive stances? One does not want to reduce the plaintiffs to a single thumbprint, even in our day and age of condensation, forensic identification, and techno-abbreviation or creative shuffling. Their relation to the complaint remains at times stealth and somewhat unruly—maybe merely personal in some forms of address. The problem of leading off with two very distinct signatories, even for the purpose of scoring some valid points, remains somewhat unmanageable, if not entirely unjustifiable. This complication will not hold me back.

How does one register a complaint? Who has the right to complain? Does the complaint issue from a place of impotence or does it have the potential to move mountains—or, more scaled down, can it arrive at any destination whatsoever (meaning: at no or, rather, all sorts of overdetermined or underestimated destinations)? Perhaps the complaint serves as a last-ditch utterance reserved for minoritized stances or diminishments—or are their envoys precisely banned from complaining, raising objections? Does authority deign to complain, and can power dispense with the urge to complain, relinquishing the need to throw down grievances? "Stop complaining, woman!" loops through internal sound systems, misogynist and unhinging. Do real men complain? Or is the complaint not radically incompatible with the worldly thrusts of any lean, mean fighting machine? What about the silent complaint? *So many questions, so little time.* When women and a child complain, they are hushed by an authoritarian glare. Routinely shutdown or merely tolerated, they bounce their complaints around the block until dinner-time.

My own engagement with the complaint, as a prevalent but largely undocumented form of saying, skids off an earlier preoccupation with the *greeting*—the problematic of the salutation that set off Heidegger when he was closing in on destinal aspects of Friedrich Hölderlin's poem, "Andenken" (Remembrance). What it means to be greeted and how being-greeted flows off a greeting from the sacred, bringing the greeted one into existence each time anew, opens an area of poetic saying that Heidegger covers with care, if also distortion. Seized by the quotidian adventure of greeting people on the streets, whether or not one "knows" them, one can test an observation that I have made repeatedly in unwritten walks of life. Like other anxious creatures, I can exhibit overfriendliness, which seems fine to me, but gets the pique of some reserved friends. In any case, I make it a point to greet others—maybe an American default position of troubled sociality, I don't know. Well-to-do people do not systematically return my greeting. Same goes for the self-involved cold fish I stupidly welcome for a split-second into my life, a searing and overextended split second. I have observed, however, that the poorest of the poor, or those whom one might consider to be stuck in miserable circumstances, tend to respond to my greeting in similar ways: Driving on the New Jersey Turnpike, asking the man in the tollbooth how he was doing, I was met with the reply, "I can't complain." The doorman at a friend's building who had broken his leg and received no worker's compensation, too, could not complain. As well as a street vendor from Nepal who stayed in his container under impossible conditions of over-heat or winter blizzards. He, too, cannot complain but effusively thanks me for the cups of coffee I bring, or the cooling lemonade. Not a grumble. I wondered about this calm, glacialized stoop of resignation—the grace of the destitute, scenes of mute compliance. Close to this experience, but matching it elsewise, my friend Peter, elegant and close to the vest of all manner of things, used to say, "Don't complain, don't explain"—the stiff-upper-lip thing, reticent and pulled together, entirely in keeping with his Irish British demeanor.

The absence of a complaint is a noteworthy event. Let me offer an untheorized example. My brother, who works in aviation, tells me that Samoan passengers were flown in abject circumstances, un-air-conditioned, unfed—add a series of "un-s" here to minimal comfort for which so-called first-worlders would clamor, issue threats, emitting from a place of entitlement, and not at all wrong to expect basic material forms of solace while flying. Not one passenger raised an objection, pressed for attention or accommodation. Not a peep. Silence, nearing the quiet buzz of auratic still shots, pervaded the plane. Let me break the description to raise a protest here.

Ach! Even at the starting gate, these reflections from the observatory of the complaint fall prey to my over-the-top misprision, a characteristic effect of the warps and distortions that I indulge when telescoping in on my friends. I feel rushed; I'm flailing. I guess, too, I am complaining. In the preface to *Daybreak*, Nietzsche rails against the hurry and flurry of today's overachievers, the "indecent and perspiring hastiness, which wants everything to 'get done at once,' including every new or old book," etc. He tags out the fast-track producers propelled by our institutions. Instead, we should read slowly, deeply, "with reservations, with doors left open."[14] Not with the door/law-slamming pace that harasses today's academic scholar and young job seeker who has to crunch pages like numbers.

Hamacher started his philological engine with the way elements of language stand up for one another, speaking for and explicating, even advocating, committed in large part to witnessing and sheltering. Yet, if I am getting this right, the defensive buildup in and around language never suffices to score stability or assure the reliability of meaning. Everywhere in his oeuvre, Hamacher famously discusses language's unreliability; in the recent work, however, I am finding on the part and parts of language more vulnerability and some willingness to intervene on its own behalf, ethically, as it were. Language attuned to its own plaintive cry, the *schreiben/Schrei* that keeps it in distress, but with more emergency supplies being delivered to fragile areas of utterance and assertion, more of a sense of *need* in play with *demand*—after all, he, Werner Hamacher, does nail theses to the door, which in Celan and Kafka, according to Derrida, means the law. Breaking down the door, the law. In the early days, when he had just begun his professorial run at Johns Hopkins, we had dinner at his house one evening, following a lecture. The kids started the music blaring, ramping up the energy around the table. We sipped soup to "Burning Down the House." Was it a stroke of irony that Talking Heads accompanied us through much of the three courses? I am remembering Ursel, Wellbery, and Nägele at the table, and I see Gasché, too—but I have a sense that he might be a drop-in from a screen memory. Propositions, in "their demand to be heard, understood, answered," propositions "belong to a language that for its own part is not structured as proposition, but as claim, as plea, wish, or desire."[15] Let me continue to underscore the predicament of want in language, proceeding from the cry, in this instance, untranslatably set in the *Theses*, as part of a longstanding plaint to which philology cables its responsive advocacy—however remote, however dimly apprehended.

Graceless Klage. I am thinking. I am puzzling. Soon the question must be faced of the relation of *thinking* to complaining. I apply for a permit for writing a provisional tract, *Was heißt (sich) Beschweren?*—What Is Called Complaining? Twinned to *What Is Called Thinking?*, the projected work asks how the complaint behaves as a call. I know, I know. Why would one want to twin anything to that name, ethically in the crapper. I have explained myself on this point and have directed harsh words elsewhere, beginning with the critical engagement of telephony as a synecdoche of technology—and eventually moving into regions of self-acknowledged *stupidity* on the part of Heidegger. Despite the grievances filed against him, the work, which in many ways exceeds its signatory instance and condemns the name it bears, continues to break open pathways.

Believe me, I am sick over the scene of disturbed transfer and the complaints I have to field due to an unavoidable commitment to thinking. This very aggravation of choices made or imposed in the tattered name of thinking is where I want to sit, in the fire of impossible connection to what hurts and sears. I am sorry and apologize to those whose sense of cleanliness and probity is offended. I dwell in life's messiness, sometimes atrocious and strictly unjustifiable. It hurts me, but I can't go clean or take on the purities, make a pitch for a cover of theoretical propriety that would mop up the stinky facets of what we face. Next to "iRony," ambivalence is my middle name.[16] In a Bataillean way and out of loyalty to the unswept portions of Being, I like to keep it dirty. Nearly everything world-historically accorded remains a source of endless aggravation for my fragile sensibility. I am reminded of what Philip Roth says in *Portnoy's Complaint.* For years, the protagonist, Alexander Portnoy, had assumed that "aggravation" was a Jewish word, a Yiddish locution. I am bound to aggravation by archaic contract. Hence the returns to Heidegger's overdrawn account and still unexpired text.

I was considering "sich beschweren," a German version of complaining on which both colloquial habit and Goethe sometime pivot. Heidegger would not show much tolerance for the insinuation of the "sich" in this form of address, even if I were to shift over to "sich beklagen," the loftier locution as these things go. Still, the queer adversity of a Heideggerian insert usefully stalls us and teaches something. Heidegger might be the anti-complainer in tone and mood, even though he bulked up on stores of *Sorge* (care). Part of the Greco-Christian stance may well have been to brake—or mask—the complaining reversion of being. Thinking has inclined toward thanking. Denkers and Dankers, thinkers and thankers do not complain, unless your name is Nietzsche and you can do both at once, will-to-power style.

Nietzsche and Dostoevsky would say that Christ on the cross details one searing complaint tossed out into history, thank you Yahweh, and there are those who continue to bicker with a sadistic Gd-the-father, but these outcries remain a matter for speculative theology. To put it in condensed form, perhaps too readably pitched, and therefore in need of interpretive tonnage, one could say, riffing off Jean-Luc Nancy, that the Christian demeanor is styled to *praise*, to offer praise in song to creation, and so strategically suited to drop the call of complaint for which Jeremiah serves as stand-out figure. In this regard, and following the protocols of reading such a claim with care and caution—I apologize for the drive-by and the way I'm throwing some of these contentions in reverse, I apologize for apologizing as if we wanted to "advance," assuming such a thing to be possible—Christian praise persists as the repression of the Jewish complaint. Both modes of address say something about the way we falter and fail to find an address, yet are turned toward the lamentable or praiseworthy near-yet-ungraspable divinity, each stance forgetting and repealing the one from which it emerges and into which it must return.

Here's how I see it from my precarious perch: Jesus of Nazareth came to us equipped with a quota of one complaint, delivered the night before the cross. The question of abandoned being, sounded on the cross, may not qualify, strictly speaking, as complaint, but opens up the darkening space of non-address for the fate of every complaint to come.

Still, the schema of assigning grammars of praise and complaint—not mine, but culturally imprinted—breaks over the rock of exaggerated simplicity. Gd breaks the seal of simplicity, issuing license for the "double dealing," as Ann Smock would say, of praise/complaint structures. Does the monotheistic deity come down on one side or the other? Gd, one could argue, complains all the time. Biblical celebrities have taken signature positions: Job, inventing a contestatory form of address, accepts; Jeremiah laments. Sarah—she laughs, also a type of complaining. I limit myself to this panorama shot, without coming in for a close-up at this time. I admit and lament the condensation: there's still far too much warp, even for my standards, which commonly tolerate glutted warps and semantic trespasses. One still needs to review and revise, with care and a refined sense of displacement, the well-demarcated projection of the Jewish culture as a *Klagekultur*, as bedrock and container of dejectionism—in other words, one must continue to tap out a perspective of Jewish culture seen as the home base of the carper, calling attention to the figure of an irremediable malcontent.

As it stands, the projection that I inadvertently retransmitted on these pages remains insufficient and mendacious, leaving out entire chapters of *Lebensfreude*—wit, inventiveness, consistent and wide-ranging reflection on the conditions of freedom. Undeniably, this projection has ignoble historical edges, and some of one's best friends, including introjected pipelines and squawk boxes, have raised the objection to Jewish-accented complaining, leading one to listen again to those cultures that claim immunity from certain behaviors and acts of grievance, and, in some sectors, how they would like to see a halt in the allegedly unceasing Jewish complaint about the Holocaust. The complaint launched against a widely held perception—that of a compulsive complaint syndrome—opens a delicate historical juncture, difficult to articulate or bear. What does it mean to demand a stop to complaint, to timetable a legitimate grievance and pencil in a final heave? I'm not sure. In some instances, without coercion or hostility backing up the insistence on cessation, it can help the one seized up by the *need* to keep the complaint alive, but a lot depends on who's asking for an end to the complaint and the right not to complain—and who's running laps as a self-designated complainer.

The "complaint" scores low ratings consistently because it comes off as aggressive, impolite—*unhöflich*, leaving victims in the quagmire of an aporetic trap, on the side of the unsavory and dubious, bound by something that overly discloses, and, so, cannot be viewed simply as relating to what is true. I purposefully swerve from the cultures of lament in order to clear the decks for the complaint, no doubt a downgrade and awkward scramble in terms of the prestige of any presentation of solemn assertion. By putting the focus on the reverberations of complaint, rather than on the sonic signatures of lament, without opposing them, I am seeking to update the fate of the lament into a modern tonality and rhetorical arrangement.

The lament carries some gravity, rises above itself to address an often inaccessible alterity. It carries a rich musical and poetic history to back it up and steer it forward. The complaint is of another order—something that the Bible itself tries to send through some anger management programs. Dropped off to fend for itself without transcendental imprinting or onto-theological breeding, the complaint squeezes out a tiny tinny voice, peeps up whiny and shrill, secondary in the lineup of contestatory uprisings that language has hosted, pushed to the back row of challenging syntactical maneuvers. The lament, as Hamacher points out, stands a paradoxical ground, for it wants its

Ach! The History of a Complaint

own abolition, hoping to stamp itself out.[17] In sum, the lament cries "I want an end to this suffering!" The desired invalidation, the self-ending of itself as lament bears down hard, even when issued from the knowing stance of dilemma and self-obstruction, confronts the hazard of not being able to put an end to its case and condition.

Not so much with the complaint, which seems, in terms of its downgrade and modernization, relentlessly reproducible, mechanically set to repeat its hollowed message, survive its expiration. One might even venture to say, though such distinctions can be only wobbly and provisional, that the lament has known itself to be affined to mourning, calling out to and, dramatically, *from* its lost object. The complaint, by preliminary contrast, sidesteps any ritual assertion of mourning. Resisting a fixed relation to loss, the complaint seems unable to mourn. Unable to let go, the complaint may well indicate a symptomatic snag and refusal, a mourning disorder. To the extent that the complaint cannot mourn but nonetheless bemoans, it shares the stances and existential allowances of melancholia and sister disorders. One thinks of the grinding machines that run the language centers of chronic complainers.

At the same time—here's the rub—melancholia aggravates and digs in, showing an end run around worldly aggravation, with the statement "I cannot complain." Because the complaint is also a release, perhaps a mere second stringer in terms of modalities of thinking, it responds and corresponds to the imperfect world of expropriation, it touches down in the neighborhood of thinking.[18] Any delivery of the complaint has something of a critical bite, profiling a commencing reflection and some subtle flex of rejection, a push of intelligent nay-saying. The complaint, running on empty or advocating world-historical change, puts up a fight against the "what-is" of life. It says a number of things, with or without the backing of truth value, putting pressure on world: that something is wrong, or that a limit has been breached, that the intolerable has made an appearance worth noting or saying "no" to, urging a pushback on its encroachments.

Thinking and criticism, while often affined, are not merely interchangeable on the philosophical ledger; sometimes they hinder or contradict each other. In some ways, Heidegger kept thinking clear of critical incursion to the extent that polemical lunges were counted out by his considerations of thinking and the regional prestige of academic disquisitions, critical approaches, scientific method were scoffed at. Nonetheless, we have to contend with the fact that a critical mind, or critical thought, even critique, launches indispensable probes on the back of the complaint—all tuned to a queasy squirm of dissatisfaction. *Ach!*

Some Daseins score well in the "what-is" of life; they are sharp and on top of things, capable, at least momentarily, of coping and surviving the onslaught of things. One doesn't have to be a Heideggerian brought up by Levinas to sense that such capable maneuvers have little to do with *thinking* and its dosage of passivities. Thinking runs on parallel tracks with the relinquishment pulsing at the core of complaint.

The victims in de Sade have no *right* to complain. Complaining would annoy the dominators, who themselves flaunt the right not to raise a complaint as they command the scene of sadistic supremacy. Why would they indulge or emit a complaint?

I took a break in order to prepare the sections on critique and complaint, meaning to show how they don't meld, yet how nonetheless they manage to inch up on each other's turf. Everyone knows how writing a piece of criticism does not involve the same gesture as launching a complaint. Right? Then I thought, wait, aren't all my launches part of an uninterrupted complaint? Yes, but . . . no, but, I whirligigged. Goethe's oeuvre, he once offered, was one big confession. What if others were given over to those sorts of rolled-up statements? How would they distill their writing to an Instagram? My writing in some ways feeds one big complaint. I recruit to this description the way Derrida picks up on Heidegger's *Schreiben/schrei*, the *cri/écrit*—a micro-event that I can't seem to shake and shray about at every possible and impossible opportunity. (I have to wonder how Heidegger takes the Yiddish reinscription of the scream/*Schrei*. Well, he should be so lucky!)

Then, in a way that I can allow myself to puzzle out when I'm off duty, I start wondering about a friend of mine, her biggest complaints, the ones that qualify her to frequent, if halfway controlled, rounds of rage. Her most frequent complaint—*not including medical complaints*—concerns—*not including how stupid and cruel and puerile the humans can be*—some avowed difficulty—*not including how some so-called intellectual positions are resentment-laden and lame, or politics unworthy of the name, or justice unserved, or racist complacence, or housing insufficiency, cruelty, indifference, and greed*—when it comes to cathecting absence. This makes her no different from so many others, also anxious creatures, coping with different forms and points of no return. Her most frequent complaint, explicitly scored, amounts, at first sight, to something quite common: "You never call!" "You never write!" "You give up no *Lebenszeichen*"—no sign of life. Her day-to-day complaints concern varying modes of non-appearance, the shrewd persecutions of an elusive friend. Where the hell have they been, these mock friends? She is getting over this, over them, she tells herself, I am healing myself of this complaint, its compulsive dogging of my being. The plaint's intensities have significantly subsided. There's still a tinge, a leftover sting to reckon with, however.

For Aristotle, the friend's lapse and lag in terms of timed responsiveness give grounds for termination. For me, it all depends on how you clock in, and since I live in dog time while others appear to exist in the temporal frenzy of a fly, we naturally come to blows. My abandonment "issues" are by now well documented, if not very unique. This "human condition" may correspond to the very nature of abandonment—one is left hanging, alone, I mean, as Benjamin says in his essay on Karl Kraus and *Die Verlassenen* (The abandoned ones), apropos of the figures on Greek vases, coldly abandoned. So, not quite unique, my total war with abandonment. Still, one feels quite unique when left on one's own like an idiot, even on the subway platform, or holding one's phone in one's hand like a phantom member, waiting for a call. One is left waiting on edge, waiting for the walled-in silence to crumble.

This glimpse at my catalog of complaining in a minor key may seem trifling indeed, subjective and contingent. (I don't usually succumb to "subjective"; I will let that slide for now, if only for the purpose of delivering a drop of provisional commonsense.) The complaint of abandonment is world-historical, even if it dwindles down to focusing a solitary figure on the subway platform. It rings an ancient bell, a death knell prior to any resurrection. Such a scene has everything to do with the call you have answered before you could speak. It may have been a stray call. As finite being, you have answered the call; if you are a Kafka baby, you are set even to answer the call not meant for you, or you find yourself one day, maybe on your birthday, called up by a jamming device that lands you in a god-forsaken castle territory, an architectural aggregate that shows up as someone else's housing project—not even the house of being, languageless. Now, OMG, I have to wonder if the complaint I have exposed, bordering on an unabating program of whines and bitches, does not constitute the most prevalent and essential instances given the ontological weight of things. *Why have you not called?* This question, the customized SCHREI to which I subscribe, has hounded me from book one; it will not shake loose. So—why haven't you?

We might consider how the complaint, companion to grievance, implies melancholia, and unleashes the energy of protest—even when it stands, in some historical instances, for the aborted revolt. I have always been fascinated by those who do not raise their little finger to protest, who dare not complain in the proud whistleblower poise of landing their complaint—admittedly, a very risky business. The non-complainers get all the credit, staying within the boundaries of coded gracefulness. *It is not graceful to complain.* My dilemma: ego-ideal wants me to be graceful. But I must complain. Sometimes I want to raise myself to the dignity of the unsounded complaint. It would be more comfortable to pull back, stop howling, go soft and compliant. Though compliancy, as Phillis Wheatley, poet of slavery's wreckage, has taught us, also bunks with the complaint following a syntax of holding back and breaking rhyme. The muted complaint holds up in the wake of a massive retraction.

The other day, in a Paris bookstore (there are practically no bookstores anymore in New York City. I want to call 3-1-1 to complain about this depraved state of affairs, the demise of noncorporate booksellers. The operators at 3-1-1 have shown me indulgence. They field my calls with some efficiency, prove to be polite and on it; they respond as if the complaint were part of a civic emergency alert. How smart of the city to divert the force of my protest by instituting this telephone line! New Yorkers need to have a pop-up address whose sole agency consists in directing their complaints. Very shrewd bit of crowd control) in the bookstore, then, there was a person, miming a child she was accompanying, a person who kept on saying "Non!" "Non, non!" This reverberating performance, loud and unceasing, interrupted my ability to select a book. Usually music interferes with my bookstore expeditions. Pierre, taking note of my irritation, pointed out to me that the child's first experience of originating "No!" is an ecstatic one, a real existential curtain-raiser: the ability to say *no* points up a great flex of *Selbstbehauptung*, self-affirmation.

It took me forever to say "no," and it's still not my forte. Hence anything with a down-thumbing inclination requires effort; the protest, the complaint, takes a lot out of me, stymying my energy—exhausting me like the hovering burden of a Kantian imperative. So categorical! Nietzsche teaches us to dance with the *Nicht*, the knot of not, part of the way he spells his name and goes down in negativity. Then comes up again, for air.

Nietzsche urges us to release the complaint from its resentimental grip. You want to complain? Then do so without any hint of resentment.

Ach! The History of a Complaint

O was ist der Mensch / what a piece of work is man. Nowadays Goethe would have agitated for a trade when deciding on a title for *The Sorrows of Young Werther*, his breakout novel. Napoleon took it along for ammo on his blood-soaked campaign of *Weltgeist* proportion, read and reread it, questioned and instructed Goethe on a thing or two. The great conqueror complained that Goethe had mismanaged the storyline but was definitely responsible for more deaths than the Napoleonic army. Everyone was struck by the work's unprecedented ballistics. Considering the tempo of the work that mimetically entrapped so many in its highly insistent suicidal rush, I wonder if Goethe today would drop "sorrows" or "suffering" for "flip-out" or something more up-to-date, more strung-out and frazzled.

Goethe handled the anxiety of *Leiden* (suffering), of course, in part because it refer us to *Leidenschaft*, passion, so that the hapless protagonist took the shuttle seasonally between suffering and passionate attachment, which often dropped him at the same station of being. *The Disconnect, Interruption, Hacking, Breakdown, Epic Fail, Final Call, Splitting, Harshed Mellow, etc., etc., of Young Werther* famously begins by declaring, on May 4, 1771, how glad the volatile protagonist is to have broken away from home. The first two paragraphs, setting up the movement and blueprint for the entire stash of letters, shift from modes of lamenting to the structure of the complaint—from *klagen* to *(sich) beschweren*, in fact to "meiner Mutter Beschwerden," sounding off on the maternal complaint.

Werther starts a correspondence with his best friend, asking after that which constitutes the human heart. As he starts up the work that will propel Goethe into world-historical stature, Werther recalls a catastrophic story that he has left behind. He had broken a girl's heart, disavowing accountability; then, after all, he admits guilt in the letter for having instigated the way Leonore was run down by rogue emotion. In the midst of the opening salvo of this text, consisting of many letters and an editorial intervention—the correspondence makes up one long suicide note, put to public notice by the notary-editor—Werther disturbs the syntax, puncturing a hole in his narrative after the word "nicht," not. He cries out ontologically, asking what (not *who*) is man, that s/he can lament. "Der Mensch" does not match exactly or only with "man," but could mean "human" or indicate "personhood," depending on the stress of context.

Werther has just put up for show the lamentable fate of a girl wronged by him in the past and whose injury, as his story unfolds, he secretly incorporates. Invaded by Leonore—in some ways a faded and vanishing memory, yet still showing up as a pinprick of conscience—he is, from the start, set to become his own victim, played by fate, infected by the compulsion to repeat. Werther, in

CHAPTER 2

any case, delicate and artistic, undertowed by guilt toward the one who precedes the text, floods his letters drop by drop with tears and uncontrolled gushes.

> Hab ich nicht—O was ist der Mensch, daß er über sich klagen darf! Ich will, lieber Freund, ich verspreche dirs, ich will mich bessern, will nicht mehr ein bißchen Übel, daß uns das Schicksal vorlegt, wiederkäuen, wie ich's immer getan habe; ich will das Gegenwärtige geniessen, und das Vergangene soll mir vergangen sein. (Erstes Buch, 8)

> Didn't I—oh what is man that he is allowed to complain about himself! I will, my dear friend, I promise you, I will improve, I will not chew over the bit of woe that fate presents us with, the way I have always done; I will enjoy the present and let bygones be bygones—*let the past stay in the past* [emphasis added].[19]

Big mistake. *I am going to put the past behind me*: stated as if Goethe had not been coached by Freud about mangled suppressions of the past, bound to assail and wreck you down the road.[20] In any case, Werther prepares the furious return of a story he thought he could leave behind at the outset. Still, not every destructive impulse is accounted for in the brakeless work. We should neither be satisfied with causality nor seduced by mere narrative coherency, especially given Goethe's syntactical breaches and spurning of logical buildup. One of Goethe's enduring sparks of insight, to be picked up by Søren Kierkegaard, fires up the *Krankheit zum Tode* motif, the sickness unto death, that pushes Werther over the edge by driving down his defenses regardless of logic, rational rebuff, or any manner of developmental projects for growing personhood. The deadly drive, in a sense driverless, is deposited in Werther like a virus, and the work itself behaves like a virus that cannot be stopped or redirected by prevalent Enlightenment policies or philosophical critique. Something in Werther relentlessly pushes him to his smashup. No theory or doctor of philosophy in the area of rational self-righting could be appointed to deter the destruction that was assigned to young Werther.

Werther's own theory of ruin begins with a big "O," sign of lament, the opening and closure, syncope, of a round of nothingness that initiates the double character of the lamenting word, which deplores its predicament: Werther laments that lament is at all allotted to us. This capacity—or send-up of incapacitation—has everything to do with the definition of man, of womanly man, the manly feminine that seizes him at moments of textual tension. The license to lament in itself constitutes the trespass in the opening pages of the novel—before anything *happens*. Why am I even allowed to lament? Does not this capacity for hoisting incapacitating statement spell disaster? The second paragraph restarts on a neighboring note, on lament's irony. Thus, ironically,

Ach! The History of a Complaint

when the second paragraph downshifts to the complaint, the scene settles in the realm of the manageable, grasped in terms of the strictly possible. Lament places the speaker, or wailer, under constraint of the impossible, provoking a backslide into unavowable catastrophe. Already on page one.

When Werther breaks away, he promises, emphatically, in the sense that Hamacher has taught us to read—I *ver-spreche*, I misspeak/promise at one and the same time, for I cannot promise, strictly speaking, but may only promise to promise and thereby skid off the promise, since the promise can only fulfill itself in the future of its assertion and not in the present to which it's proffered. This means, according to strict logic and grammatical prescription, that the promise can never be fulfilled, not now—Werther promises to put an end to the lament, rhetorically breaking into a lament—O—, canceling and initiating his writing of disaster, but never mind, let us not tag him out in letter I merely because he breaks his promise about stopping with the lament already, lamenting that he laments, ironizing his dilemma, promising never to do so again as he's doing it again before having started, dropping into bleak irony.—O—.

I have misquoted—or, rather, misappropriated; I took a misstep in thinking through to the end what is happening in the phrasing of the lament. *I took the question for a question*—again, one of Heidegger's, Derrida's, Hamacher's themes, dealing with the philosophical compulsion to question. Wait. Maybe my misstep is merely a matter of grammatical adjustment, and not indicative of full-throttle Goethean anacoluthic eccentricity. Maybe the culture of the question rings differently in German and English. Give me a close-up of the emergent lament. This is important. The better part of my argument hangs on a diacritical mark, merde! The break-in sentence ends in point of fact on an *exclamation mark*, not a *question mark*. I suppose we could say that the refusal to yield a question mark falls in line with Hamlet's utterance, "What a piece of work is man!"—quite different from "What a piece of work is man?"—I take the liberty of inventing a new folio to support this instance: a revelatory force is put behind the assertion. The flow of Shakespeare's language steers the observation away from a questioning pose, whereas Werther, echoing and diverting this sense of things, is caught somewhere between the question and the assertion. Man is the lamenting animal, yes? Or, what is it that allows one to lament? Is this the end of man, where one breaks off from the human, cut from the determinations of language, primed to become a howling creature? What even permits the human to lament, a quality or act that transpierces the properly human being of the human? The lament not only brings out the improper, but tips toward the inhuman, introducing the inoperative zone of the "human animal." (Let us remember that *Werther* was on the nameless monster's reading list in Mary Shelley's *Frankenstein*.) This moment of original

CHAPTER 2

complaint—he complains that he laments—leads off the textual encounter and marks the spot where Werther tenders his resignation, makes the promise to cease lament in a pull toward Enlightenment perfectibility: I promise to improve myself. I shall stop lamenting. We understand that lament for Werther presses and depends on repetition, opening up the uncontrolled domain of surrender and prepossession. Werther's promise? To stop tapping out the same story over and again, to stop obsessing on the little bit of malevolence that fate has thrown at him. That's who he used to be. Now he will—stay loyal to *now*, "stay in the present," enjoy only the present moment as he finishes with a past that must remain in the past. Except, except that the pain of the past keeps being called back into the present, repeating itself on compulsion.

Nonetheless, Werther's first letter contours a promissory note stating that the past is past, I mean, grammatically, that the past has passed, from now on it stays in the past, I will enjoy the present, a determined position that entails suppressing lament. Let's not even go to the Derridean sticking point of the repression of writing that Werther's vow requisitions. He writes that he will stay present, off repetition, implying that he will not kick into writing. His task makes him attend to as he gives it up (much as he gives up painting in favor of the purported fullness of being), opening and closing a range of writing indissociable from lamentation. This book, the envoy promises, will not be a lamentation. It will be a book without writing. I promise.—O—

The complaint presupposes an address, probably the wrong one.

Any good Nietzschean would comprehend by now that at least two valences uphold the complaint. Even a bad Nietzschean must concede this point. There's good complaining and bad complaining, the issuance of a noble and a decadent complaint. These can be further fissured around Freudian tracks that cover all sorts of minor scaling of the complaint as culture, behavioral grid, cult strength, medical description, legal notification, cultural queasiness (the so-called "Discontents" squatting in cultural *Unbehagen*), lamentable weakness and narcissistic soft spot. The constant complainer, whimpering with no off switch, grinding down on world, can come from a place of weakness, wearing away any vitality that life has to offer, whining to exhaustion, shutting down responsiveness regardless of the push-off point from referential injury. On the other hand, following the lineage of Nietzsche's "noble traitor," one could imagine the *bold complainers* who muster up courage to say what wrongs our being-in-common and lights up the bright sense of justice, who risk incivility in the name of civility, taking to the transfeminist lookout post, the in-your-face act-uppers, and those who take to the streets. The ability to wield a complaint in the face of mute indifference or oppressive silencers can advocate life's capacity to power up and adjust vivaciously.[21] In this regard, the bold complainer squares off with a needling detractor as a life-affirmer, a Nietzschean warrior of resistance that legislates and affirms new addresses, new names, aims. Ever building up his spans and pathways, different tones of future philosophizing, Nietzsche makes room for a new class of affirmative disablers.

These opposing stances of complaint collapse into and support each other, contaminate and cross over into the fields of their adversarial type. I refrain from saying that the low-powered, constant whiner is *not* the most noble, even though we culturally pitch against all forms of ingratitude no matter how dire the conditions are from which they siren up. This is where Nietzsche comes in strongly, for the weak may mask the strongest perspectives, covering over the most powerful dispositions, whereas the seemingly strong use props of mendacity to accomplish their takeovers. Can the complaint reinforce advocacy for righteousness in the strong, good, Nietzschean sense allotted to things? Or, conversely but not absolutely: to what extent does the milieu and mark of complaint deplete and extinguish any bump of breakthrough joy? These are Nietzschean questions that kick in today according to their inherently strict yet untimely schedule, soliciting with nagging precision a time-released set of responses.

Though this may seem to come out of left field or from the orchestra pit, music is a player in the clash of complaint cultures. Keeping time, music comes out of the blue, returning furtively, at times, to the blues, which travel between lament and complaint, ever reverberating the plaintive cry lodged in classical to reggae registers of sounding off. The unceasing hums of distress—genres and subtly played subgenres of the musically pitched complaint—come in many forms. Bob Dylan and his progeny throw down one big plaintive report after another. Apart from hip-hop constellations and rap broadcasts, punk movements and their successors place high among the more overt venues for lodging a whole series of complaints, as perhaps is the case with the greater part of the rock 'n' roll inventory, still awaiting the Nietzschean evaluative grid as music and noise-articulations mutate persistently. The appeal to or of music does not announce an arbitrary application, for Nietzsche came on the scene in the spirit of music—and pharmacy. He eventually downgraded Wagner to bad drugs, illicitly scored and harmful to the vitality of those who addictively listen. Nietzsche was keeping his own scoreboard, marking its character and measuring the worth of musical returns. He makes the very definition of humankind dependent on rhythm, but the essential character of rhythm was an ancient Greek thing that can be pursued in the work of Philippe Lacoue-Labarthe.

Complaints carry good and bad tonalities, worthy and derisory qualities in terms of their launch pad and aims. A good complaint would be prepped with the energy of critique, enabling a Nietzschean-genealogical scan and sense of how things have deteriorated or overreached, according to what sorts of subterranean logic or seismic shifts in grammar and being. Nietzsche, in ready complicity with Freud, has a sharp sense for the profit margins of destructive histories. Who, they ask, are the secret beneficiaries of a certain constellation of incidents or belief clusters? Who is served by traditional safeguards and the sticking points of normativity? What are the decoys or beards or undeclared blood sports waged in support of certain occurrences or rolled in for the prevention of beneficent, if disjunctive, life-forms of growth and kinship?

A well-aimed complaint can change the course of historical wrongdoing, putting in place an ethical 3-1-1 call. Such a disruption of inane consensus begins its essential chain by showing attunement to tradition without norm, to the way language plays you, cracking open the delusional playbooks that tend to hold sway over entire warps of attitude (what Husserl calls *Einstellung*). The Bible has booked a strong inventory of social injustice. Yet a cynical practice of bad translation, a steady dephilologization, I would say, has been notoriously used by death-driven haters such as the Christian Right to launch destructive complaints against social minorities and designated groups of construed deviants. As if Gd were clear and readable—and spoke English!—on any day of creation. I wish to stand as plaintiff here on the side of a *right to opacity*, operating a scrambling machine meant to ensure specific forms of social justice.[22]

Let us call up Babel.

For many years, I have worked in seminar on the bare signifier *trans-*, which accounts for so many of the highly invested movements and transfigurations of theoretical note to which we find ourselves commonly tied. Alongside the many possible trajectories, illicit and altogether conventional, of the *trans-*, the transferential implications of the work of translation ranks high on the list of its potentiating qualities.

In the "Tours de Babel" essay that some of us continue to study, Derrida, passing through or as Benjamin, opens up the eventfulness of our babelization, the many transgressions and boundary assaults that led to punishing

Ach! The History of a Complaint

paybacks, exposing the divine reactivity to the push for transparency, *one language*.[23] Someone registered a complaint, of biblical proportions: *"I don't think so,"* Yaweh said, kicking down the first skyscraper. Or, rather, turning it into a condemned site, a generator of *"deshem*ination," Derrida says, turning on the name of the *shem*, releasing its propensity for disseminating into far-flung approximations. Henceforth, to fast forward, translation ruled, bringing home our broken relation to sense and meaning. Why is this particular story of divine grievance, a tipping point of the complaint, important for us today? How has the story of Babel been forgotten or debabelized as Gd's words are yanked into ever-regressing territories of national religious anxieties and their destructive analogs? The greater part of the lexicon of contemporary forms of injustice stems from Bible-thumping quoting activity. Even "in God we trust" has no footing in the book of books. For the Bible has uprooted trust as it says something about the very quotability of its phrasing and the way complaints are lodged in its name, according to the way it pages us.

Benjamin set this understanding on us, and Derrida cleared the way: Babel means that you *cannot*, under any circumstances, say, "because the Bible says so." One is prohibited from saying anything with the secured sense of biblical injunction or assertion, because transparency is itself under biblical lock: the words are constitutively scrambled. Installed and at its core, the Bible trembles with rage, under gag order, because Gd Him/Her/Itself has launched the *trans-*, and forbidden any settlement with assured intention or meaning or election or sanction or homophobic announcement or clear-cut statement to the extent that it, the Bible, has incorporated a trans-machine, altering, transferring, transvaluating, transposing, and translating from the ground up, endlessly. Traumatic norming comes into play only in the mode of delayed reactivity, at the site of discredited utterance, a gift of divine violence. Let me add my blessing to this self-violating miracle: *Thank you, Gd. Thank you for giving us Babel, baby Babel, as your language of choice, thank you for the gift of unreadability, for the complaint that was thundered on the myth of transparency, the urge toward one meaning,* monography—*and for enjoining the task of the translator.*

Thank you for the irreparable damage you gifted us with, without which we would have license to think and say that we know.[24]

Protest movements of note have been dealt severe blows and in significant ways threatened with complete shutdown. Nonetheless, one finds forms, however insufficient and limited, to swarm egregious outbreaks of injustice with agitated protestation. Whether or not creative and daredevilish, as in Oregon's "Shell no!" manifestations or Cranfield and Slade's *10 Riot Songs* album, or with a Black Lives Matter demonstration or the dazzle of the Bernie Sanders presidential campaign, the Women's March, or Mohammed Ali's poetry of resistance—and all the subgenres of protest that we are capable of working up in this country—civic forms of grievance often hit a brick wall or must cool off precipitously, suffer police action and various excuses for "crowd control."

Being a political activist in the United States of America looks different than, and is at variance with, neighboring patterns of intervention, outrage, plaint, and petition. French folks seem to know how to get in the streets and rumble with the discursive and material shutdowns of power. They can even make a difference, kick up dust in the face of oppressive measures and disturbing decrees. Not always, but sometimes. In this country, by contrast, we're more like Kantian theorists, the ones profiled in the *Perpetual Peace* treaty: essentially on their own, philosophers/theorists fire blank shots, for no one cares what they have to say, and they barely make a dent in public policy. They advocate without reinforcements or coercive persuasion. Maybe someone will pick up the discursive drift and, if so, probably the wrong party or only in a mangled way, which is inevitable: permanent scramble. That's the American way, even nowadays, when "deconstruction" is hijacked by the far right as a designation for constitutional degradation and civic injury. But this sorry state of affairs lays a lot of responsibility on us to shoot off and remain vigilant in the most unexpected, least measurable ways. We are honor-bound to fire away. I will not belabor the point. Obviously, when philosophers weigh in on politics, the results can be disastrous. So I am not entirely opposed to a nearly universal restraining order on the philosophical compulsion to intervene on so-called political turf. Nor do I welcome the death threats that ensue when someone or other accidentally reads something. Some of us however are different from the others, I tell myself. We should have a special pass. Take my ability to analyze phenomena with extreme patience and neurotic exactitude. *I can be trusted*: I could make democracy work, and reroute capital in serious ways. Every day I sit at my desk waiting for the call to action, prepared to offer theoretical counsel and psychoanalytic acumen, perhaps a philosophical background check on all sorts of currencies and events that are about to happen or fail to take place. I could warn nations to avoid treacherous zones of phallogocentric compulsion and paleonymic reprisals. My knowledge could help prevent wars. "Warum Krieg?" (Why war?), as Freud and Einstein said to each other in their correspondence, passing the torch, thinking already of me. I could bring substance to health reform and help along with healing traumatic wounds of desperate circumstances, unrelenting surveillance techniques and searing displacements. But no one calls me, not even accidentally, from one of the lowest offices of the West Wing administrators. I waited around in vain during the Obama years,

Ach! The History of a Complaint

ready to explicate false moves and create safeguards for our fragile democratic institutions. I foresaw the calamity of vulgar lawlessness and catachrestic misogyny—who grabs *"by* the pussy"? What or where is that? There's no doubt about it: I could have analyzed disavowal and its discontents, averted disaster with my critical acumen. But I sat in solitary, like other demystifying tools, cast aside by the deciders. This waiting around for nothing, too, constitutes a task, I suppose, a calling—a service, perhaps, in the sense of being laid off often described by Kafka and Robert Walser. Well, thank Gd that Kant understood my predicament and addressed it to my satisfaction. At least we have that, I tell myself.

Look, Kant or no Kant, I don't like to think of myself as a complainer—such a job description does not suit my sense of honor or humor, and falters when it's supposed to match up with my off-the-rack elegance or responsible state of alert. The mission statement concerning the complaint fails to flatter my militant sensibility—it seems not to go far enough when shooting up a dummy target or sounding social outrage—even though Goethe Himself offers substantial backup for such an investigation and stance of preparedness. Now I'm wondering: What got me riled up enough in the first place about the paraconcept of grievance, or propelled me to probe the contours of civic grief? What about these topoi and their thronging themes had me forego a single day of so-called free time in order to attend to the urgent claims of complaint culture? Now I'm thinking, maybe I need to explain myself after all? Let me make the effort at least to give a sense of where I'm coming from. Why do I write about some things and not others? What are the essential stressors? What in my history am I unable to shake loose?

I suppose that a lot of the thematic pressure in this study arises from a kind of "rights of nerves" dictum handed down to us by Walter Benjamin and Karl Kraus. One is moved along in one's relentless study by things or quasi-events that can deter and destroy the scholar-artist, disable the thinker, and confound the philosopher or fervent social activist—to the point at least of shaking confidence in the sliver of a world that may have seemed secured for a while.

Writing, goaded in part by nerve states, is sponsored by the noise of existential shattering, psychic moroseness, by what enervates and "fragilizes," as the French would say. For instance, when things became difficult or irrespirable for me on the West or East Coasts, I started some of my inscriptions, held them down to page or paper, to paperless scratch notes (let me spare you further autobiographical details such as why I ended up hating Berkeley, which, for the most part, nonetheless escapes me since, truth be told, I live in the *inoccurence* of my existence and, obstinately detached from my own history, I have to concede the point: Berkeley has charming qualities even in my absence and

CHAPTER 2

I needed a job after my years of wandering and I was overly grateful to those who recused themselves on decisive committees and, on good days, muted their theory-bashing habits so that I could stay on)—In the absence of solid footing one must be even more responsible to one's elusive history and to those who have thrown the brunt of their own stories into some of the stakes that were named or semi-forgotten. *Ach!* It is not easy to pinpoint one's starting point or to account for one's flailing self, hence the difficult yet necessary alignments with discourses of responsibility. I have always worried about the debilitated subject (a type of destitution, shorthand for a grim metaphysical power outage), reflective in the end of my own state of enervation. It is hard to go on, day after day, when the power or persuasion is down. Even so, whether—or not—a traumatized being can hold on to the events that are said to constitute a life, she must nonetheless give talks (sometimes), lead a professional life, and make her way through the desert of practical reason's apparent requirements.

For instance, as one can infer from the enduring chip on this shoulder, it was never easy looking for a job. No matter how well I cleaned up, I was never an obvious choice or sell for an academic career. I should think that others would meet with less obstruction. How could one not complain about the scandalous difficulty that young scholars face today trying to land a job, even the highly exploitative ones for which they are forced to be grateful? When it was my turn to find a home base, after some years at the University of Virginia, Riverside, and Berkeley, I was for a spell more or less blacklisted and had to calibrate institutional expectations, de-monsterize and dial myself down. At the same time, I could not simply forge a proper university ID in order to get low-grade security clearance. Who was I kidding? The deliberations with debilitated self were intense: I could present a restrained version of myself, and maybe the hiring committees would vote for me. I had to be my own cheerleading squad. Yes, I could be a viable candidate for a university position, I would tell myself. Yes we can! Why not? Look at the others who've made it through . . .

If you put on your allegorical ears, you will tune in to an institutional track and attack in these pages, in some ways muted like the death drive. The anxiety was always high. Looking back on the assembly line of frazzled nerve endings—I was impelled to produce work in the factory of damaged nerves—I note that a lot of my writing was motivated, from the start, by attacks on immigrant populations that continue to this day in all the countries I visit, even the most seemingly enlightened ones. The writers I select, from the eighteenth century to our now-time, have had something to say about the consistency of this phobic stance. Hence, I felt compelled to study some of the related motifs of expropriated being (or, in strict Heideggerian, *ex-appropriated* being), their political and theoretical implications.

Ach! The History of a Complaint

I try to take these texts to the mat, struggling with their sometimes indefensible edges and peculiar war cry, their logic of injury. My own itinerary includes substantial visitations with wildly incompatible malcontents from, say, Nietzsche, genealogical faultfinder, to Husserl, who sent up smoke signals that I am still trying to decipher, to Heidegger, who bellyached about how everything went downhill after the pre-Socratics, and Valerie Solanas, chronic grouser of the ends of man. Every one of the thinkers and innovators with whom I put in time and to whose frame of urgency I succumbed, including Derrida, Nancy, Dennis Cooper, Kathy Acker, Edouard Glissant, James Baldwin, a host of filmmakers, psychoanalysts, videographers, and poets, addressed life-threatening loopholes, calamitous defense mechanisms, conceptual glitches of vital theoretical gravity, and struggled with core survival issues. I took their complaints seriously.

I have spent years in the archives and have trained myself with little indulgence. (I stop myself for several minutes, wondering why I feel compelled to offer a training video—should I delete? Leave it in? What's my point? All college equivalency strivers can turn up the same measure of themselves and their pursuits. I'll leave it in, see what happens. Or will it wreck everything? It could bring a certain amount of ruin. So, big deal, I tell myself, I'm a workaholic, who cares if loading up on language has engaged a sacrificial economy, a struggle to which one donates one's body, one's health, forcing me to push on with a compromised immune system. Who gives a crap if every day is a struggle of dramatic proportions in soma and psyche? Every working-class American, nearly every student and early-stage professional puts in preposterous hours for scant returns—I won't mention those whose struggle is so dire that they can't even sacrifice themselves, we're all involved in miserable overload, but others can't choose their neurotic suppliers of stress so freely.) I devote equal time to the Greeks and the geeks, the losers who are destructive of world, of what's left of world, and their sniveling complaints, as well as the ostensibly winning teams and themes of abiding insight. Configuring something like an account of the writing habit, often obscure and harassing, I realize that I take and read and reflect on complaints all year round, day in, day out.

"The Lord giveth, the Lord taketh away." Gd does not have to hear Job's plaintive appeal; the monotheistic deity does not have to *repair*. Gd gives; Gd takes. The providential economy is part of an *argument of force*. The reparative experience belongs elsewhere. Jeremiah's lamentations are made in the mode of catastrophic nostalgia.

At the same time, the biblical complaint is never *refuted*. The rapport de force says something like this: "I'm stronger, you need to shut up." The supreme attitude trickles down, laying siege to all angles of relatedness where the weaker party's complaint is closed down amidst the shrapnel of divine violence.

The second paragraph of the May 4 letter shifts down from lament to complaint. The rhetoric of lament, which has dominated the opening paragraph, fizzles, collapsing on itself, and gives space to the negotiating stances that complaint can encourage. Writing to his interlocutor, Werther commissions his friend to tell Mother that he has looked after her business interests. He has spoken with his aunt, hardly the evil *Weib*, bad vibe and woman, that she was made out to be. Werther has discharged his task by conveying to his aunt his mother's complaints about a withheld inheritance. Reasons were given, misunderstandings resolved, their part of inheritance assured. Werther concludes the paragraph by stating that misunderstanding and indolence contribute far more to the world's ills than ruse and malevolence. The conclusion, very Goethe-to-Eckermann in style and dictum, diverts a prevailing perspective on habits that invite calamity. As often happens, Goethe powers down on what drives aggression, on deeds that might be attached to evil or conspiratorial stratagem. World-class harm happens by way of sloth, by way of lazy transmission, misunderstanding—part of a grammar of negligence and rhetorical oversight. In order to get a handle on calamity, Goethe downshifts to an exegetics of irritation, minor disturbance or a quality of glitching capable of bringing major world-disorder. Minor dents in articulation and perspective serve gradually to mark a pileup of unchecked ineptitude, disregard, escalating indifference to a pitch of endangering hazard.

Goethe preferred slow-burn ethics to prescriptive assertion; this was his way of moving beyond good and evil. Even more to the point, his gaze stays with a reflection that he locates *prior* to any good and evil. The syntagm, "good and evil," for him, provides in the end too facile an evaluative grid. The fuel for getting *beyond* good and evil was available to Goethe as what comes prior to good, to its derivatives such as evil, affording him the time he needed to move at a radically slow but undeterred pace. (Or "beyond," as Derrida observes in terms of Freud, is never really beyond, and no one gets *beyond* the pleasure principle, always lagging behind itself. Another story, but not far behind.) Goethe sparked the Freudian principle and corresponded with Nietzschean moves to the point of mapping them. He flew beneath philosophical radars to capture alternative causalities and valuations, indicating slower forms of registering meaning. Thus the tropes of sloth or inactivity could trigger massive reactivity, fearsome consequence, as in *Elective Affinities*, where everything starts up with a slowdown, when a friend loses his job. Losing work is not a result of sloth

Ach! The History of a Complaint

or slowdown, but it produces such effects. The fact of having an intimate, a companion or neighbor, out of work puts ethical pressure on the couple in the novel, even on their garden. The opening question or "issue" confronts the existential hole dug by a listless friend: what is your responsibility when a friend ceases to thrive, depleted by the frozen stances of unemployment—a problematic that travels in one way or another in the German language works of Schlegel, Hegel, Kafka, Walser, and others.[25]

In Goethe, the one who falls off the labor lines, unhitching from qualities that labor contributes to the creation of a world, is considerably endangered, prone to a structureless drop. Even leisure time depends essentially on the provisions of work—they belong together, reciprocally replenishing. Goethe tries to keep his characters busy and purposefully distracted. What Levinas calls "sabbatical existence" in many ways undermines the life-capacity of the young storm and stresser. Early on, when Werther stops mediating his mother's business affairs, tosses the sketchbook, he starts foundering, spinning into alienated leisure, as it were. At loose ends, he starts reading junk like *Ossian*, only to be carried away by the suicidal push that had from the start thrown him together with poor Leonore. For Werther, it is not clear that it could have been otherwise, because nothing seems equipped to redirect this impulse, over which Goethe scandalously suspended sentence—neither good nor evil, certainly not *beyond* posited valuation, but a stalled discussion on suicide in a permanent sidebar of impossible negotiations. Werther is already gone when he arrives on the scene, following the impertinent logic of non-presence and writing, rendered by an impossible grammar of being: "Wie froh ich bin, daß ich weg bin!" How happy I am that I'm gone.—Sure, one can and must translate this opening/closing statement into English more or less as "since I have gone or gotten away," but Goethe puts it all in the present tense: being gone, going away, writing from and solely in terms of this being-away. I write to the extent that I am already gone, a specter of my history, a proxy of the split away part, whose self-departure I lament.

The paradox of the lament is that it always wants to do away with itself, put down the lamenting subject and its unappeasable causalities. The lamenting subject goes down like a rabid dog. Well, maybe not like a "subject," nor like a "rabid dog"—this figure comes from Lyotard, and means to underscore how we handled, or failed to handle, Nazi Germany as historical calamity: it was put down like a rabid dog. *No working through,* if that seems possible. No coming to terms in a severe and lucid and worthy way, not on the part of the majority of Europeans. This does not mean that strides have not been made, or that the rigors of restraint and understanding were always entirely voided. Germany has come a long way, and continues marking the unmarkable without

CHAPTER 2

the complacency of having worked through an impenetrable wall of grievance. Hamacher, in his way, on another register, questions our ability truly to "work through" anything. Wait. How did we get from *Werther* to Nazi Germany? What kind of a slippage have I provoked or allowed to transpire? I can see how the theme of inheritance, the way it abounds in *Werther*, has pushed me this far. But, still. My pathology, my obsession; I apologize. I guess these stutters bespeak *my* ability/disability to work through. Perhaps the lament itself, as structure and appeal, offers an access route—even though any such route must be barred, and the pathology is not entirely mine but irreversibly bequeathed on one and all. Whether that call is accepted is another matter.

Lament seeks its own end, as Werther articulates explicitly. He promises, as we said, to finish off the lament, he laments, in order to disinstall the past. A logically tall order. What concerns this maneuver now, implicating the fate of the text, is that letter 1 has inscribed the end in terms of a subgenre it has selected as object for overcoming, the *Klage*. Like Werther, the text has injected itself with a poisonous intrusion that may go into latency but will reemerge to reclaim the textual body. The lament that Werther has promised to void is, from the start, overtaking him and the text that seeks to contain and spill the traumatic storyline in *Werther*. The irony of this suicide pill is that the protagonist has wanted to switch subgenres: if he had been able to sustain the attitude of complaint, Werther could have taken on the world, instead of directing an oversized libidinized aggression back to himself. That is a big *maybe*. Goethe, in any case, walks away famously unscathed, ready for more trouble down the road. Though I do not want to pop open another lost file at this point, I will indicate, for the philologists of the future, that the *complaint*, manageable and on the side of life, belongs to the domain of the maternal, whereas the lament in *Werther* stays in pursuit of the lost paternal metaphor. Some call the elusive figurality that heads up the quest, as address and source of appeal, "God-the-father."

That Goethe chisels down the megaconcepts of a prescriptive ethics is something showcased by *Werther* in the famous section on *Laune* (mood). One is responsible for one's moods, for the way one upholds *Mitsein* and goes about the practice of social justice every time one faces others. One must desist from fatiguing the interlocutor and friend with utterances borne of foul humor, avoid the unleashing of corrosive complaints. Temperamental downturns can affect entire galaxies of being. Bitch-moan, bitch-moan, blah-nag-blah-nag. Goethe throws injunctive halts at the sullen bouts of temperamental indecency: cease and desist these dispositions, turn away from this field of representation. *It is within your power* to stop approaching the tipping point of bad sociality: the invasive arrogance of presenting and pressing and pushing a rotten mood. On the Goethean charts the unconcealed bad mood, the belligerent disposition that it presupposes, is responsible for ruthless social destruction: a core complaint on Goethe's playlist. The subtle edges of Goethe's irony should not be lost on us: according to his argument, mood can and must be ethically penalized. Suicide, however, as extreme measure and limit case of making a complaint stick, a finitizing way of leaving a plaint behind, gets a free ethical pass, shivering through the remnants of language as a push and pathology that cannot be judged, much less condemned—except by clerics and other churchgoers, such as those who cleave to the State.

Flaubert went to court for picking up this line of thought.
The book was thrown
     at *Madame Bovary*,
        it went to court
           and not even Baudelaire
            could bail out the
              suicide writer,
    —a realist, the unrelenting griper: let us understand Flaubert
       as stylized modernity's chronic complainer.

Werner trat herein, und als er seinen Freund mit den bekannten Heften beschäftigt sah, rief er aus: Bist du schon wieder über diesen Papieren? Ich wette, du hast nicht die Absicht, eins oder das andere zu vollenden! Du siehst sie durch und wieder durch und beginnst allenfalls etwas Neues.
Wilhelm Meisters Lehrjahre, book 1, chapter 10.

Werner came in, and seeing his friend busied with his manuscripts, said: "Are you poring over those things again? I bet you don't intend to finish any of them. You'll just look through them again and again—and then start something new."[26]

Werner, the good friend, shows up for the protagonist. Addressee of the letters Wilhelm sends out in the *Lehrjahre* (apprenticeship), the treasured friend remains unseen in his place of remoteness, much like Georg's "friend from Russia" in Kafka's *Judgment*. Werner picks up the slack where the protagonist cannot stabilize a perspective or mark out the boundaries of speculation. Werner—grounded, bright and skilled with life's pragmatic edges, capable of counting, masterful in critically discounting—puts down some superegoical tracks in the novel. Werner instructs and critiques. He knows his subject, he has

CHAPTER 2

prepared an entire genome map of Wilhelm, the ever-straying friend, prone to flopping as he's *bild*-ing his *Bildung*, going under and making ethical comebacks, scraping through. When Wilhelm spaces out or drops into poetic aneconomies, their exchange gives Werner some leverage. He tries to pull Wilhelm toward a shareable world, to the upside of running and calculable economies, in alignment with the peaceful management of commerce, mindful of fiscal advantage, gaining on generalized types and psychological solidity.

As in a number of his prose works, Goethe brings speculative acumen to the subject of human activity (*Tätigkeit*), to the way it and we get organized nonviolently, by fixing the way endangerment and the allotment of destructive acts change currency and can be converted to monetary transfers. At least that was Goethe's speculative wish fulfillment: *a girl can dream!* Goethe thought it could work—that the work could work and sideswipe a history of cruelty. Read back to us, Goethe's intervention runs today as one long complaint, an *Anklage* or accusation in terms of the way business in fact has been conducted—or rather, derailed from possible affiliation with its philosophical origins and poetic stamina.

In the days before totalitarian corporatism held sway, prior to the Western lockdown on the cold vaults of venture capitalism, Goethe asked Werner to voice his theoretical exuberance on the matter of revenue, the broad circulation and pumps of *money*, the funds and foundations of a certain type of pursuit-in-common, linked, however tenuously, to the pursuit of happiness. Today this sort of apologia may seem off the boards, largely obsolesced and rundown in terms of the eighteenth-century ideal of bustling business poetics. Yet, certainly now, when declared over and out, dirty and fast, the speculative prompts of high finance deserve a hearing, especially given what Goethe and Schlegel brought to the table—the a prioris of the relations between gold and *reelle Sprache* (language of the real), the conversion and translation from gold to paper money in the second part of *Faust*, and Goethe's investments in the depathologizing potential of organized cash flow and balanced governance. Werner speaks for the prevalent modalities of "Spedition und Spekulation," drawing charts of expenditure and speculation that are meant to promote prosperity "und Wohlbefinden" (141), general well-being, at the pulse of the world body's *Kreislauf* (circulation). The world is posited as a body that needs to keep pumping and moving, creating and exchanging values that are "leicht und schnell zu verschaffen," like a quickening pulse that announces the swift movement of energy. Qualities of justice and price fairness, even fair trade, align. There is no "rechtmäßigeren Erwerb" or "*billigere Eroberung*" "als den Handel" (there is no equitable acquisition or cheaper conquest than trade

Ach! The History of a Complaint

practices) according to Werner, who sharpens his worldliness and *Verstand* (intelligence, reason) on his friendship with Wilhelm.

The logic that prompts Werner's theorizations proves to be in the service of the world's thriving body, vibrant and alert, oriented toward its well-being by the poetic exercises of commerce and peace. Poetry steers the course of business away from mere privative interests, endowing it with rhythm and reflection, a certain prowess restrained only by the dignity of means. The market, meant to supplant the spillover of world-class aggression, subdues and converts the currency of bloodlust, can quash or reassign the determined maneuvers of clashing armies. Goethe was resolved to root out, or at least to reroute, hostile stances and vulgar appetite for accumulation by means of the world market and its underlying metaphysics of exchange. At the same time, according to an implicit hierarchical score sheet kept by the Bildungsroman, Werner's place may scan as a subsidiary of Wilhelm's messy positing and positions, his passions of destruction. Unless Werner, ever converting values and changing masks, comes out on top. He will have tutored Wilhelm, brought him into the vicinity of ethical being, following the development monitored by *Bildung*. Werner is not a member of the *Turmgesellschaft*, the control tower that supervises Wilhelm's every move in the novel. But Wilhelm is under the control of many, and Werner remains a powerful player, partner and existential administrator of the highest life-stakes. Wilhelm resists his education, yet Werner may have the upper hand—even if his manipulations seem at times underhanded. The value of his commentary on business and free commerce remains strongly supported by the novel's tactics.

Eventually, however, the great militarist, or *"militerary"* commanding officer, Heinrich von Kleist, will catch up with Goethe's philosophy of business in order to show the revengeful underpinnings of the market and its cutthroat, if often transcendentally set, transactions. The disruption of justice by the preeminence in social structuring of business calculations and commercial claims—representations of failed equivalency—thematically emerges in the domain of Kleist's passionate depictions.[27]

In an ironic swerve that ties friendship to the poetic stock market, Werner, when offering his boardlike presentation, refers to his "geschätzer Freund," his treasured friend, leaving it undecidable whether Wilhelm, when appraised by his devoted friend, transcends market valuation or derives his worth from an economy stubbornly tethered to commerce, to the freeing of funds and production of value on which the market classically thrives. Does one always avoid assessing the market value of one's friendships? In a sub-Goethean and pre-deconstructive sense, I can only hope so; but, sometimes, contaminated and saturated by overburdening precepts of capital and use, one just fails to register how the valuing of friendship measures up to the immeasurable, or is prompted by unconscious columns of calculation. Can friendship, even the most lofty in nature, escape such calculations? The complaint of friendship hesitates to grow economies of an evaluative cast, but does this not amount to a naive dissimulation of the returns of worthiness? I do not hesitate to divest such estimations, but still . . . . O, my friends!

In order to be in a position to complain, one must presume a *right* to something—to a better deal, a better world, an improved material or phenomenological arrangement with things tied to our fractured world. Not everyone has been granted title or privilege to such a language of defaulted equity. On the plantation or in the Bible or, among trafficked women or in lockdown, hunger bitten and in poverty—the unfree lack the ground to sound a complaint. Existentially disenfranchised, bereft and frozen in place, terrorized, the destitute and spurned stifle the grammar of the plaint. One can barely say "I," and certainly not "don't" or any of the other liberatory "no"s. Nonetheless, sometimes a riot of censure breaks out, the accumulated despair leverages a social physics of pushback. Indignation calls it.

The discourse of sacrifice steals away the possibility of complaint, buffering the plaintive theater that speaks out, or writes in. Sacrifice, by means of another logic, throws in the towel of dissidence.

Samuel Weber shows up at the first launch of the complaint project. We're at a night session in Saas Fee, Switzerland, where we have finished teaching our June classes in 2014. There's some exhaustion, but giddiness as well. The general assembly brings everyone together, and the numbness, by some existential fluke, transfers energy and gets socialized. I try to settle into my discomfort zone.

Knowing Sam will be there provokes a double reaction from the sensitive ones, my internalized anxiety pins: the sheer joy of having his ear, finely tuned and receptive, induces the jitters, signing the provocation of wild and jumpy yelps of fear. What if the esteemed friend finds me *stupid?*—part of an age-old primal pang associated with acts of self-exposure. The self-decimator switches on and the ambivalence comes roaring forth: like I need the extra, superegoically-fueled pressure, like I really have to submit myself to his hardnosed critical *écoute* at this stage and age, *stell Dir vor*, go figure! I ram archaically into German expressions of dismay, maybe incorporating my grandmother

Ach! The History of a Complaint

or some strong protesters in the tradition to which I'm unconsciously tied, kind of forever. Like Benjamin I am related to Heinrich Heine, but he was for real related, moving in and out of superegoical correctional zones. He's going to nab me, Sam, I mean subtly. He'll display a quizzical face, frown; maybe even he'll want to throw up his hands and stop me in my tracks, I just know it. So much for my gratitude to this irreproachable landsman and a history of serious-friendly relations, as Hölderlin would say: all his saving qualities left in the dust!

I project my own store of aggression onto the hapless friend, someone who has never shown me so much as an iota of undermining affect. But it's never too late for him to kickstart the negating side of his fine mind, I bully myself into thinking. Look out! Yet, Sam, given the opportunity to tag me out, shows restraint and lets me slide all the way down the slippery signifying chain. In fact, while I deliver, his smile soon reassures me and lends my voice some texture. He won't come after me is the sense I get, before the inevitable deflations crowd out the manic Alpine high.

Well, a few minutes of *Selbstbehauptung* (self-assertion) are better than none; I'll take it. During Q&A, the audience has things to say and invents some viable sidebars: a student from Belgrade, Andreas, asks me to develop the thought of the *silent complaint*, to see if I can pass the mic to those who cannot or choose not to sound a complaint: sounding out the multitude of those who "prefer not to." I circuit my response through Derrida on Foucault, remembering the pitfalls Derrida considers of presuming to *speak for* those who will not speak up, reflecting a frayed part of an advocatory ethics. What kind of violence occurs when you take up the cause and causalities of another? This will become an issue of consequence for Hannah Arendt, especially when the notion of compassion creeps in, driving all modern revolutions, as we examine in the following chapters. There is a tendential urge among the socially attuned to speak up for others, an imperative to do so, despite all and any aporetic deterrence. No doubt it comes from a good place that however remains outrageously self-appointed and complicated to pull off. Your action may well be called for, but you cannot get away with such appropriation unscathed. You're going in there, where you do not belong or have any jurisdiction; nonetheless, you have been called there, summoned. You have gained entry to the ethical dilemma of heeding the aphonic complaint.

The lecture milled a few other questions, one that flagged Rousseau as chronic complainer: Rousseau, citizen of Geneva, dwelled in the neighborhood of our Alps. He feels close by, still murmuring, even today. We regularly obtain travel passes to the borders he created with paranoid discourse, at least if you're waiting it out in my language sector. Where does paranoia take over from the complainer's rut? Or, does his brand of "l'anguish" rather bubble up from an outpost of paranoiac insight, a heightened sense of historical alert, or even—to follow Freud to the letter on paranoid excess—does it owe its emergence to homosexual repression? How does complaining pick up the scattered relay of repression and desire? I trek through the fields created in Q&A, understanding that I will get back to some of these prods and luminous deterrents. Sam raises a point that will stay with me for a long time. Turning to Benjamin's essay on Karl Kraus—one of my start-up texts in academic adolescence, which I no longer command—he refers to the moment when Nature and the world of things begin to complain, and asks me to reflect on the structure of complaint in a non-anthropomorphic sense. I reflect on the way being yields the complaint, readies and relies on grievance, banks on finitude. Our shared temporal predicament wipes down deluded states of non-grievance. Yet, all pleasure states crave eternity, Nietzsche admonishes, making us will another relation to time and being. Life-affirming and resolutely yes-saying in his way, Nietzsche tries to countermand the complaint of being. How does he manage? By launching a different arsenal of complaints, clearing out targets that stand in the way of rigorous affirmation. A day later, on the bus to the train station in Visp, I hear a student say to his neighbor how rigorous, pitch-perfect, "awesome" Sam's class had been this summer. The student was returning to his *Wohngemeinschaft* in Berlin, to a communal living arrangement; I am off to conduct research in Paris for the next month: these tickets to ride recall Benjaminian trajectories, I tell myself, Paris and Berlin, Berlin and Paris; then I feel the portal darken as the Alps diminish, becoming a snapshot from afar, an obstacle course of unmasterable memories. I will call Sam to tell him what I heard on the bus on the way down. Everyone needs witnessing, I tell myself; maybe, though, some folks don't. They're differently armored. Sometimes they give the impression of a steadier cathexis, more confidence with their object-love and worldly accords. Still, no one should be left to the deflating solitude of the occasional complaint that comes in to deck you for days and weeks, or Gd forbid, the full-blown grievance—barely precise, but on sinister target, a smart missile somehow equipped to find you at your lowest point—that now pops up with consternating regularity in universities and other contentious spaces of discursive free fall.

Ach! I complain about—and once in a blue moon to—my students, internally, at least, saying how hard I work for them, the endless preps and rewrites of lectures, unacknowledged letters of recommendation, doctoral training and thesis edits, job marketeering under impossible circumstances, how I knock myself out on their behalf: and what do I get in return? An occasional grievance, a far-flung postcard from the disgruntled. I exaggerate. In any case, it's

Ach! The History of a Complaint

on me. Most students have shown grace and gratitude; most have completed their work with me. But what is it about the stray *envoi* of faultfinding that continues to sear a psychic soft spot? Is the corrective compulsion they betray not also a shadow of my own propensity for waving around the complaint? How bitterly I complained about my teachers and schools, the stupidity to which I was exposed! Maybe I should stifle my own species of restless indignation before going after others, less malicious in their plaintive habitats, less ready to murder their benefactors. At least I didn't act on it, I tell myself. Besides, what kind of signs of thanks should one expect from those who must disavow their debts? *Ach!* By now I should have transferred all my accounts to the Cordelian aptitude columns for listing "nothing," maybe rejoining the ranks of the noncomplainer *in extremis*, the dutiful daughter and meek earth dweller. Yes, I would prefer to snuff out entirely in uncomplaining submission or, at the limit of saying and signing, of singing-signing, raise my voice in praise. For, despite all the noise, I am a true submissive. I submit to my time here and understand the terms of the contract: "no one said it would be easy," and so forth.

Deserving its own dossier and inventory, the medical complaint calls for a concise treatment of body, institution, and language. Psychoanalysis deals routinely with complaints. In most cases and studies, the delivery of a complaint functions as the "open sesame" of a psychoanalytic encounter. According to psychoanalyst Anne Dufourmantelle, the complaint made during the analytic work initiates a wager, poses a dilemma, and defies analytic arbitration. The complaint, she warns, should not be confounded with the *demande*, and actually dismantles the scene and coordinates of analysis, throwing the analyst into crisis. Neither *demande* nor reliable description, the complaint throws a wrench into the system, no matter how nonsystematic and pliant it proves to be. The complaint serves to show the impotence of the other. In conversation, Anne has said that she felt diminished by the subversive function of the complaint in analysis, shining a harsh light on the bareness of our being-there, together, in the scene of a critical encounter, working-through and remembering, flailing through distortion and denial, pressed on by language that subjects us.

In his work, *La Fin de la plainte*, another analyst, François Roustang, tries to mark an end to the complaint, a way out of the debilitating and repetitive stances held in place by the complaining subject. According to the analyst, the complaint must be brought to an end; it must complete its rounds, even if this means redescribing the analytic experience. Analysis should not be used as pretext for extending the life cycle of the complaint and its strategic epistemological underpinnings.

CHAPTER 2

Roustang offers interpretations of Narcissus and Psyche in light of the "illusion of healing by means of self-knowledge." What Narcissus teaches us is that self-knowledge can be fatal. Locked in embrace with himself, "Narcisse 1er," Narcissus the first, proves to be a paranoid dictator, having lost all distance, blinded to any possible sense of alterity and differentiation. There are other ascensions of Narcissus, including "Narcisse II," second or secondary, who is essentially inexistent. The Narcisses rallied by Roustang are "champions de la plainte" (champions of the complaint), and the analyst goes after them ferociously.[28] I admit that the encounter with such severity, his uncompromising pushback on the complaining subject, have taken me by surprise.

At first I was startled by the severe beating, or at least bad rap sheet that Dr. Roustang gives the complaint, the subject that ticks off a mechanism of grievance as well as ticking off the analyst. I myself come equipped with critical takedown switches, but my technologies sift and sort, quibble, return on the back of ambivalence to bureaucracies of doubt. No such quiver here. This guy would decimate me if I went to him, vulnerable and raw. OK, maybe he's not talking to or about me, and my customized stock of problems. I'm not so sure that I'm all that narcissistically wrought to the point of needing paring down (I'm not kidding—if anything, I need periodically to *renarcissize*, but that's another story). From the start, he seemed harsh to me. I was developing from page 1 a negative transference. But he's not my analyst, so I dial it down, bracket the misgivings. I can always return the disparaging volley with scholarly determination, detached and cold, I tell myself. But the "rights of nerves" rarely prompt me to be detached and cold. Should his relentless pursuit really be taken at face value, though?

Then I remember the legions of narcissistic snivelers that have come my way, always hankering after more, rarely in touch with or jolted by the spark of alterity, except for what has existentially bamboozled them en route to my phone number or office or table. I have had entire conversations with those who not once asked how I was doing, what I was doing, if I was even capable of doing, my face practically dropped on the desk, fists pounding, I was in so many ways crawling. But now I am complaining again. Pardon me.

Still, Roustang really sticks it to "les plaints qui se prolongent au-delà de la décence d'un chagrin ou d'un deuil se développent comme un cancer qui va tout dévorer" since, instead of proliferating like cellular life in the service of growth, "elles prolifèrent sur le vide de l'intérêt pour soi" (the complaints that go on and on, exceeding the decency of the time of distress or grief, developing like a cancer that devours everything, proliferating in the void of self-interest).[29] In some respects, this guy tops Claudius, counting down the right and restricted period of proper mourning. He has no patience with what he sees as a senseless emptying borne of self-involvement—a precarious position for an analyst to occupy. He must know the risks he is taking, because he is smart as a whip, and was, I'm told, on all accounts a worthy critic and practitioner of psychoanalysis. I've heard from a friend who used to go to him to air her complaint that he was an excellent analyst. Another friend found him to be on the harsh side of rigorous. I suppose that only an analyst would authorize and specify the sense of decency and measure when it comes to timing one's period of grief or pain, but, really, what a smackdown. I'm smarting! That part of my superego permanently occupied by Derrida wonders: He's a little off, no?—Who dares to hold a stopwatch over suffering, the time of catastrophic wounding? Of course, it would be nice to stop the pain, call it a day, but to call it a cancerous growth owing to self-indulgence? Yes, and no. No—and yes. He really has it in for *les Narcisses*.

I'm not that far behind him on this assessment, I must admit. They have become unbearable to me: I would love to unstick them from my skin—grand reception area. Champions of the complaint, "les Narcisses ferment les yeux à ce parcours fatal et tentent de justifier par une répétition inlassable la direction erronée qu'ils ont prise. Ils pensent soulager la souffrance qui s'exhale de leur recherche folle, alors qu'ils s'enferment dans ce don't ils prétendent sortir. Il n'ya plus d'issue pour eux que l'appel à la pitié ou à la compassion" (The Narcissi close their eyes to the fatal course on which they embark, attempting to justify by unrelieved repetition the wrong path taken. They think they can subdue the suffering that emanates from their mad search, but in fact they lock themselves into what they claim to overcome. There is no exit for them other than an appeal to pity or compassion).[30]

Eckart says that all of Protestantism comprises one long complaint, a ceaseless session of *meckering*, carping. This contention made Peter laugh when I told him about the conversation. He added that Luther's nailing the list of grievances on the church door of Wittenburg starts off the complainant's movement—a fracture in Christianity linked to the Reformation, a sort-of cover-up term. On a more personal note, Peter reminds me that I used to despise complainers—the whiners and snivelers, the scores of kvetsches and chronic grumblers. I don't remember complaining about this sector of Dasein, but can believe it. I worked hard at emulating ego-ideal poses of obduracy, at most allowing for softening Zen practices of non-preference: sheer acceptance, allow, allow, moments when one wishes nothing to be, move, or posit otherwise: non-preference. I would be neither dissatisfied nor satisfied—no fear, no hope, just lean into the emptiness. But enough about me and the fog of histories remembered.

Mariano says that in Buenos Aires, the opening salvo of sociality consists in massive complaining. It's simply not polite to break into a social encounter without ragging on your parents, lovers, the friends who populate your existence. This initiatory clearinghouse makes space for newcomers. I like it. Nothing irks me more than having to hear the puerile gush of family-hugging, lover-bedazzled opening rounds of assertion. Such an embrace of preapproved world defies my comprehension. I will go to Buenos Aires and make new friends.

The unmovable event. For Roustang, the complaint issues from one who wants to keep intact her *chagrin*, if only to avoid confronting it head on. In a way, he rebukes the complaint for not becoming a lamentation, a rite of passage—in fact, for not *becoming*. The complaint, he argues, ought to have given way to an aesthetic *mise en forme* of pain, a reorganization of the beauty of expression trying to catch up with a disorder perceived in its first stages as irreparable, an elegy meant to begin the work of closing a mourning period. But to the extent that the complaint persists, it remains instead a repetitive fixation that feeds chagrin rather than exhausting its course. The complaint that does not finish itself off or move up the ladder of formal transformation increases pain, opening only on a condition of depression that, with each day, is more irremediable. In this way the complaint complies only with the refusal of an imposed reality—something that may have overwhelmed my existence and relational systems, a terrible event, disruptive and inassimilable.

Faced with the unmovable event, I become tired, depleted, unable to effect the existential and material modifications required of me if I am to change things: I remain in the rote of the complaint, over and over again, preferring to deny that something has happened to me, to my world of structured accommodations, specific grammars of avoidance. The event "insists," however, for it won't go away. When the complaint runs out the clock, stabilizing only its concourse, it has become a way to evade facing the event. Instead, Roustang argues, one can regret its occurrence and encroachment, one can deplore attendant facts; one wants, wishes for, demands a time and place when things were different. Continual complaining means that I have been unable to appropriate the overwhelming event and assume responsibility in some way for its onslaught and implications. This is when fault is assigned to another, be it destiny, society, heredity, the genitors: my messed-up parents. "La plainte en vient à porter plainte et à se répandre en accusations" (The complaint shows up to register a complaint and to spread out in the form of accusations).[31]

In a way that proves critical, judgment is suspended by the complaint and condemnation staved off as the event continues to develop consequences. One develops a pervasive sense of encroachment: one feels shaken down, squeezed and surrounded by enemies, and begins permanently adopting the figure of one persecuted. As much as the complaint resembles a rebuttal to injustice, evoking recrimination, maybe indulging a subtle Nietzschean dose of vengeance—Nietzsche claims to detect a subtle dose of vengeance in every complaint in the *Untimely Meditations*—nothing of the sort will rise up or amount to much, for the subject of complaint remains obstinate, stuck in process with the faulty understanding that the order of things must change, and not "mes propres sentiments" (my own feelings).[32] What happens is that a state of division reigns where no reconciliation becomes possible. Complaint has existential takeover plans, attaching to everything and nothing, crowding out life's capacity to endow and enrich.

One of the sticking points of complaint, according to Roustang, is found in the way it blocks out forms of consolation or overcoming. The complaint issues from the stunted lifeline of childhood wounding. Something happened—and has not ceased to happen, continues to hurt—that cannot be ignored by an analyst or therapist who needs to consider how the complaint "était le fruit de l'impossibilité de vivre" (was the fruit of the impossibility of living), arising as it does as the impossibility of living life at an early age: the wounding struck so deeply that it prohibited any new growth. In this area of being, obstinacy holds intact an infantile part of the self. The complaint is an effect of the refusal to grow up, or it expresses, at least, the subject's regret over having grown up. Staying in place, dissatisfied and stunted—this still shot keeps one hooked on the cherished self of childhood that remains frozen in a pout. The complaining subject is thus protected from plunging into the pain of growth spurts, which limits the astonishing abundance of life's donations, so readily available, according to the therapist, as part of the very risky prompts of overflowing generosity, free-floating gratuity, and the adventurous frontiers of friendship and love. Resentment, reproaches, requiring that others give us what, in principal, we cannot receive—these stymied uprisings are held in place by the complainant closed in on himself.

Roustang profiles two relations to the stall of being on which he appears to hang the complaint. They prove contradictory and rich. On the one hand, the therapist is enjoined to induce mobility, pull the complainant out of the ditch. This pullout and push cannot be accomplished by turning away from the emptiness to which the complaint attests. The narcissistically retrograde patient, running at top speed on empty, needs to learn how to *wait*. Maybe in French this directive becomes more eloquent, for the patient needs to *patienter*, to assume her patience-ness. (I add this disclaimer: Roustang would be unlikely to approve this Freudo-Heidegger inflection of being that waits; moreover, he has long ago booked out of psychoanalysis, a practice that he believes feeds the complaint. I resume.) The patient needs to assume his patience-ness the way one assumes one's castration (ditto on the unlikeliness of obtaining Roustang's approval on a concern with castration as moment of truth). The patient needs to show patience, to assume "une attente dépouillée" (a bare sense of waiting) that resembles despair. Emptiness itself, the voided space of our existence, is what goads the breath and breeze to enable movement in existence. Roustang admittedly goes far here, to the Far East, in order to stir up some movement, seeking to locate a syntax of light but firm prompting, a tug that would let things and beings touch, get in touch with one another, giving them over to "l'unité d'une caresse" (the caress's unity), an existential tap both French and Asian. A force that comes from yonder yet stays with us, a pulse from elsewhere that prompts and gently prods; this is what the Chinese call Tao.

However, remodeling existence so that it releases from the tether of complaint is not a given. The complaint does not let up of itself, often tantalizing the complainer into complacent standstill. Nothing moves or budges, nothing unsticks from the standpoint of narcissistic tenacity. Toward the end of the work, Roustang therefore offers another approach. Pushing off from the "plainte muertrière," a kind of lethal complaint, condemned to stasis ("il se condamne à ne plus se mouvoir"), repeating incessantly the same grievances, the therapist Roustang chooses to follow a path not taken.[33]

How does one break into the closed circuit of the narcissistic economy? One way is to deploy *disrespect*—"l'irrespect inclus dans l'impératif" (the disrespect inherent to the imperative).[34] There is no way to avoid a rhetoric or pose of disrespect in the address to an apprentice, student, or patient. This nettling structure becomes apparent in hypnosis, to which Roustang returns, which induces the subject to heteronomize, to learn to situate "la dependence comme source de l'indépendance" (dependence as springboard for independence).[35] At the same time, the narcissist must learn to make the leap that is freeing on her own, outside herself, for no one else can fend for the event of self-freeing that comes out of relatedness. The therapist's radical incapacity to free up the analysand in place of the other comes to the fore, and in the aporetic retreat the chronic complainer becomes unbound, prompted by the "suprême irrespect" of the imperative. The very setup of the encounter and its impotent inflections serve the purpose of shaking up the hold of narcissistic stagnancy.

Ach! The History of a Complaint

The asymmetrical relatedness presupposed by the scene and sentence, "You will now close your eyes," means that the subject has sought and yielded to a commanding other, one who has broken the narcissistic seal by giving an order, delivering an instruction to the now suggestible subject.

The staging of heteronomy cracks the sealing fantasy of independence, breaking open the myth of some individualistic autonomy by instituting the diverting fields of heteronomy. Such a mutation in relation, and toward relation, is effected by a disrespecting move on the self-enclosed sufferer that comes about as a kind of slap of "snap out of it," bringing the sufferer abruptly to relationality and world. In Freud, differently set and otherwise marked up, the movement from narcissism to identification introduces the possibility of a just politics.[36] For Freud the narcissi must be able to get over themselves, identify with others, if the political were ever to hold sway. But group psychology and the sorry state of mankind left Freud pessimistic about the prospects for such a leap.

Roustang, who has distanced himself from Freud but still remains in some disrespects on course, looks for a detox remedy for unbridled narcissism, cipher of our era. What can serve as "cure de désintoxication narcissique" (rehab for toxic narcissism)? How can one desituate narcissism, the suicidal inclination of self-internment? Roustang seeks "un autre type de sensorialité" (another type of sensoriality), a spacing of being that would make room for replunging into field of the unconscious, if only to find some relation to it, simply by being there and getting one's bearings, without fulfilling the prophecy to which Liriope, mother of Narcissus, was privy. When Liriope, in Ovid's *Metamorphoses*, asks the oracle if her son's life will span to old age, the response is distinct: "Si se non nouerit," if he does not know himself. Roustang interprets the oracle as saying that the condition for longevity rests on the injunction *not to know oneself*, not to know who one is, for such knowledge signs off on a death sentence: "L'autoconnaissance est fatale" (self-knowledge is fatal).[37]

Under such constraints and prohibitive conditions, how can the plaint of the narcissist, the worried comprehension of Liriope, be stilled? Sometimes, the way to disrupt narcissistic burrowing, archeological and specular in nature, is to thread the narcissist through an experience of stupidity, or by the sheer idiocy of non-experience, a reduction or mineralization of being condensed into inanimate thereness. In other words, the narcissist needs to be cupped in a place already sketched out in such phrases as "I feel heavy, like a stone," "I cannot move; I feel as dense as a slab of concrete, as thick as wood."

A lot depends on *placing* the narcissistic body, letting it take its place in world—something that is not assured or easy to attain. In order to achieve movement, the narcissist may need to go through a phase of stupefying thereness, allowing for nothing but the stupefaction and stupidity of hunkering down in existence. The sheer lassitude of being-there that the analyst seeks to encourage may be the opposite of nomadic transversals or schizoid mobility, no matter how stationary their itineraries remain. Becoming-thing, petrified, emptied, and still, the complainer neutralizes, drops heavy into life, a recovering complainer fettered neither by the pause of stupor nor by the myth of ecstatic emancipation.

Ach!

The Trouble with Deconstruction

To learn to live *with* ghosts, in the upkeep, the conversation, the company, or the companionship, in the commerce without commerce of ghosts. To live otherwise, and better. No, not better, but more justly. But *with them*. No *being-with* the other, no *socius* without this *with* that makes *being-with* in general more enigmatic than ever for us. And this being-with specters would also be, not only but also, a *politics* of memory, of inheritance, and of generations.
—Jacques Derrida, "Exordium"

For a while I argued that I had no choice when it came to Derrida. That's only partially true, for one makes choices and stands by them, even when faced with a no-brainer. Still, it's not as if I could have signed up with Habermas when I set out for obedience school, nor could I have landed plausibly in one of the more authoritarian ports of call! Do not think that I was not tempted to attach to an authoritarian master or school, dreaming of being taken in hand, trained in a "methodology," taught how to fail and rebound, opportunely manicured by analytical philosophy or, in that other field, refined by thematic reading skills and targeted for a fairly straightforward job. Some part of me wanted to join a secured group, settle into a Kantian comfort zone that consists in blowing off an excess of risk and following the evolving academic orders, become part of the university's sifting and sorting systems, defensively fitted for scholarly armature. (Kant wants us to get over comfortable choices that imply for him immaturity. He urges that we enroll in the program of Enlightenment, which, still ongoing, is seldom risk free or in the thrall of external recognition.) Still, "choosing Derrida" means something, at least, to me. Among other things—among poses of readiness and calculated passivities, beyond the helpful fictions of agency and decisive decree, in terms of *ethos* and scaled-back conformities—it means that one has made a commitment, established a line, however fractured, of responsible address. Even when something comes at you that seems destined for someone else or rings up a wholly different set of coordinates and identity markers, constellating a different type of call altogether.

I complain about the indirection of an eventual call, even and especially the Heideggerian *Gewissensruf*, in other works that probe limits of ethical commitment and record the intellectual shakedown. Knowing when to take a call never amounts to a stabilizing act, but incurs all sorts of hesitations and damage, running up a considerable existential tab. Is it meant for you? Kafka gives us cues about how to take or decline the call, redirect its intentions. The phrase "this call is *not* for you" requires, for instance, on behalf of the purported receiver, a capacity for desistance, a sense of when to back down and, the other way around, a surge of determination when it comes to stepping up. All in all, one is not sure, when assuming responsibility for the call, whether one has been blindly led to do so, urged on by delusional prompts or projection, if at all that call was meant for me (or someone hitching a ride with or in me, or beside myself), or an entirely other destinee. Nor can one be certain about what goads the reach for a call—a primal impulse, whatever—one can simply not be certain, especially when the nerves lead off, as in the case of those triggered by Benjamin and the way he formulated the "rights of nerves." The call comes in many forms, and one can quickly find oneself wrung and strung up, shaken to the core. And so, like characters in key narratives who, when struck, become transformed or are roused, suddenly awakened, I was shaken, one day, by an address—perhaps by the way Derrida, flipping full transference, once turned to me and spoke out, asking my name. He reported the particulars of that encounter, the initiatory startle, in *The Post Card*, and I bounced it back, according to a different switchboard, in *The Telephone Book*.[1]

Let us say, provisionally, that I did not refuse this call. Nor did he leave me stranded or entirely unanswered. I am struck to this day by the windfall that had him take my call, for I arrived on the scene having read him, prepared to mime and rhyme, to imitate without properly duplicating—yet copying him nonetheless on every memoed sign, "mad about language," prepared for the pursuit of likeness on the level of the signifier. As with Freud's Rat Man, who showed up at the analyst's door having browsed through some texts bearing his signature, I had my reading list in hand when turning myself in to his authority in order to be coached, if not delivered. He decided to bite, or buy, or at least not say good-bye to one of his future translators and ever terminable-interminable disciple. My membership spelled out different terms than that of others, at least in the fine print. On a number of fraught occasions he seemed to terminate me, but, on the whole, I sprang back like a cartoon character. I abided by the asymmetry that our bond implied from the start, withholding any reciprocal rejoinders that might have been provoked by the minimal yet straightforward allotment of harshness that was turned on me.

For the most part, I was meant, I suppose, to profile a stance of one who could be a Derridean without imitating Derrida, but also without disavowing his oversized "influence" on me when I downloaded his lessons. Nowadays, when I'm on my beat, maintaining the original commitment to a teacher involves a series of practices, some of which include regularly checking in with his declared allies as well as keeping up with a class of nonresentful litigators—those, at least, who sized the tasks that he set, who determined their breadth seriously enough to take them on and run with them.

Any masterful teacher probably provokes strikes of ambivalence, moments when the rest of us cannot entirely tell friend from foe, though Derrida admittedly claimed to know the enemy and, conversely, to our coltish consternation, went easy on those who engaged lamely. Sometimes, when he turned on someone whose ambivalence crossed the line, I permitted myself to talk him down, and to this day I am eaten with remorse, wondering if he got it right in the first place and I was being too Californian, looking at the "bright side" of aggrieved commentaries lobbed over to his side of thinking. Despite regional disagreements on matters of friendship and acuity, my membership was not, to my knowledge, revoked. To a startlingly large degree, we shared the same "friends" and created family resemblance among implausible congruencies. Some features of filiation are easy enough to detect. They can be summed up and made into recognizable checkoff points: we share the reading lists that he more or less invented and protected; the distrustful habit of nabbing intentions and rhetorical feints are giveaways, making those trained by Derrida instantly detectable—though we cannot be the only ones motored by infinite hermeneutic suspicion, or am I mistaken? Also, in some instances, the particular brand of humor, a certain level of warmth and acceptance, sometimes naively apportioned, can be viewed as a marker.

As a group—though I could not name them all, and don't have them on speed dial—Derrideans, at least in my imaginary roll call, go after the same sleeper margins or syntactical bluffs that abound in texts but that tend, by necessity, to remain concealed. Striking out on "our own," we nonetheless have a penchant to stick to the discoveries and textual lineups that Derrida cued up for his readership. Some of his own choices have become classics, prompting further mutations and unpredictable appropriations. I am not sure that Benjamin's "Kritik der Gewalt," the now-famous "Critique of Violence," would have enjoyed such a prominent run in our circuits if Derrida had not gone after the mystical foundation of authority in his way. Ditto Carl Schmitt, and countless others. Not that popularity counts in our circles, on the con-

CHAPTER 3

trary and yet, to a certain extent notoriety of text and title tend to happen to a certain degree. In the main, overexposure and its anticipated tipping point in vulgarity are scorned, so one is already traversing aporetic terrain when going down the Derridean reading list in terms of the recondite pop charts. Still, I give points to those who rescue a difficult text from oblivion to make it speak to us. It speaks!

Which brings me to the question—or complaint—of making such a choice, of resolving upon a mentor, *your teacher*—in some regards, choosing your weapon. How does the type of teacher one chooses become fateful, more determining than one can forecast at the outset, even when the deal tanks (I, for one—or many—have been tanked as many times as thanked) and negative transference becomes the rule of the day, the non-relation of choice? Jung and Freud became locked in that kind of wrestle, each knotted up, fitted to reproach the other, a name-place of permanent grievance. I used to tell my students that they sail out under our flag, and it's hard to switch teams after a certain point, though—here's the rub—you get extra points for doing so: just look at anyone who's turned on their teacher; or, ask Nietzsche when he booked on Wagner, or lesser pupils who bailed and lived to tell about it. But, in all sobriety, I'd want to create a sector to cover a brand of grievance linked to complaints that attach to structuring forms of teaching. How long does the attachment to the teaching body last, under what circumstances and in which time zones? In this context, I would like to analyze the type of traumatic invasiveness that has you carry those who are non-present, yet remain ever beckoning, even superegoically enthroned. Perhaps I should reintroduce myself at this instance, if only to offer a snapshot of melancholic review.

To that end, let me give you an echography of my regulated state of being, a reflective scan of so-called mind/body, to the extent, at least, that I have the right access code for the purposes of obtaining such a readout. In the past several semesters, I was in the organizing phases of a commemorative exigency. Psychically—and, without fail, somatically—I started preparing to make myself battle ready, if necessary, for a memorializing event. Being a Derridean still requires that one, at strategic checkpoints and invested junctures, bring up the sentinels to defend certain positions and positings, and to assume one's institutional guard. Perhaps not everywhere, for there must be one or two institutions, where, under enlightened leadership, terrific advances have been made and miraculated in terms of accommodating critical thought and its often unforeseen offshoots, departments, and institutions where the DOA tagging placed on theoretical thought can be easily overcome or set aside. Those universities, or pockets sewn into them, become the momentary comfort zone for those who know only a typology of irksome prods and provocation that,

The Trouble with Deconstruction

at best, throw you for a loop or start eating at the most sensitive parts of your *being-toward-death*. At worst you dance around with worry, the way Kafka did around the telephone, pinged by an alarming series of intrusions into your so-called work spaces, where one sets up the effort to think and play along, to listen, ward off, and write, to dress yourself properly enough to show up in the classroom to teach, and write.

A lot of people remain anxious about echoing Derrida, miming his rhetorical feints and sounding off in his dominant key. Not that many can carry it off or convincingly pinch-hit for his articulations. I'm more Winckelmanian about the whole problem of reflecting off your teacher, because I guess somewhere I believe that, in order to be great (if that's the way to pitch the stakes), one needs to imitate the Greeks, which maps in me as "Derrida." I myself do not seek to be classified as "great," not so deluded yet, or maybe I cannot remake some of the masculinist idols and metaphysical mystifications of aiming for "originality" or the rhetoric of "no one ever noticed this before in Benjamin or Nietzsche or in the work of fill in the blank"—a pathology that Derrida saw in Giorgio Agamben's stated wish to be the first to nail or even discover a given philosopheme or strategy or problem cluster or conceptual range of consequence. Agamben always wanted to be the head of the class, the first to clear a particular historical runway. But I don't necessarily see that tendency as limited to Giorgio, who may be among the first to say out loud that he means to be ahead of every significant curve, in front of every train of thought and denounced wreckage. The tendency to score a first, to break down some walls, no doubt is part of the staple of professional hazards shared especially among the philosophically minded, no matter how traditionally bound they may be. Freud stole a base here or there, as did Derrida himself. Still, genuine originality implies monstrosity, a good degree of unrecognizability, as does, according to another algorithm, the compulsively mimetic reflex. I go to Lacoue-Labarthe for getting a handle on that slice in the history of thought and mimetology.

The way Lacoue and Nancy have echoed and bounced off Derrida might stand as exemplary for us today, their fearless honoring of a teacher and his oeuvre, which does not mean that there was no static on the line or unsettled disputes here and there. They hung in there, with each other and with him, striking out on their own, staying near, marking off proximities in the distance of an unbeatable intimacy. Derrida wrote on them and they on him, differently but vaguely echoing the way Deleuze and Foucault primed each other in friendship and epochal designation of the other's breakthrough discoveries. It was different with our guy. Derrida did not spare them his critical estimates, any of them, including his disciples, though he accorded übergenerosity to a handful of them. Usually he was on the alert. I wonder whether there's ever a time of immunity, a pass allowing a great teacher to let some things slide, releasing problematic misappropriations with which the exemplary student leaves home. Should the teacher ever dress down an offspring's work, reprove and publicly register a complaint? Conversely, should a teacher acclaim, withholding critical reprobation, even when her nerves are shot? We know that students do, and possibly should, shoot down their teachers Brutus-style, when the masters harden into an icon, become authoritarian or power blind. Is the test of power, the press of justice ever concluded? When is one or the other given a free pass, or are such tests from the get-go impossible to evaluate, at all times bottoming out as inconclusive? What happens when the student effects a breakaway, pushed on by an imaginary spree of *originality*?

With his work on the paradoxes of parergonal logic, translation and related transit systems in Benjamin, supplementarity, the hymen, and so many other run-throughs that continue to bring us out of our paleonymic stagnation, Derrida was able to shift the grounds of purported originality and orient us toward more difficult areas of shade-ins, echoes, secondary and excremental margins. What does it mean to be a Derridean, to dwell in his shadow, to be prone to conducting spectral colloquies in the halting throes of an infinite conversation? Not something that I take for granted, and so many have dropped off or too quickly assimilated, caved in to the ongoing criticism, smoothed over the edges, understood, grafted, introjected without discernible remainder or quiver.

On bad days, Derrida haunts and hounds me, dissatisfied with me, downturning the domestic approval ratings that I seek from him ever and again. On better days, and these are many, he holds me up and pushes me on, I imagine, to finish aspects of his own work. I am one of the few who does not struggle with the possibility that I am no more than an invention of his, an effect of his oeuvre or merely a lone, if mutant, French theorist with a Germanic sense of duty driven by an unrelenting and cruel Superego, but enough about my idiomatic *Geistesgeschichte*, the course of an intellectual history, a spirit's chronicle. I said—*theory*, that I practice French theory, or rather German philosophy with a French accent: when one doesn't have to decide or tell between philosophy and literature in a rigorously taut, tensed way. I said "me," I said "I," but these markers have been faded and are barely overhauled remnants, mere grammatical conveniences so that my sentence can get some feet, go on its ways. I don't remember ever putting up a fight against the idea that she is, very possibly, an echo of Jackie Derrida. Others still argue with their predica-

The Trouble with Deconstruction

ment and CVs, needing to have signatory rights cut off from their incubators and teachers; they struggle with their dreams of emancipation and myths of autonomy, or sometimes very understandably they have to run away from home base with not a small amount of bruising and coerced branding. Still others cut themselves loose and go in earnest search of their "own" voices and deliberate styles. I understand only too well this impulse to cut one's own profile, to insure against identity theft of any kind. I understand that they want an intractable signature, the homeland-created and self-referring work. I see things differently—I mean, the same. But maybe I'm kidding myself when in self-deprecating rapture, maybe the irony does not lift off.

At best, a highly tensed echo machine, a mash of reiteration with a pronounced talent for receiving the other, transmitting with only a little distortion and next-generation flaws, I do not share the concerns of those who need to make their mark as if it could be sewn up, sent and delivered, with a certificate of originality. But it's no one's fault that I come equipped with inordinately sensitive receivers and favor conditions that allow for secondariness, simulators and mock-ups, promoting excremental outgrowths of the other. Quite frankly, I was brought up to be a receptor, a thoroughbred replicator. Hence the endless reflections on non-presence in terms of telephone, medial connectors, non-prescriptive ethics, drugs. I have been tracing and tracking that which withdraws from day one. Heidegger says, "Entzug ist Ereignis," withdrawal is event. This recessionary draft speaks to my upbringing, or what Kafka calls, in his "Letter to Father," my *downbringing*. An echo chamber and simulator, a knock-off of the real deal, temping for the other, I know how to step down, let myself be used by the inspiriting breath coming from an undefinable Somewhere, the *unWo* (the unWhere) of which Celan writes. I was ruthlessly tethered to that *unWo*, which approached in many forms and improbable figurations, some desperately familiar, alien familiar, drop dead in-your-face alien-familiar. In terms of zoography, I wanted to be the animal that followed him, his puppy, in *animots*-mimetic ways, aping him, on some beats parroting, or doing whatever it would take to be teacher's pet, close but not too invasive, keeping my lynx eye on the daily fluctuations of my stocks and the shares I put in, pulling back strategically while readying myself for the embraces and pats that I sought from him.

Once he asked me to write an abstract for the imminent publication of one of his articles. I applied myself to imitating his style but curbing its textual intricacies—so replicating the genre constituting an abstract, an abstraction of Derrida. A few months later, upon publication, he quietly told me with a grin, half-embarrassed, half triumphal, that Paul de Man had gone out of his way to compliment the abstract—who knew?!—that the abstract—itself

CHAPTER 3

a copy or Instagram of the essay in question—had won the day for being exemplary, a tour de force of condensation and precise delivery, capturing the essential gist and ground of the Derridean argument. We know that de Man had a thing for paraphrase, which he showed to be notoriously untenable—he had his students produce, or rather, *fail* to produce, paraphrases as dislocating exercises. You may think it's fairly easy to follow an assignment that requires you to paraphrase an argument, but it's a resistant and only ever frustrating venture. I swelled up with a bubble of pride when learning that I had scored well on a related speech act, the triumph of my life—acing an abstract—and asked whether he told de Man that I had produced that little gem. And so I find out that Derrida hadn't told de Man: it was a compliment he wanted to keep for himself, *Carte postale* wrong destination-style, right destination maybe, if you consider that I imitated him, doubling down on his idiomatic habits and rhetorical finesse, siphoning off his text and inimitable mannerisms. But the calculations don't stop there: Derrida preferred to keep the compliment possibly meant for me, the abstract writer, to himself, for himself, deflecting off me, or rather his momentary double and ghost writer, on him, wanting something that was and was not mine, having originated in any case with him, the doubly expropriated sliver of a text, but that he wanted to have signed and nailed to de Man's door. A little abstract that bound us and to which we both narcissistically attached. Rebounding off de Man's compliment—you should all know that Professor de Man was spare in his compliments, cutting and putting down his most sophisticated students—the abstract bloated in significance and became the property that we tugged-of-war over. In a related incident, trying to score points with the frugal and withholding friend and counterpart, Jacques told me that all he ever had wanted to do was to "seduce" Paul de Man, bag his approbation, an intention and borrowed kickstart that I annexed according to my own narcissistic metrics.

So why do I bring the drama of the abstract to your door, I wonder? On some level of urgent need, I suppose that I am tracing the contours of a loss, a sense of loss that I recognized from day one of the encounter, the first encounter having been organized around a tiny colloquium—seven or eight people, I had stumbled in, don't ask, I think Professor Rainer Nägele was to blame, he put me on the wrong or *right* trail—a discussion on Celan, with the widow and literary executor, Giselle Celan, present with the *Nachlass* (posthumous works) in conversation with Derrida. My first encounter with Derrida, recorded in *La carte postale*, gave me to understand how the *contre* becomes irrevocably attached to the *rencontre*, the *gegen* to the *Begegnung*, the "towards" to the "meeting," and all the counters of our encounters, most tender though they mostly were. On some remote level, instigated by the touchy theme of echo and mimetic tendency in writing and institutional circumstance, framed by academic rivalry and artistic valorization, I may have decided to come forward to issue a complaint, to hear myself complaining, if only to negotiate, if minimally, with the severe returns of the plaint from which I cannot, on my own, detach and separate. *Ach, ach!* Not a pretty picture!

Am I honestly complaining about the authorship of an abstract? *Do abstracts even have authors?* And who in her right mind would come forward to make claims on forgotten, miserably inessential abstracts that Mr. Paul de Man, for whatever over- or underdetermined reasons, may have tossed, one fine day, at the great philosopher and his shadow? How did I, once again, get caught in a vain snag that jacks up the narcissistic habit of complaint? I am certainly down with this task, though.

As companion species to all narcissists, starting with my mother, I have grown on the training grounds of narcissistic crushing machines, where I squeak and peek and, on good days, echo out from the master grids of articulation and wayward assertion—whatever they serve up, I can recalibrate. Don't get me wrong. This is a proud position. For I am Josefine, Queen of the Mausvolk, fueled on Benjaminian melancholia. My spectral reverberation, while making no pretense of assured arrival, still gets airplay in the Shakespearean sense where *air* and *heir* coincide to the point of consternation and game-changing anguish. Who can anoint herself Derrida's heir? I breathe his air. I surfed his hair. His legacy, still in many ways to be constituted, cannot simply be taken for granted, and it is as if my teacher and mentor, my friend ("O my friends!") is coldly rumored to have left his body more than ten years ago. A chronically disturbed observer of departure dates, I do not only keep a spectral calendar but continue to engage the beloved teacher, a live feed, more closely instructuring than ever before. My Hamletian heritage allows for regular visitations and midnight consults.

My own—if one can still say "my own " after all the grafts, theoretical homesteading, rewrites, chowdowns, and borrowing plans—my own involvement with radical mimetology and the styles associated with echoing the master began with a close-up of Eckermann, Goethe's schizonoaic companion who finished the master's autobiography, wrote in his—the other's—hand, copied him in so many ways, and continued to hold his conversations with Goethe in nightly séances after the great poet's death, in a room overpopulated with birds, forty avian creatures including birds of prey, where I found my name inscribed—*avis*—but that's another story of signature and crypt.

The metapsychological fact of birds is something that I have already explored, including reflections on their involvement with phallus and pecker,

CHAPTER 3

augury or divine figuration, even the eerie and disfiguring place they maintain in Hitchcock's filmic insight and psychic flow chart.[2] Eckermann depended on his houseguests, the birds, as he echoed and replayed Goethe's oeuvre, which fell to him, as his task to complete, without ever finishing. "Le petit Docteur Eckermann," as he was called, steadily began to take on the morphology of the other species and began to look like a bird. This feature is noted by nearly every one who went to meet him, including George Eliot, who diagnosed him rightly as an undead, still taking dictation from Goethe, producing the rich volume of a remotely echoing text.

Echo consorts with the ghostly above, reverberating according to another rhythm of being and its spectral flipside. At one point Derrida expressed the wish to be Echo—perhaps an ironic toss between his narcissistic overcapacity and something that I would situate in terms of effects of the phantom and haunted sites, the troubled arrival of the *envois* that he continues to send us by all sorts of deviated and partly blocked routes.

In the interest of somewhat fuller disclosure, I should probably not avoid the following angle. Sidelined and routinely downplayed, Echo may stand as the figure of a minority, yet, in the end, she rules. Derrida, ahead of the reading curve, has shown some suspicion with regard to Echo's self-positioning. He did not exactly buy the pose that she strikes of fixed secondariness. Don't count her out, for Echo pulls a fast one. He, at any rate, was onto her, close to the heals of her stratagems. In the "Oligarchies: Naming, Enumeration, Counting" section of *Politics of Friendship*, when Derrida closes in on a conflict in the philosophy of *philein* in the Aristotelian thought of friendship, he also takes the "call of dissymmetry" that Aristotle in a number of cases refuses.[3] Derrida addresses the question of "the 'oneself' thus out of joint with its own existence," when the self falls apart in the effort to befriend itself—or not—and still assure the testamentary structure of friendship.[4] Can I stand up for myself? Do I count?

Well, Derrida could count on me to be his Echo, that goes without saying. But, on closer examination, he pulls her away from narcissism as commonly understood, for Echo pops up suddenly as "celle qui prend la parole aux mots de l'autre"—a complicated phrase that says two things (but of course, twice and two simultaneously), thus raising the stakes of where in the doubled meaning to locate her performativity and trespass: the translation runs the phrasing in this way, at once as "she who speaks from, and steals the words of the other"; and "she who takes the other at his word." In both cases she is on the take, a word thief, whose "very freedom prec[edes] the first syllables of Narcissus, his mourning and his grief."[5] Echo not only supplies the "last word of the last will and testament" of friendship, sealing the deal of friendship and its remembrance, but, to the extent that she raids the narcissistic language trove

The Trouble with Deconstruction

before he can name his grief and say his pain, she robs him of "his" language that was never simply his, but always on the way to dispossessive extradition, latching on to the first taker, Echo.

No matter how diminished, forgettable, or secondary, there is something of the quality of preemptiveness in all the fields and connectors that take off from Echo, who swoops down to snatch the first word and run, or fly, or hunker down with it, lap it up. This relation to language, to friendship, to their outfolding into the areas of justice and politics is responsible for "another experience of the possible," says Derrida. For it breaks all "ipseity apart in advance, ruining in advance that which it makes possible: narcissism and self-exemplarity."[6] Echo raids the narcissistic stronghold from the get-go, plunders the self that would be adequate to itself, disrupting the ground on which politics is built and justice sought. Derrida cautiously announces this essential disturbance as the good news of a different possible experience of justice, another possible political arrangement, freeing up some of the totalities that have led to no good in our shared histories.

Elsewhere I have tried to see, in terms of Freud, Lacoue-Labarthe, and Nancy, whether narcissism could ever give way to identification, the beginning of the political in the pursuit of justice.[7] Echo, then, usurps from the start, which is to say, when there is still nothing much to seize upon but the onslaught of grief, a pang that still seeks its word. The reverberative remainder remains her signature, loyal and self-dissolving, yet, if I've understood correctly, she cannot be trusted, as she is meant to purloin and poach where the phallus once held steady, filching boundaries between other and self, an instigator and guardian spirit at once, bossy and receptive, even caring. Echo redirects Hamletian readiness, taking calls, handling them, before they go out. Such incoming calls, their spectral inferrals, are fielded by the Echoes among us, the Echo-manns and vibes.

After his great interlocutor's unavowable demise, Eckermann continued to converse with him and allow Goethe's oversized visit in dreams.

Since his rumored departure, I was beset with dreams, some of which I reported to Marguerite Derrida, as if pleading with her to pull me out of a ditch, existential and oneiric, as often, in the past, she had done. Sometimes, in conversation with her, I could supply the "answers" and do the work of dream interpretation myself. In late July, around his birthday, I dreamt, for instance, that Derrida had seen Philippe Lacoue-Labarthe at 4:00 a.m. in a Parisian garage, for office hours. In the dream I was puzzled that Jacques would want to give Philippe office hours when I thought they were somewhat estranged at that time. My anxiety, high on the Richter scale, tremulously pitched in the dream as I cried out, "Why 4 in the morning?—That is too early," especially since I'd instructed him to stay healthy and replenish, stop exhausting himself. I asked myself after awakening, why the horror around 4:00 a.m.? My rapid response *Traumdeutung* would be that "4" matches 2004, and it was too early for Derrida to leave, at the age of seventy-four. It was too early for Philippe to depart, to have Jacques depart and separate. They left too soon, each one uniquely too soon.

Around that time I remembered having argued with Bill Regier whether I could keep the teenagey mark "4-ever" in my chapter on Flaubert. After all, the book was titled *Stupidity*, why did I have to follow the style sheet when I was down-styling, moving to a section on graffiti, a type of scrawl that Derrida, by the way, did not appreciate on the walls we passed in the 'burbs. During our walks in Ris Orangis, when he was still well enough to take them, move his energy, we'd pass suburban scribble patches and I'd try to entertain Marguerite and my teacher with disquisitions on defacement and public traces. That did not fly.

"What should be understood by the end?," asks Derrida, recalling Seneca, who wonders why man—and not the animal—always dies before his time, while also understanding that he dies *immaturus*, immaturely and prematurely. In *Aporias*, Derrida tracks dying's prematurity to Seneca's rhythm of absolute imminence, the imminence of death at every instant. "This imminence of disappearance that is by essence premature seals the union of the possible and impossible, of fear and desire, and mortality and immortality, in being-to-death."[8]

Wanting to support and secure his legacy, though I was never certain what such a call to action might entail, or what it essentially means, yet prodded by a sense of duty—what does it mean to help constitute a legacy?—I complained bitterly when I saw that the *New York Times* published a corrosive obituary. *Who does that?* If the form and cast of the obituary were merely old news, a rerun of ancient history, my complaint would not resurge at this time. The complaints against Derrida have cast a shadow, and maybe such stains are unavoidable, though with time they should have worn off. Nonetheless, they tend to establish a fissure from the ground up, even if we assume that our work by now and earnest interpretive jaunts have covered falsifiable territory.

Whether or not warranted, provable or just, the complaint sometimes wedges disturbingly and colors the way utterance returns to us. Perhaps I am slower to recover from injury than others, and I dwell without rest or reprieve on the consequences of the unjustifiable. The murderous vulgarity of the continuing complaints of the Unreaders was staggering. One destructive cliché after another was flung at Derrida's memory. After the initial shock subsided, the malevolent dismissals gave food for thought, returning me to Lacan's discussion of double deaths in "The Ethics of Psychoanalysis," when the first corpse does not suffice for the purpose of absorbing a certain level of rage, when the angered go after what is already dead, but not yet dead enough. I slipped into other identities to get some bearing, affining myself to Antigone, for I did feel the need to follow him into the double vault of a solitary seal constructed by the city's chronicle, the *Times*. An injunction hung over my head.

Sometimes one is called up. One can hit the snooze button, but I was the kind of wreck always on the alert, a first responder ahead of the call, ready for it, sprung by anticipatory bereavement from the starting line. I realized also that impiety and distortion were more than ways of desecrating his memory, supplying also an inadvertent mechanism for keeping Derrida alive, if as a contestable monument of consequential breakthrough. I mean, who complains about a thinker that one has not read? Should I settle into a place of a legacy watch, I wondered, or would that be too controlling of a fate over which one cannot simply hold vigil round the clock or know exactly what one is securing? Keeping up with Derrida's places and atopoi, clocking the pace of his subtle disappearances and returns, is a daily practice. O time!

I was trained for this, I tell myself, I am a descendent of Diotima, the other sister of Antigone and Ismene, and I carry traits of some of the meaner versions of watchdogs, classical women rebels—those who, with one and the same stroke, stir trouble *and* protect a sacred grove of memory. I drape myself over a declining legacy, installing a loudspeaker from one of its remote corners, reading out. Not that he *needs* me. I answer a call, but it does not originate, I tell myself, from a place of need. That which calls me springs from a more complicated combination of urge and calculation. I think of the way Rousseau suffered from the mutilation of his legacy, the way the newspapers ran his obituary ahead of the race to the finish. The solitary walker was crushed by the rumors newspapers carried, the downplay and adversarial warp that were spread in the flavor of the day, that of derisive scorn. Maybe works can take such hits and redirect the complaints addressed to them. On the off chance that some works, on the contrary, are fragile and need accompaniment through the temporal zones they must yet traverse, maybe a tugboat, I keep my watch.

To this day I try to gauge the windfall that Derrida entails for those of us who are oriented toward philosophical reflection and poetic modes of disarticulation, historical disinscription, and rhetorical variances in Saying. His books keep me company, the archive expands into uncanny holding pens, the spur to attend to my teaching stirs me, forcing this Dasein to come to grips, to show up for him. I have been in a reflective stupor since his so-called demise, sitting by a pool of reflection, as I contemplate how he became what he is: the trainer, the coach and mentor, to the history of nerves a horse whisperer and, on firewalled or stalled days, my ghost-dunked wake-up call. In terms of schooling, Derrida taught us to be on the lookout for what lies beneath philosophical radars, eludes the phenomenological capture, diverts the subtle rumble of being. He had us attentive to evental edges that had no proper home base or accountability in the great systems of philosophy and law—accent, tone, inflection, loose screws, semanticized ploys, micrological operations, nano-palpitations in syntactical maneuvers, the fine print attached to upended contract and covenant, the nuance of an apostrophic ethics: Who is being addressed? By what ghostly broadcast system? He has urged us to consider: What hails or eludes testimonial positionality? How to case the House of Being and, keeping it real—or phantomal—how to accommodate parasitical utterance or nab performative fraudulence? The list is long, and he left no doubt that performativity was viewed by Derrida with suspicion. Performativity plays too smoothly with far too large an apportionment of positing swagger.

Well, we cannot dwell on the aporias of performative speech acts forever, even though the complainer is one of its prime perps in another sense of making sense of things. If only the complaint could change the groundswell from which an injury has emerged—an injury that does not make it to the finals scored by the lament! Let me offer what I can, retelling the event of an encounter and the type of plaintive stances that it has thus far provoked. I register what happened only to the extent that a traumatized being, barely grounded, can put together a story or be cautious with memory.

Once upon a time I sought him out, in need of a teacher, academic deprogramming (put together by what I'd call a sort of deprogrammatology), seeking instruction that comprised at the same time a tough-as-nails training. I went after him. Booked out of Virginia and went to Paris, deciding to scrap my so-called educational duties, restart. My training brought yields that cannot entirely be counted up, but I can offer a brief tally of what has stayed with me, become theoretical habit. I followed Derrida to learn how to deliver a number of blows to regimens, grammars, and limits against which we crashed according to programmed philosophical protocols, without entertaining for one minute that one could overcome or overtake these fundamental constraints. The world-class optimism of *Überwindung*, overcoming, had been left in the dust. One fought at the limits of metaphysics, in the intervallic moments of certain expositions and fragilities.

I watched Derrida deliver smackdowns of highly invested assumptions; he taught us how to get a close-up of marginal predicaments and occurrences, even *inoccurences*, undocumented *Bedeutungs*-shifts, fluctuations in meaning, evicted from philosophical premises. He also oriented us to major historical events and their unpredictable undertows. In the Californian heat these lessons, or training sessions, led me, in the early '90s, to analyze the Rodney King trial, a prototype of unrelenting police attacks on Black bodies. I probed the legal justifications sent up to cover the unleashing of such a magnitude of policing violence, how the language of repressive acts had to do with specific projections onto bodies of color cast in the rhetoric of ghostly entities. Something had interrupted a broad-based understanding of medial representation, the relation of technology to law. I came at the problem of criminal phantomization first by attempting to reconfigure the question of how to read the interruption—a motif in Derrida's reading of Levinas.

At the time, I considered why, in a generalized manner, television had become the locus for a certain type of self-interrogation of the body politic and legal recourse (I had watched televised congressional hearings with Derrida: without being naive about intent or outcome, he expressed admiration for the way Americans put themselves and their flaws up for review in a popular forum, the intrusive query supplied by television). I wondered, in this context, what it means that television polices or, in strategic moments, blanks out the world as representation, stops showing or telling by a form of broadcast that crushes reference. Crisis-prone, yet unable to tell what it sees, television is inundated with stories of policing and judicial narrative, insistently absorbs Walter Benjamin's phantom body of the police, engages the historical and hermeneutic capacity for switching on cold and hot cases, ever running the traumatic story that cannot and yet must be told in television's relentless production of corpses. Derrida—and Blanchot—have taught me to watch for the neutral gleam, the blind eye of televisual metaphysics. Maybe they taught me more than how to watch TV, or the way TV watches itself watching by means of aleatory, guerilla video and other internal alterities that medial technologies house and host like so many disgruntled ghosts, plaintive, menacing, or merely distressed.

So the title I gave this chapter is "The Trouble with Deconstruction." Derrida has taught us so much about how to read and situate titles that I feel obligated to comment where I think I've been heading under this heading, or beheading. Today more than ever, Derrida's thought on beheading imposes ethical strictures on us, to think about politics and capital, the provocation of decapitation, in ways that he modeled. Let me mark while turning the page without forgetting this thematic cluster of traumatic proportion, in so many ways referentially anchored and tremendously disturbing to heads of state when they put their heads together and, in one case in particular, pull their heads out of their asses.

The title, "The Trouble with Deconstruction," refers in the first place to Derrida's expression of dissatisfaction with the term as an adequate lever to describe what he was doing. He more or less, more than less, discarded it fairly early on after giving it some air time in conjunction with Heideggerian *Abbau* (demolition, dismantling). However, Lacoue-Labarthe stays with the term precisely because of its fragile span and troubled shelf-life. Derrida gives it another chance, as late as *Aporias*, parenthetically resurrecting a moment in *Psyché: Inventions de l'autre*, "where deconstruction [no quotation marks] is explicitly defined as a certain aporetic experience of the impossible," before proceeding to the step (*pas*) and paralysis of the nondialectizable contradiction and anniversary or birth and death date that only happens by effacing itself in *Schibboleth pour Paul Celan*.[9] Derrida does not entirely write off deconstruction—it comes barreling back in, unexpectedly, by means of *Rams*, where it is enrolled as the name for struggle: deconstruction, says Derrida here, is a struggle. For whom? For him, for us, for all who take the trouble to read, as a mode of textual engagement and ethical pressure zone: it instigates political struggle and relentless democratic probes. Above all, it entails a struggle at life's limits, like the sacrificial ram rebelling against all persecutions by and of substitution.

Apart from its reappearance in *Rams*, "deconstruction" appears to have run its course; it sinks back again, without entirely disappearing. Even so, he lets it live out a certain exhausted history that rears up again only sporadically, at strategic moments of agonistic encounter, such as the encounter with Gadamer, who heads up Team Hermeneutics. Thereafter, the uses and mentions of deconstruction survive here and there mostly on a citational jag when, for instance, Derrida starts memorializing and quoting his own works in his later texts. When you translated him in the later years he started supplying footnotes, not trusting, I think, that his many works and crucial passages would be summoned up by his readers and translators on their sole initiative. He became more hypomnesiac by the book, feeding our memory disorder, concerned about the stability and staying power of the enormous archive that bore his signature. As a term or cipher, "deconstruction" was not to be simply eliminated or quarantined under quotation marks, stunted in citational lockdown, but kept around as a sort of remembrance, a discounted memento not altogether shunned, yet quietly living out its usefulness and mention-value in unprotected regions of thinking. I'm not sure what kind of an orphaned figure it cuts. A relative of Isaac, benched and replaced, a remainder unsacrificed, emptied out? Taken out of the game but still pressing its moves, it is neither obsolesced nor stripped down and junked, permitting only of a problematic closure, a kind of gift/*Gift* that keeps on giving even as it is more or less taken off the table, withdrawn. The other guy says "Entzug ist Ereignis," withdrawal is event, however. And so I stick with it because deconstruction—with or without quotation marks, mark it, Horatio—shows up more often than not nowadays as a bully-point, a target zone for nonreaders and anti- and infraphilosophical hate speech. I wear it, I live with it, I eat it, I *schreiben schrei* it: DECONSTRUCTION!

Part of its disseminative swell touches the title's relation to cinema and the limits of seeing, the problem of and with finitude, our *Sein-zum-Tode*, being-toward death.

Let me open some dossiers for further consideration. "The Trouble with Deconstruction" is meant, above all, to call up Hitchcock's film, *The Trouble with Harry*, whose body resists the serial attempts at burial, turning up and returning time and again to make trouble. The body of Derrida's works appears to share a similar fate, showing up only to be serially cut out of the picture and undead. The status of a harried burial started off a facet of deconstruction on its tattered yet determined career path. Deconstruction was tagged DOA, rising from the start with the menacing qualities of an originary ghost, up there with Hamlet's father, visor down, difficult to read, handing down impossible assignments, ordering—or pleading with—us to "Remember me!" Let us continue. According to my own playlist of things put out there, essays and books idiolectically cast, "The Trouble with Deconstruction" is also meant to recall a prior essay by me, pivoted on Kafka's desistance in his undeliverable letter to his father, bearing the title, according to my CV, "Trouble in Parricide"—perhaps not unlinked from my ongoing, if untranslatable relation to Jacques Derrida. I have gotten in trouble with colleagues and friends, believe it or not, for *not being parricidal enough* regarding the great mentor and master-teacher. Recently, though I am not tallying from the vantage of a comparative analysis—I know from Levinas too much about the crime of substitution to think that I can get away with murder (or parricide) on this score; sometimes, though, it's unavoidable to substitute one for the other and scramble the honor code of singularity, and so one pulls a fast one and *substitues (substikills)* my autocomplete wrote—if only to get a furtive point across. I have violated theoretical codes before. I don't like to do so, but sometimes, as said and unsaid, it's necessary to commit the crime of substitution—you lose one person, one pet, one job, and you think of all the others that left, they take a number, they all pile in, singularity fans out, can't hold it together, replacement parts of lost objects, bound to fail on the rebound, but who's counting, who's binding?

In this spirit of criminal substituting, I recall a story for you. Recently I organized a colloquium and lecture performance to commemorate the passing of my friend, Friedrich Kittler. It turned out that a number of speakers arrived with the attitude of destructive complacency, part of a *Stimmung*, demeanor, or frame of negative transference. This troubled relation to the teacher after his demise, before and after his demise, may seem quite shocking, but remains as Derrida would insist, the law: "c'est la loi" he would say to me when I'd cry that yet another student flipped on me. Trouble on the line of transference is the norm, even if you've been the good breast of *Germanistik*, handled their emergency calls, monitored and encouraged their emergent language spurts, diapered them academically, and so on and so forth, *ach!*

If we stay momentarily with the transferential edges of trouble, we should remember that, in the French language, *trouble* also indicates a heart's agitation, as when you're crushing on someone. You are troubled, turned toward this other who closes out, by means of thrill and thrall, all the others—a distraction, creating inner turmoil. But trouble in my title timed in on the screen, the memory screen, in other ways as well.

Who could forget the *trouble* that Derrida got me out of time and again? The letters of recommendation, the place offered at the dinner table, the consults on Heidegger's thought of proximity, the first responder's rush to the distress of unemployment and injuries of institutional misogyny, and the soothing backup in face of other relentless markdowns? Mark it, Horatio! There would have been little place for a chronically profiled misfit like me in the university without him. He pulled me out of trouble, ended significant obstruction, broke down some doors—continue to remember, please, that in his reading of Celan, doors are laws—he kicked down some doors and created around me, us, I thought and felt, the fantasy at least of a regulatory ideal, an "it gets better" energy of futurity and resolve, when he put into play, for example— one among many, for example—an unconditional university, a fantasy strong enough that I could maybe fake it until I maybe make it while continuing to prize, like my man, no, my "I'm not a man, I'm dynamite" Nietzsche, the value of adjusting to my fate and that of others—the *capacity* to fake it and affirm faking it in the sense of donning the mask, appropriating the will to fiction, throwing off historically burdening obstacles to any path and *Holzweg*, while honoring histories of the unsaid. For this and so much more, I thank and think my teacher, Derrida, to this day.

Let me slow myself down to settle with some truth value at this juncture. Trouble came in different packages, multiple deliveries, at the wrong and right addresses that I gave out. It is not the case that I was *not* in trouble with him at times. Once, in a fit, a bad fit, he was so mad at me that he called me the Number One enemy of deconstruction. *I was the trouble with deconstruction?!* I am still trying to wrap my head around that one. It sure makes you wonder, wounder. But this memo came up later in the process and distress of writing this chapter. How could I have forgotten and repressed the scathing *Anklage,* the accusation that came my way? When writing I fall, I barely scrape by in terms of my thrownness, *Geworfenheit*; memories deblock, I ask the inner locator to find what determines and overdetermines certain decisions and slowdowns. Superego feasts on my vulnerability, goading me on, haranguing and bitch-slapping me as I try to get the words down. Repression unleashes: I can't go on, I must go on. Let me dust myself off. What initially motivated this title, inescapably off pitch, was a less unconsciously encrusted consideration and set of references than I have enumerated. Thinking I was writing in a different key, I was unaware of hidden prompters. I was set off, more innocently, perhaps, and in neutral, by Hitchcock's pedagogical and Oedipedagogical scripts, the connection established by *Rope* where Jimmy Stewart plays the role of every failing teacher of theory who must deal with a dead body, the fate of writing, and, even more to the point, by *The Trouble with Harry*—but also, don't kill me, eventually, linking these films to Woody Allen's explicit use of the term using the same proper name, *Deconstructing Harry.* "Harry" by the way means "rules the home" in Norse, and in Teutonic the meaning of the name is "war chief," while in English the name means "home or house protector." At the same time, I know the limits of reading names, for Derrida, who often played his name against meaning, taught us not to fall into the semanticizing trap, the lure, of reducing a name into meaning. I can't help it. He protected the question. He protected the house, the ever obsolescing hospitality of the house of being, language. In ways, meaningful and untranslatable for me, he kept watch over the deracinating grid of our thrownness.

Ach! I fake it 'til I make it, day in, day out, I pretend–make it. In the meantime, I tap out, type in and file complaints, I reset the plaintive cry, the *Klage,* and sharpen the accusatory stance, the *Anklage,* day in, day out, unable to desist from my own tightly circumscribed circle of grievance, the ongoing hum of bickering and moaning that I take and dole out. Here and there I catch a rumble from the philosophical bleachers, I witness in near-catatonic shutdown how my sound system produces noise, the dissonant echo of lament as I stagger. *Ach!* I am attached to the *ach* of *Sprache,* the ache of speech, the way Friedrich Kittler breaks it down. I turn the same question over in my head, expand its focus, then restrict its scope, only to open it up again. Back and forth, all day long, and during the bumps of insomniac countdowns: Should I complain about this or that, the way this one treats me? Will they hear me? Should I answer some insolent complaints that have come my way, not the highway?

What does it mean to lodge a complaint, something that is philosophically devalued yet part of the repertory of critical feints?

Secretly, I attach the *ach* of Sp-*rache* to *Rache*, the word for revenge, ever since my mother would pound the living room floor in our immigrants' Washington Heights apartment singing—and, more terrifyingly still, mouthing, distorting her face as if she had stepped out of a Francis Bacon portrait in menacing self-dislocation—the Queen of the Night's aria, "Der Hölle Rache," hell's vengeance, the wrath of hell, one of Mozart's last airs as he was fading out. As sweet as Mozart can be, the sonic intrusion was hell for a child: a minor's vendetta was in the making, way prior to the shrills and cracked trills of puberty. The boys I knew, they went through the confusion of voice change as they pulled up. They blushed at the voice, what passed for a voice but burped up a drumfire of self-estrangement, one's ownmost maladjustment, making me wonder how embarrassing it was for them to have one's own rebel voice drop, squeak, bump into upper registers while falling into pubescence, that cracked voice, disqualified from the tryouts of lament.[10] Could Hamlet be played in broken pitch, a minor's key, I wonder, losing command of direction and voice while the spectral newscast booms?

I don't know about you, but I have heard a number of complaints batted by those who have not read him, or have bumped their heads against one or another of Derrida's demonstrations, cursing at times the shifts of focus and outrageous expanses for which his signature was responsible. That there *was* a focus, and that one had to bear down on the way a work worked it or turned against itself, sought hesitant refuge on the borders of an erroneous track and engaged the mystifications of others, did not elicit gratitude or mindfulness with regard to the search for another logic, but rather opened the gates of grievance. Why so? Let me try to answer to the greater part of the complaining instinct without becoming defensive or issuing too many counterclaims. Let me call up what it has meant to read, how we had to behave and discipline ourselves, deconstructively.

We had to read, even "overread" and "read into" micrological maneuvers, muted and great histories, dig in minute syntactical mines, to come up against a tipping point of meaning, a narrative blip or ethical fault line. Deconstruction made one's life-and-works miserable at times, putting you in relentless pursuit of semantic or diacritical loopholes and the "defective cornerstone" of a circumscribed problem, political articulation, ethical reflection or hermeneutic-theological districting traditions, upending material reliance on evidence or demonstration, making one converse with sciences of unknowing or phenomenological prestige and check off systematic quirks in cognitive description and epistemic circumscription. Nothing can be taken for granted (not even the "grant" or gift in the granted), so much is thrown into question (if the *question* still holds, after Heidegger's takedown). And so forth and so *da*.

One doesn't have to look far beyond the universities and creative sites to see the ongoing battles waging, even as a distant rumble of resistance to reading and textual struggle makes itself heard in those places hosting critical thought on all levels of discernment, journalistic appropriation, popular makeovers, and social activism. I sometimes surprise myself by my own scholarly demeanor, even in the streets, when in protest at the desk or around the block. I love being a scholar, its intense standoff with perspectives that challenge our slice of tranquility and commitments, the endless study; even so, deconstruction tightens the screws, puts you on the nightshift, upping the paranoiac ante—making you responsible for a text's very survival, tapping through the night for survivors, as if language mattered and one false move or attempt at setting things right in a nonadolescent instant of lucidity could make a difference in our battered world, such as it stands, fissured and wobbly, on its sorry-assed axis and axiologies. *Ach!* I want the distress to stop.

Complaints on the subject of deconstruction—an embattled term, which is why, out of theoretical spite as well as, undeniably, an uncontrolled surfeit of loyalty, I still use it—take on different allures of dismissive feints and assertive put downs, but they rarely come across as convincing to me. What is one really complaining about when stubbing one's intellectual toe on "deconstruction-*ism*"—the warp that adds bulk and vacuity to the song of the vexed plaintive. Deconstruction—a term or name that has followed a plan of affirmation and erasure—does not belong to the species of thought that culminate in an "ism."[11] The add-on of "ism" helps congeal a scientific system that deconstructive operations disable, keeping things open to internal filtering and constant change, open-ended verification and hypothetical floats—building on the experimental disposition for which Nietzsche advocated in a rigorously consistent way.

Even those friendly, for the most part, to critical thought issue grievances against Derrida, mistaking, to take one instance, his engagement with Benjamin for a misfiring of a number of contingently invested concepts. I cannot take on the entire Bureau of Complaints that has been erected around Jacques Derrida's work, though I would like to be agile and witty enough to do so, like a tennis player returning balls served by an unstoppable practice machine. But I'm not sure this plan would improve my game. Such an assignment of repair and redemption, grandiose yet unconvincing, represents of course a real temptation for me, maybe even a task, part of the esteem due to an object of mourning.

CHAPTER 3

I could sign up for the job if only I were able—or in a position—to field all the complaints addressed to the name of Derrida! I am trying to imagine the kind of CV I would have to generate in order to make myself a viable candidate for this calling. Let me just say that the complaints I have collected, which were not deliberately directed to me, but randomly sprayed with a limited number of talking points and the compulsive resolve of shutdown (one often wonders why; why the need to shut down a whole sector of thinking, breathtaking and mind-blowing, what is the hidden threat here?), recharge the same themes. Perhaps I can retrieve some of the offenses, to the extent that they still, in some furtive way, abide: deconstruction, still seen as being too difficult, is ticketed for straining boundaries and credulity with its wide-ranging swoops and micrological reading habits training on where significance drains off and insignificance takes the day; it is identified, moreover, with clichéd knockoffs charging obscurity, relativism, Eurocentrism, nihilistic purchase, queer recounts of positions, deviant figures, and it has been discredited in some institutional outlets for philosophizing sans method. In a dreadful cast, it has been identified with the deadly distortions of the Alt-Right. The rebound of castigation and appropriation belongs to an ambivalent history of philosophical writing, a machine that makes it possible for a Hegel or Nietzsche—and Marx—to fall to right- *and* left-wing usages. Yet some of the Alt-Right branches despise "deconstruction" because of its continued Eurocentric focus and destruction of identity. Sound familiar?

Each of the charges pointed at deconstruction can be and has been answered, but as a registered symptomatologist I wonder rather why the complaint repeatedly takes on a recognizable shape. If you feel that you've heard this already, that is because Echo, in this sense, conforms to the nature of the complaint, or one of its dominant tendencies, consisting in replaying an unbroken record of the same accusation—a reverberation that tends to keep a living vivacity sapped of energy, in time warp.

The nature of complaints made against deconstruction or the name of Derrida (or, for that matter, against more or less declared allies such as psychoanalysis or the name of Freud) discloses something about the character of the complaining disposition when reaching its limits and becoming a distorting accusation, an attack, where *Klage* snaps into *Anklage*, accusation, turning violent, with the expectation of building a resentful life of its own.

The process repeats a prior complaint, nagging at credulity, hammering these imputations to the point of wearing down the contesting—or muzzled— recipient. In order to sound the accusatory note, complaint must simplify and exaggerate, round matters into incriminating bites that can be hurled time and again. These features of the complaint, when it assumes the role of recrimina-

The Trouble with Deconstruction

tion and accusation, make us ask if there can be such a thing as a *reasonable complaint*, or must all acts of complaining bend to the leveling techniques of simplicity? Even "good " complaining, the kind that steadies the railing of protest, the seasoned outcry, must find a way to level down a relation to language, deliver catchy slogans, inculpate with a knack for snappy and downsized language usage. In this regard, anything that intervenes to complicate our relation to language, to recall the pressure zones of non-relation and semantic breakdown, risks becoming the *object* of complaint. To the point and often blunt, the complaint complains about complications, beginning with those lodged in the very language that allows for its rambunctious itineraries.

Derrida, whom we did not know to be much of a complainer, though he smarted and raged when unjustly attacked, somehow put me on the lookout for the ambiguous fate of the complaint—not a necessarily elegant mode of address or easily accommodating ethical stance, often feminized and devalued, unable to prevail when it comes to significant philosophical showdowns. The complaint does not necessarily cover his own itineraries or radical breakdowns, but his work spurred us to shadow the margins of philosophy, no matter how minoritarian the neighborhood of thought. One lies in wait for the tipping point to disclose itself, or the flip, when the stakes noiselessly mount and new forms of meaning and address push forward. One waits and waits, and sometimes nothing of significance darts out at you or calls for attention. Still, I am planted in the field of the complaint, since forever, maybe, and it is my way of running with the *cri/écrit* on which I was suckled.

I have argued here that all of *Werther* pivots on the difference asserted and collapsed by Goethe between complaint—*Beschwerde*—and lament—*Klage* ("Was ist der Mensch, daß er klagen darf!" What is mankind that it may complain/lament?), the start-up engine, I dare say and condense, of the suicide rush and ghostly undertow that haunts this work. *Ach!*

What is a complaint? I obsessively ask, Who has the right to complain—or not to complain, even to shut down the other's complaint? Women and children and minorities are constantly seen to complain, maintaining a shrieky, clamorous, *noisy*, and so illicit relation to language, to being—the way minorities and Jews have been linked to noise in musical precincts and world-class kvetching, the minoritized howl, in other areas that represents yet another story.[12] *Ach!* I stick to the boisterous clamor of my subject, though it ever and always has to be scaled ambivalently, for complaints appear to carry good *and* bad tonalities, worthy and derisory qualities in terms of their launch pad and aims.

CHAPTER 3

Let us consider under what conditions, if at all, it is possible to dial down the *Mecker*-machine, the nattering mechanism, in a gesture that may well deliver an echography of the philosophical impulse, close to the Benjaminian starting gate of the *rights of nerves*: if the complaint is also what motivates or impels thought, this is in part because it recalls what burns you up, kicking off the whole regimen of writing that cries itself into a nocturnal howl. However probing and "abstract," Benjamin stayed close to the somatic instigators of thought. There were no detectable anti-noise machines accompanying the way he struggled with the themes and inquiries that beset his sensibility, the motivating push of his writing drive. Ever since Benjamin and his constellated cohort, one asks, concerning the unrelenting writing edge, "What makes one isolate, go into writing lockdown, launch against all odds a dissenting screed/scream with all existential bets off the table?" Scanning histories of the great complainers (though the greater part were transvaulated and not always pushed onto the stage as such), one wonders what impelled them to register an affecting complaint, to go up against a wall of indifference. Perhaps they sought to enter into negotiations with an advocatory ethics, defending even objects and things squeezed by inert being, lined by unfairness.

The complaint, aware of its own thinness, struck by its essential incompetence when it comes to changing the world, nonetheless attests to its capacity to bemoan the frugal share allotted to a demeaned being—sensing another predicament, another person, Dasein or figure, living or dead, maybe half-dead, stupefied or frozen. Sometimes, despite its meager means, the complaint manages to act as part of the lexicon championing a destitute other, whether on the outside or comprised as innermost hostage. When detached or reprieved from the narcissistic trap, a registering complaint can suddenly show the minor efficacy of fretting over one straggler—or a lost population—that, hard to locate, may inhabit the ego, as Maria Torok and Nicolas Abraham would say, forming a crypt.

The problem of locating the psychic seat of the complaint, its provenance, signals a need, still pressing, to return to the precepts of cryptonymy in order to explore the effects of the phantom, the way phantomal dissatisfaction ventriloquates and agitates, ceaselessly sounding complaints, crossing over to an existential no-man's land. We learn that, if they speak, the dead come through invisible channels clutching dossiers of unfinished business, breaking through the static barrier in the mode of complaint. Whether by remote control or voice systems lodged in someone's head, these phantoms hold in custody one who is enjoined to act on the complaint, perhaps resolve or disable its encroaching menace, maybe simply hear it out without the ability or impulse to repair, without proper access to reparative justice. I'm not sure where the complaint falls here—on the expectation of justice or with the firm knowledge that justice will not be rendered, leaving one in the slow-burn fury of unrequited engagement. I receive a lot of complaints, not necessarily aimed at me, not always, and I try to track them down to their phantomal source and subterranean histories. But, enough with the logic of tempered destruction and ghostly clamor. Can we let it go, for now, and clear the spectral channels? I can do that, I think. I have been a crypt dweller for long enough. *Wait.* Is "enough" the right word?

In fact, yes, I can let it go: I am disciplined and do not need to chase every passing ghostly theme or paraconcept that suggests itself furtively, if with justifiable insistence; I have gone to obedience school, received restraining orders and have learned the lessons of Heidegger's thought linking *heeding* to *obedience*, with the understanding that you are always listening for the *hören* in *Gehorsamkeit*. Still, my fantasy inventory makes me wonder if perhaps it wouldn't be worthy and necessary now to run in another direction, and go back over the crypt formation to which the chronic complainer is bound. Let me table this impulse for the time being. Instead, I'll indulge another option, equally imposing, and promise to straighten up, offer an *argument*, which is more or less what I signed up for, even if it should invite rhetorical flatlining—something by-the-book arguments often do, *ach!*—and a bit of thematic overkill.

Let me return to another aspect of Derrida's capacity for reading and greeting shadows, with the understanding that the ability to greet is part of our crisis today, as the world convulses over the pressure of opening borders and spaces for the unwelcome, the growing surge of the undocumented, and the United States absorbs the phantasm of a wall meant to seal off neighboring populations. The thought of *greeting* in more recent philosophical scrolls and controversies attunes us to the way Hannah Arendt writes in her work about welcoming the stranger, throwing a lifeline to the tattered refugee, but also to how Heidegger's reading of Hölderlin's hymn, "Andenken" ("Remembrance"), remains adamant about the importance of poetic acts of greeting.

After I started working, with some anxiety, on the motif of the greeting in Hölderlin and Heidegger, I found that Derrida took the greeting, the aspect of unconditional hospitality implicit in the greeting, seriously, creating dossiers of the *salut*, the salutation and its attendant healing protocols. The greeting, in Heidegger, and differently tuned in Arendt, pivots on and sharpens the ability both to welcome and to say good-bye, so that something can at all arrive, restart, and open—indicating as well the ability to dwell with and say good-bye to metaphysical thought blockages and a trail of historical snags. The denial of such blockages and snares frequently prevents us from throwing open the

CHAPTER 3

gates that hold back others who cut in, in some ways seizing one's acquired sense of space, giving the distorted impression even of encroaching on time and the apportioned share of temporal existence. The way a greeting relates us to the unrelatable, shifting some of the inherited grounds of what can be shared—of what traditionally passes for the unshareable—serves as the starting point for carrying, when called upon to do so, the weakened, deracinated other, without encouraging the presumption of one's own towering stability or existential coherence. One carries without assuring one's own courage and stamina to stand strong.

By the same token, the motif of the greeting inserts a *distance* where there was an imaginary squeeze of encroachment, so that the other, paradoxically, can show up as a sufferable disruption. I understand that one cannot simply "speak for oneself" as a self-alienated or socially minoritized being; nor can one present oneself as "the other," as some proponents of critical thought and art expression have been tempted to do. Derrida has been stern about the error of such self-representations that consist in whining about oneself as other. Still, I have my stash of complaints and moments when I have felt othered, ethnically sidelined. One of my most bitter complaints, as an instigation to the sprawling sense of injustice, regards the failure of someone I recognize to greet me on the street, in the elevator, in social or asocial media. What does it mean to refuse a greeting? In terms of philosophical and language theory, I mean. According to the master poets whose oeuvre depends on the ability to greet, the impetus to trope and hope for a responsive alterity's spark of recognition, however subtle or illusory, is crucial to poetic saying. The way I handle a complaint when it becomes registered in my psyche does not always live up to the mandate of the poetic vigil. I phase into sulking. Then, I go after it and turn the particulars of a perceived slight into a theoretical work, at best a poetic exultation.

You are helping me with the exigency of taking Abschied—*the struggle with taking leave, seeking permission to abort and cut my losses. I'm still not sure I can make it, at least in terms of separating off from the object of complaint.*

Consistently marking the difference between Benjamin's *Zerstörung* and Heidegger's *Destruktion*—two modalities of destruction and clearing the way—Derrida shows the way things shake down, breaking apart, even as they remain vital to our understanding, to our grasp of life's crucial motors, impulses, and dependencies. He develops, in this regard, an understanding of the disturbed side of hospitality by sifting through its sunny-side up, cheerful facets and examines the corruption inherent to its persistent contemporary demeanor. At what point do the virtues of hospitable welcoming operate destructively, tipping over to become a vice? Nietzsche has warned that even the greatest virtues, when not held in check, turn the vise and become techniques of social wrongdoing. We carry these twists and turns of history, burdened by their latent content. The most innocuous histories, when repressed, can leak out in inauspicious ways, just when you thought it was safe to embrace a concept or sign on with a tradition-bound narrative. Even the most innocent of virtues may come from a bad place and continue to pump venomous inference. Derrida rarely lets such histories slide by, but ventures after them to see what gives them viability and metaphysical cover. Thus the levers of "hospitality" and "forgiveness" come up for scrutiny—paraconcepts by which history itself is motored and time restarts. The testamentary theater of forgiveness—the drama of last-ditch deathbed solicitations and donations of the forgiving word—let time and beseecher pass. But have we ever forgiven, especially when the slogan "forgive and forget" creeps onto the scene? If you must forget, you cannot forgive. The great poet, Heinrich Heine, famously gripes that it is simply not in mortal mankind's job description to dole out forgiveness. That suprahuman exertion goes to Gd only. Heine, for his part, prefers not to, and sees no other option than to remain resolutely unforgiving, unrequited and contracted to the bandwidth of complaint.

Subjecting traditions, grammars, and the ethical assuredness of acts and meanings of hospitality to a genealogical purge, Derrida focalizes the bodies of women who have served to nail hospitality in place—Lot's daughters, who are offered up, in recurrent memory drops, to a specially appointed gang of guests to whom all is due. The stripped-down schema of giving it all up to the one invited to "make yourself at home," blurring the lines between guest, even ghost, and traumatic intrusion, forces us to reevaluate the meaning behind acts apparently innocent and socially valued, backing up a whole syntax of hospitable gestures and exposures based on violation. Derrida goes to such lengths not in order to set aside the urgency of hospitality, but to explore if we are *capable* of hospitality, of honoring unconditional hospitality, which may be a wash in so far as it exceeds implicit limits of opening up to alterity without setting normed caps on what we give to the guest/intruder. Who gets to be hospitable, under what conditions, and what is the level of toleration for admitting the overstepping other? The advent of the other bears persecutory potential, but also stands as a figure of liberatory potential, opening up spaces with grace—or grudge. But even this view of the liberatory potential of the other poses a problem for the Derridean meridian, for it subjects the other to a calculative grid, measuring the value and step of the sacred encroacher, its exploitative capacity to yield some kind of benefit or interest. The other should be expected to give—*nothing*, a genuine gift. This commitment to thinking the hospitable void and its implied critical instabilities makes us revisit (for the purpose of obtaining visiting rights, permits, as well as documents, programs, maps for resettling, migrating, existential and material renewal, for reviewing the plight of the undocumented, the *sans papiers* and refugees) the theoretical underpinnings of obstinate discourses on and against immigration, their fault lines, mythologies, fear factors, vocabularies of violation, and metaphysical support systems.

Let's face it. Some of us would not have survived professionally (in some cases existentially, in my case, phenomenologically) had Derrida not lit up institutional corridors. His authority—always in crisis and object of bitter dispute, ongoing complaint and, in the day, many a teacher's pet peeve—let in the strays, those labeled as deviant, including the discursively marginalized columns that have included literature and psychoanalysis. He was not the only one, but he delivered the strongest voice to advocate for the inclusion of those fields that were deemed unassured, lacking in conviction or prestige, cognitively impaired, even unmanly. He never let up on his commitment to the poetic word, particularly when it met with resistance in the realm of philosophical immovables. Derrida was not intimidated by the fractures exposed by poetry and other minorities allowed to squat in the house of philosophy: the mute exhaustion of language, an unreadable outcry propelled by the poetic stagger, a stutter in the ability to say or feel—these unaccounted-for stray shots gave Derrida free range over a number of imponderables. Together with Deleuze, but according to different schedules, he opened the gates to drugs and stupidity—things, if indeed these are things, that qualified barely as themes or dignified pursuits, but surrendered to thought the feel of philosophical quicksand. The way it grappled with the violence of incomprehension made literature a source for another turn of knowledge. For instance, it draws close to the other side of knowledge, in feints of hapless ignorance, challenging masculinist and sure-footed philosophical maneuvers. Literature drives philosophy out of its self-acclaimed certitudes. Staring down empirical or dogmaticist grounding, it shakes the philosophical assertion when it makes worlds or de-creates being in crucial ways. Derrida has taught us about the unannounced perils of closed systems of knowledge, the historical cost of truth, all sorts of referential strongholds and the dogged mystifications of authority. It may seem odd provisionally to conclude a reflection on his teaching with a plunge into the darkness of unknowing, but I see few other options for us.

Elsewhere I have argued that the denial of stupidity in philosophy and politics, in terms of ethical failure, makes knowledge incomplete, untrustworthy. Though I do not always score the highest grades, I have been trained to ferret out trouble, hunt down the blind spots and faulty premises, founding mendacities

The Trouble with Deconstruction

and stumbling blocks of the conceptual infrastructures to which we continually appeal. Some of us troubleshoot, advised by literature. Fearless about immersing itself in modalities of stupidity as theme, object, or grounding fiction, literature revels in breaking down forms of idiocy and their secret yield of insight. Ever since psychoanalysis—with its heavy reliance on literary insight— helped point the way to the unconscious, a dark reserve of obscured self-knowledge, we are obliged to seek those dimensions of being that remain locked in incomprehension, remote from our ability to grasp or take action or be certain about the prescriptive bait we habitually take and are prone to act upon.

Derrida confronted stupidity as a paraconceptual lever later in his curriculum and seemed amused by the way I describe, via Kant, the problem of rendering oneself ridiculous, a side issue to those who gain in popularity even as their texts remain obscure to most readers. Such a dubious upswing in popularity risks a plunge into vulgarity, an inescapable dumbing down. For a number of us, the engagement with stupidity goes in another direction, since it is like pulling the handle of an emergency brake, part of an ethical call of desperation. So much that happens in the realm of politics reviles yet compulsively repeats ignorance, is based on presumed foundations of knowledge—on axioms supposedly tried, tested, and approved by cognitive corroborative schemata that appear to have become dependable.

But stupidity accompanies the fundamental *unreliability* of language's positing habits, disclosing in its own bumbling way the scandal of routinely faltering assumptions, the way the promise of meaning has been chronically mismanaged. The refusal to consider stupidity as a theoretical challenge poses a problem for all thought and thinking processes, their inherently disruptive procedures—compromising everything that aligns with thought and thinking. For how can one genuinely apply oneself to the task of thinking if one blindly moves along points of obscurity, points or positions that are regularly covered up, conceptually redacted or forgotten? Yet, stupidity is not merely the opposite of thought. To the extent that thinking plunges into the night of nonknowledge, a wide range of surprise attacks ensue, bringing about not only what oppresses, but also unanticipated *délices*, the tremors of sensation that incite newness, stirring everything that we can't be sure of—the unrecognizable, the future, mutations in being, unaccountable aggressions, the ceaseless dreariness of worry, and the sparkle of caress, such as Derrida, Levinas, and Nancy, countless poets and novelists, artists, activists, and homebodies, unleash.

To the extent that thinking is prone to abandoning itself to deflated expectancy and extreme forms of self-questioning, it belongs to a fold in stupidity's dossier. As Robert Musil, Roland Barthes, Thomas Pynchon, Albert Einstein, and others note, stupidity functions somewhat like a smart missile encrypted with your address that can get you at any point, taking down all hopes of intelligent discovery or rhetorical finesse. One is *always* prey to stupidity's onslaught, for it disables and is locked into all thought, owning every bit of writing, even when you feel you are at a great remove from the disturbing erosions of which stupidity unhesitatingly proves capable.

Trained by Derrida, sometimes you think that you are called to a task, that you are skilled or fitted or sufficiently bookish to handle it, that you have received the proper and sufficient instruction and reboot. But, as in Kafka's depiction of Abraham, you discover that, in fact, you are not up to the task; rather, you discover the extent to which you are vulnerable to ridicule and reprobation. Ridiculous and exposed, you are largely incapacitated when facing some of the work's greatest challenges. You're overcome by serious strictures that must be taken into account, even by the cowboys riding philosophical thought with swagger. Elusive and inappropriable as any history of stupidity must be, it continues to provoke my scholarly curiosity and determination, inciting yet reducing my sense of theoretical acumen. *Ach!* I try to see where it produces violations in our *Mitsein* or the forms we have of being-together, where sheer stupidity becomes responsible for ethical breaches—but also for a surprising openness in the way we encounter the world and the pained existence that it contains. Sometimes "ignorance is bliss." I do not want to ignore such enticing hypotheses, the way we are increasingly exposed to not knowing what the heck is going on in any possibly affirmative sense, when control is relinquished and pretense of mastery derailed or provisionally suspended.

Before closing these remarks that are meant to invite and encourage further reading of Derrida and, on some hesitations, to cut me some slack, I would like to report on an event that caught me off guard, left me stupefied, returning me to the snares of stupidity. One of the last gifts that Jacques Derrida offered—he still keeps them coming, as his works will continue to be published by Éditions Galilée and its off-site affiliates for the next forty years!—entailed a seminar held at the European Graduate School in 2004. The philosopher was ailing at the time, too tired to make the trek into the sublime Alpine regions where we normally congregate, so we came to him, in Paris. We gathered in the loft of one of the students and began our work with Derrida's thought.

After the director of the school, Wolfgang Schirmacher, and Derrida exchanged a few words, I gave a brief presentation, introducing and situating the occasion according to the protocols of scholarly presentation, and even though I've done so a thousand times, I was trembling with anxiety, hoping to do justice to the great teacher and beloved mentor. Then there was a moment where everything went silent: we were, as a group, tensely, expectantly, oriented toward his language, awaiting his lecture. He had been advised to prepare for

The Trouble with Deconstruction

a session on forgiveness. Instead, Derrida dealt another hand. That's when we learned that he had decided to address the paraconcept of *stupidity*, which, I'll admit, put me off balance, since it meant, at that moment, that in some way he would be engaging the book I had just published on that very topic. Derrida's decision to turn his thought toward stupidity presented me with something like a crushing blow, maybe what others would be able to take in as an honor, whatever. (Cards on the table, full disclosure: given my paranoid infrastructure, I also, in the back of my mind, worried that he was out to get me, snuff me out in some inescapable way that I surely deserved.) I was very close to my teacher. He had the power to uplift but also to decimate his students, even though he practiced, for the most part, gentler forms of pedagogy. He did not aim to humiliate or bring harm to his disciples. He flourished when we were on top of our game, delivering with what looked to him like respectable skill and athletic focus.

Still, the effects of his decisions were not always in his control. Derrida had taught us that trauma is not only a result of damage done or anticipated, but can be tied to happiness as well. That's more or less what I felt, traumatized in the precincts of Derridean scrutiny—lucky and screwed. It's not easy to describe what happens to a Dasein when a venerated teacher reads and produces a commentary close to the heart of one's writing, no matter how critically apt or protectively caretaking and generous it turns out to be. But my fears were inflated. In some ways I was just a conduit to another set of relations: the true seat of address, one could say, was shared by Deleuze and the other Jacques, Monsieur Lacan. There were a few sidebars with Heidegger as well.

At some junctures of his elaboration of the problem posed by stupidity, all of Metaphysics was called to approach the bench. It looked like I was just a start-up engine for an acute *Auseinandersetzung*, a coming to terms—or blows— with the still traditional premises that Deleuze, Lacan, and Heidegger hold when it comes to the string of signifiers constituting animality, bestiality, *bêtise*, the French word, though off-scale, for "stupidity." Derrida involved my work on stupidity, inviting some of its strands to participate in the arguments that run through his book, *The Sovereign and the Beast*, which was also meant to be the topic for the last seminar we planned together for his annual visit to New York University. Surely, one cannot escape the edges of irony when I think, with quivers, that Derrida engaged me on the subject of stupidity, *ach!* . . . In conversation he liked to recall the section on "the ridiculous philosopher"—a qualm initiated by Kant—where *Stupidity* describes the way the philosopher necessarily is subject to exposure and specific forms of devalorization, a kind of public nuisance and untamable freak of nature. *Ach!* There is so much more to

CHAPTER 3

say about the way the philosophical being must self-efface, downgrade herself, morph ceaselessly, and dive for cover.

Perhaps I have said too much already as I stumbled blindly into the reopening of this case study that in so many ways has involved the history of thought, but also entails the calculable-incalculables that lead up to choosing Derrida. Perhaps Daseins like me are mere remnants of an arduous process of integration. In the best of cases we are cast off like boosters after a rocket launch and abandoned without gravity. Still, regardless of how I figure or disfigure myself—as rocket-launching equipmentality or obsolesced author-function floating off into estranged space—let me at least remember, finally, the way Derrida's work called for a darker radiance, keeping us abreast of an unrelenting pace of faltering, attuned to unconscious rumbles, and adapting the persistent stagger around neglected corners of obscurity. Some movements of thought no longer embrace mythemes attached to Enlightenment, effecting instead a retreat of confidence that poses problems for a recalcitrant readership. At times in his work, Derrida's passages through truth-bearing philosophies have felt the strain and isolation of snuffing out the light, leaving maybe only a flicker to commemorate the times and promise of the heliotrope and the white metaphor.

The Obscure Ravishment

Much like my schizonaic companion species, Johann Peter Eckermann, and Freud's Hamletian patient, aka the Rat Man, I still take midnight calls from JD and tell him jokes that I've saved up, meant to put a smile on his visored face.

I also ask his forgiveness.

Ach! I don't think he would approve the pathos of forgiveness-begging, a fatal flaw in the chronically guilty, Kafka-mantled readership. Don't overshoot, I tell myself, leave it alone. Don't ask his forgiveness—it's too late. Or, let the memory of a friendship adjudicate the plea. Leave it be. A recurring motif that he has brought home involves the complicated experience of friendship. I run with this, still exploring how to relate to a teacher (friend or foe, parricidal bait, object of desire, marker of the *"envie* de vomir," as he said, pointing out that one *wants* to throw up: who knows? What's a teacher, or in Blanchot, what's the difference between a master and teacher, who or what instructs, intrusively, covertly, with traumatic impact, with and without mercy— one day you' re in the doghouse and out of teacher's pet zone, the next day you're a lapdog, if you're lucky, primed eventually to stand as show dog)—I'm talking about the asymmetrical relatedness to teacher, the uplifting humiliations and momentary approval ratings: all this necessarily places one on the limits of an Oedipedagogy and other complexes that I harbor to this day. Not far off from the hidden facets of aggressive coexistence, a liability of masterful teaching. I would propose now to read a number of other texts by Derrida, compelling and provoking further reflection, inviting debate. Yet I am disciplined, I can and must stop, I can end—Nietzsche teaches that everything depends on knowing how to end, that cadence reveals the essence of man—I believe that I have shown discipline here, I can end the complaint of the disciple, though I admit to having allowed for rogue sequencing and superseding my own sense of limits—I am disciplined and do not need to chase down ever more persuasive tropologies, newer intelligibilities, stand tougher tests of loyalty—or maybe I do, of course I do—

To the extent that I try to contain a song of remembrance in a book, I would like to indicate what it means to seek refuge here, in a contested and possibly obsolesced—and certainly undead—form of exposition or phrasing. How is the struggle with the book, its assumptions and historicity, part and parcel of deconstruction's legacy? Derrida's engagement with thought made him explore the conditions that continue to bind us to the book, even when it has been ripped apart by historical mandate and technical mutation. Despite a movement of steady obsolescence to which it has been submitted, the book has managed a set of survival techniques. Derrida gave us archive fever, a contagion that inventoried for us the attendant phantasmata of keeping, incinerating, storing, sending off, eating, reclaiming, shredding, and dispersing the book, resignifying at each turn of the page the archi-*biblios* and historical recounting. There is no doubt that in some ways his work, cued up by the errant *Carte postale*, gave up on the book and crashed against library walls and their institutional containment policies.

Flailing against the very concept, if this is a concept, of library could not have been an easy stance to hold for a "man of letters" and erudite reading systems, a sublime creature of our bildopedic culture. Granted, his corpus, as he might say, was always up against the book. He made us tear into the question of the book, beginning with the essay "Jabès and the Question of the Book" and rebooting, time and again the book of books—I mean, *Of Grammatology*, in addition to casing, together with Blanchot, the sovereign closural moves made by nearly all books, even as they are breaking out of their boundaried determinations. Still, he gave consideration to what it means for the Jewish people to be tagged as "the people of the book." Here, too, he eventually showed ambivalence and signs of recoil. In the context of his work on the poet Jabès, the book, with its overload transcendence, made him wince once or twice. His struggle with overbooking a cathexis seemed real to me. He was not the only one to effect this constant turnaround with an unbreakable attachment: "Little by little the book will finish me."[13]

The book, whether cherished or abominated, whether a solid and lasting pat of his relays or obsolesced from day one, laden with metaphysical significance and—from day two—biodegradable, interfered in significant ways with his *écriture-* and text-bound thought; yet, he, too, was bound by the book whose remaindered essence his work disrupted. Perhaps he was even seduced by the way books aimed to shore up any number of disseminative spills, tranquilizing and controlling rogue itineraries, coding untrackable complaint systems and closing deals with sovereign resolve. The master thinker decided that he couldn't book his own autobiography and invited an alien, Geoffrey Bennington, to do the circumfessing for him! This inclusion of alterity, a programmed foreign body, was his way of practicing allothanatography and getting it right, killing it. Then there was me—there were others, but then there was me—at his door (let us remember that "door" in my mother tongue, Derridean, means "law"). I was at the door, like a cat, her claws out, fine print, scratching to be let in. *Ach!* I think of all the revolving and slamming doors I encountered institutionally, whirligging in and out of jobs, kicked to the curb—I will not go over the slams again. . . . But, let's face it, I was at this door, adoring, much like Freud's Dora in search of a mentor. My adoration of Derrida, too often over the top, with nearly no trace of readable ambivalence. It may have caused me a good deal of trouble, I can no longer tell—one of the troubles of deconstruction. Now that I have my footnote in the door, at least in terms of this narrative, and I'm sticking to my story, I'll remember his teaching without the spice of complaint. Though our playbook allows for grievance among friends, one cannot forget how Derrida airlifted some of us out of areas of constriction where we lay, demobilized, held back by sentinels guarding forbidden sites, overseeing relentless rounds of academic humiliation. As soon as I could—not that I really had a choice—I, like others, booked out of normative, punishing academics and headed for deconstructive troubleshooting zones. Of course, one cannot simply book and bail, one was still bound by norms, protocols, rules of encagement in the university. My writing habits earned me a lot of trouble in the beginning, made some nervous and me a nervous wreck, got me kicked out of my chosen field before I was called back in the game. I suppose that the struggle with writing, the constant negotiation with institutional codes is part of an attempt to answer the calls of deconstruction in the outfield of thinking, if that is still possible—and, somehow, against all odds, it must be so.

The Trouble with Deconstruction

A Pass of Friendship

notre plus juste prose
et si nous sommes capables de respecter l'imprononçable

our prose most just
and if we were capable of respecting the unpronounceable
—*Phillippe Lacoue-Labarthe, Phrase*

Typically American. I am not going to begin by throwing shade at the work. Certainly, I would not be the first scholar or receptor, the first morph of Diotima, to line up behind a work that I cannot claim to resuscitate or over which I cannot entirely jubilate. So many commentators (an old Kafkan term) have become companion species to that which they cannot properly carry. I can't say if such reticence to recuperate and polish a recessive object calls up penalty material—whether it's fair play to knock a text placed in your custody, or if you are not rather duty-bound to go the extra mile, to make it luminous where it lapses or exhausts its initiatory verve, breaking an implicit contract not to give up on itself, to push through despite the staggering odds and all the wagers set down in unconscious counsel against one's own work. In short, should one not stifle complaints you may entertain about the gist of the thing, your adopted text?—all texts are placed in foster care, as Goethe almost told Eckermann on one of their walks, when the shared object became the cuckoo's nesting habits and giveaways.[1] I pause.

Sometimes the stall or cancellation policy is an effect of the work itself, though hard to account for or deal out. Still, when a text is placed in my custody, should I not be stepping up to defend the perceived flaw as a necessity, or at least make it my business to determine that necessity in keeping with the good faith of hermeneutic labor? At the same time, should a text to which I am infinitely responsible have me in a dogmatic stranglehold? *Ach*, I am perplexed about the degree of adherence required of me, its absolutist orientation, even where it is not a matter of "liking" the text, endorsing its principles or cheerleading for its game-changing greatness. Some texts don't seem to need you and remain impervious to your approach. Others run like cats under a sofa, relying on your patience and soft-pitched coaxing to bring them back out. It's not easy to maintain relationships with difficult texts, and I have to assume that, no matter how much they hammer at you, it's not right to go behind their backs to complain about this or that annoying habit, structural disturbance, or conceptual pitfall. Still, one wants to come clean and find its unsteady pivot, maybe go in there and fix something. *Ach!* The aporias of duty, of friendship and duty: running on a fast spin cycle through betrayal and abetting, backstabbing and backing—one sometimes opts for becoming a flunky of the text-in-error or arranges for an intrusive correctional stance, risking inelegance and the arrogant standoff. Allowing for the exposure of one's own theoretical rigidity, one becomes innocent and guilty at once: doubling down on interpretive injustice, one abandons the beloved text to its greatest vulnerabilities.

On the whole, I try to stay close to the work, honor its stubborn commitments and posture of defiance, yet let myself go rogue when a breakaway seems warranted. Lacoue complained to friends that he had identified in his work and life too closely with Hölderlin. This reflection, besides prophesying a collapse, foretells the history of being capable of upset, a concept that will become important to his work. Keeping a "dangerous proximity" to the poet's fate (Blanchot's fraught term when considering Hölderlin), Philippe sent himself and his friends a warning signal that kept them vigilant throughout. One feared his Hölderlinian capture. His attachment to the great poet cost him, disturbing his sense of serenity when he managed to get himself grounded, minimally centered. When sizing the damage of mimetic compulsion and prohibition, of what it meant to imitate the ancients, our predecessors, Lacoue was precise and relentless. The way he ran mimetology and detected the failings of myth in politics made it possible for many of us to return to German texts that had been counted out for reasons of Nazi contamination and scandalous appropriation.

Still, at points along the way, this one lets me down. I wonder, is this my doing? Have I failed the test of reading, of friendship? Perhaps I falter at the fault line of textual complication, the way it conceals its aims; or, is this on him?—a charge I would not lightly ponder with regard to a work that commands my attention, to which I repair, as if answering a call. For I tend to seize on works without much regard for momentary flicker zones, unshaken when light dims or a concept arises that seems off. Still, I am drawn to Lacoue-Labarthe's *Phrase* by some sort of duty, and also by the conviction that it takes care of its own cleanup, that it is perfectly capable of accounting for its stealth moves, the way

A Pass of Friendship

it staggers with rollers of tremendous ambivalence so that my own trashing instincts, at times irrepressible, can give it a rest, idling in standstill. The surplus of hermeneutic aggression with which I've been gifted should not always be showcased, exposing the way I trash and thrash, disturbing the serenity of a book-braced text. Wait. Such trash-diction seems admittedly severe, in some respects unwarranted and possibly crude, even though in my vocabulary "trash" and "litterature" remain closely allied, belong to a thinking of remains, of what cannot be rescued but maintains on its own asthmatic steam minimal staying power. However, at this point it would be prudent to snuff out the trashing instinct, an app that every critical mind no doubt comes equipped with. It is not clear to me what in *Phrase* deactivates my capacity to advance, making it difficult for me to connect in the full embrace that makes the reader exult, take a run at or *with* a text, or at least be taken for a run into the fresh air of its brisk discovery.

In our shared history, I have logged in time when I liked to follow him around like a puppy, joyful and connected, even when, yanking, he had shortened my leash. It's true that Philippe yanked me, here and there breaking my stride. Once in Berkeley I told him—I would never do this again, by the way, reveal a nascent text, offer a sneak peek at a baby about to emerge, far too vulnerable to pokes, jokes, or criticism, no matter how sedately conferred. It cut to the quick. I will have been forever unprepared for his gentle yet resolute misgivings about the direction I was taking with regard to psychoanalytic modalities of intervention—I told him one afternoon over coffee and language of my plans for interpreting the Rat Man, tightly threading the case of obsessional neurosis. He stared at me over his glasses, as he would do when registering an incoming jostle, and then laughed. *Lacoue-Labarthe laughed:* this in itself constitutes an occurrence of note. I was familiar with his smile, but here he seemed to be laughing at me. Is there something unforgiven in the remembered urgency of the philosopher's laughter? Am I still spooked and permanently restive around that memory? He also offered a benevolent laugh—but that was different—when, a year or so later, he read my "Narcossism" section. Once, making good use of our time together, I had asked for a blurb for a forthcoming book. He said, to my astonishment and chagrin, that he would first have to read the galleys. Lacoue-Labarthe did not read English. Bill said we needed the blurb yesterday. Unlike Nancy, who asks you to start him off, this one stuck to his ethos and required that we find time to read the entire text before he would sign on.

"But you don't read English, Philippe, darling!"

"You will read and translate for me."

"The whole book?"

"Yes!"

"Who has time for this? I have three classes to teach and a buttload of meetings every single day this week."

"We'll make time."

Now I realize what a blessed occasion that was, reading and explaining to him for hours upon hours, quivering and then shaking with delight when he smiled his approval, signaled complicity and, "Yes, yes, go on. Wait. Did you really write that, or are you making it up?" He agreed that *Rausch*, rush, and philosophical scenes of ecstatic opening, stupor, crashes ought to be pursued in terms of Nazi Germany and less Nazi regions of thought. I had jumped off Derrida's addictive rummaging in Plato's pharmacy into another region of mind-altering reflections.

At another time, after a lecture on Heidegger at Berkeley, when that philosophy department started trashing me, Philippe declared solemnly at the end of that ordeal that I had been "sovereign." He raised me up, even when I was puny, and also, to boot, all punked out, wearing spikes and some Jewish neo-Nazi outfit. This one time, post-blurb and pre-Heidegger lecture, the situation was jinxed, or something. Things didn't go so smoothly when I was presenting the newest sketch for a text in the making. This was different, searing and disturbing to my overdelicate frame. He said that my go at Freud's case study was "typiquement Américain." Wait. *Whaaatt??* "Yes. Very Yankee."—Very *what?!*

I may have jumped the gun when defending against a perceived insult, swiftly closing up the Batmobile, my armor, my *amour de soi*, but, whatever, this curious appraisal breached and hurt my heart-space, stalled the work, and ended up making "The Sujet Suppositaire" even more outrageous and anal-militaristically fixated than it had set out to be, exceeding its own negotiated sense of limit and minimal worry for decency.[2] Pushed to a limit of narcissistic accommodation, I returned defiant, a regressed and rebellious teenager.

Anyway, it is very often the case that my work breaks into endopsychic perception, so, for instance, if my reflections are drawn to a problem area of psychoanalytic utterance, "In den After, dürfte ich ergänzen" ("Into his anus, I helped him out"—this is how Freud finishes the patient's sentence), then I find myself taking it up the ass: the very thing or *Unding* I'm writing about explodes into the reality-tested world, trying to run for it, escape the constrictive pages that frame its possibility. Relentless and persecuting, it also gets up in my grill. Writing creates strange destinations and unassigned deviations, makes things happen and rouse out of a subterranean slumber. At the time, I was determined to theorize Freud's analytic performativity, the way the text turns on itself as he cooperates with the beloved analysand who occupies the case of the Rat Man.

A Pass of Friendship

The patient was unable to finish a phrase, and Freud offers to help him with it. The phrase is so striking that it invites one to think of the irony of psychoanalytic intervention, where language lands and restructures the analyzed body. The fact that Freud "guesses" at the phrase not only reasserts the triggered signifier "Ratte" (rat) to the extent that the word for guessing in German is "erratten": it also offers an allegory of the psychoanalytic hermeneutics that collapses on itself as it moves forward (or, as the case may be, upward). Both Lacan and Edward Glover drew significant theoretical dividends from the way Freud conducted and wrote the case, restructuring Hamlet, but I chose to launch from the way he "helps" his patient say what troubles him—particularly since psychoanalysis, so invested in helping out and relieving the condition of essential helplessness, the start-up condition of *Hilflosigkeit*, slips as it invents the language of intervention. Freud proceeds from the overdetermined anus, unsymbolizable, yet established as a site for the inscribed mappings that bring us back to the chain-reactive issue of money, donation, theories of the gift, and the human difficulty of parting with money.

Nowadays, upon reflection, I am not so sure that Lacoue meant to rip me a new one when calling my unborn essay a typically American thing. Maybe he didn't intend to cut off my lifeline—in other words, hit me with a caesura or one of the other stops and stalls, pained suspensions, for which his sense of scandal and key signature moves were going. At the time, anxious and pleasantly—for the other, I'm assuming—*pleasantly* self-doubting, being nabbed as American or, for Christ's sake, lined up as *typically* American, after all my protests, European hideouts and background checks, not to mention the Middle Eastern grafts, my Anglo-Princetonian pretensions, Californian implants, Latin American transferences, when people—including especially Richard Rorty, in a memorable slam—were telling me that in my writing I'm too hard on America, too relentless in my criticism, the unceasing attack on its racist heritage and F-factors (Adorno's fascisoid markers) check-off lists: after all this inmixation and immigrant *Wut*—the rage of the immigrant, the rounds of faking it 'til making it, never sure of making it and if there's a momentary reprieve from all that immigrant anxiety, and you're almost making it, against all odds, the fear befalls you that it can all be taken away and was fake in the first and last places anyway. How could Mr. *Typography* declare me or any part of my work, especially its most scandalous foray into Freudian precincts of anality and *Geld*, yes, how could Mr. *Typography* typecast and deplore me as typically anything, much less, for pity's sake, typically American? *You didn't say that.*

Yes, Philippe, you did; you said it; in fact, it goes further than me, if that is imaginable: you uploaded a number of anti-Americanisms, and, for his part,

CHAPTER 4

Jean-Luc has declared that Americans don't know what love is; really, the French have a monopoly, or should I say "polyopoly" on love? You told me that I didn't know what love is—a statement that has mystified and preoccupied me. I'm not saying you're wrong. Still, right or wrong, you may have wronged me—a pass of friendship.

Well, at the time of security blanketing the quivering essay, you said that shit about me being typically American and tripped me up, calmly executing a restraining order. For pity's sake! You also say in *Phrase* that when one asks for pity, one is stymied in the halt of non-address. Whom is one addressing when making a plea for mercy, urging pity? ("Ou demander pitié, mais à personne, en vain").[3] But I didn't want to hear any more (*mort*) such nonsense from Mr. Moral Upperhand. At least he didn't say "typically Jewish"—he wouldn't, he was a philo-Semite to the end—or, as my mother continues to hiss in my delicate ear when something unsavory goes down that she puts on me or indicates the neighbor she detests, "typically female!" There was a time when Philippe exempted *les Juives* from the onus of American backlash. Jewish women could not be demoted to Americanisms of any stripe, not even the stars. Once he said that I resided, in his imaginary, in the place reserved for Hannah Arendt, an ID that I still illicitly carry.

Don't worry. The disclosures that I've made of the cloud cluster of friendship do not aim to represent satisfied payback or one or another of the versions of vengeance served on a cold platter, or any closural fiction that could soothe or console the one left behind. My younger self is invited to please get off the platform. The immaturity of my complaints about the departed friend is *ahurissant*, as he used to say, "stupefying." I hope that what could pass for aggressive emancipatory moves—freeing myself from the grip of overtime mourning disorder, flaunting my faux independence—opens some dossiers worth noting, despite the way they organize around singularized memory bubbles. Others have the good taste to conceal their complaints, or they find discreet outlets for grievance. I, on the other hand, compulsively seeking justice, call in the witnessing body of unwitting thirdness to adjudicate my complaint—with the proviso that I play myself as guilty, as thoroughly undeserving of the friend, subverting any chance of convoking a benevolent judgment. The act of breaking into a perfectly reasoned commentary (I can confirm that discursive reliability was on its way) in order to key into the grievance behind grieving renders me more unsavory, on the side of guilt, I fear and know. I am a provocateur of my own downfall, always handing down emergency supplies of incriminating evidence against myself. Others ask the dear reader for sympathy. One way or another, lassoing affect, this gesture sums up the *demande* of the writing being. I however

A Pass of Friendship

make the compassionating embrace impossible, spraying myself with reader repellant, shooing away any fiction of community that, at the same time, I desperately try to convene.

Starting myself off with a grievance against the widely admired friend—he really was a friend to me and my considerable lost causes, the proliferating causes of loss, which he often nailed and subdued—puts me in the wrong, no matter how many corroborations for my complaints I could wrestle from other common friends, comrades, and commentators. *Ach, ach!* Plus, addressing the absent one, I bring back his superegoical mass, the sense of being answerable to his nonresponse. But language falters, darkening the portal. The one who complains, no matter how cautiously aligned with the measured exigency of *justesse*, is bowed by the deadweight of enunciation.

Like others of its kind, this plaint makes up part of a self-exposition that cannot catch up with its choices, not even that of choosing to speak of *Phrase*. It is not clear to me whether Philippe offered criticism at all when he flashed the American flag at my flailing essay—whether he was simply cautioning or prudent, a true friend who stops you in your tracks, manhandling you. (According to Montaigne, the supplement of violence would volunteer the sign of true friendship, stepping up its *jouissance*, where complicity allows for manhandling; who could begrudge a friend the occasional smackdown, a go at you with no patronizing or coddling, just a good, bright smack, as in its typically American slapstick usage or the conversion of passion, when only context can tell, if at all, whether its action entails a slap or a kiss, a smack of both lips *smack, smack,* or a whack?)—or maybe (*maybe*, but here, let's face it, I'm kidding myself; still, I stand firm on the "a girl can dream" motivator), maybe the American flip-off was in the end *affirming*. For he did like America in some ways, I tell myself: he loved jazz and admired the Black cultures that he encountered here; he was soothed, even enlivened, to the extent possible for him, by the hospitality, the largesse that America had shown the visiting philosopher and his interlocutors of choice—Lyotard, Derrida, Foucault, whom he met at Berkeley, Ann Smock, Denis Hollier, Marie-Hélène Huet, the many others.

Well, still. I'm having trouble letting go. That particular phrase flicked at the nascent work continues to leave a scar, a buzz of unreadability, even though it may have exerted the privilege, or exposed the insouciance of friendship. But I am not *insouciante*. Nor was he. He was dashed from the start. That must have been where we connected, on the premises of brokenness and the unflagging alert of anxiety. I am a walking, OK, a barely walking, anxiety disorder; the curator at the Louvre called me a *grande angoissée*—like Friedrich Kittler, she added, to my astonishment. I did not know Friedrich to be a *grand angoissé*, but that is another story, though they did know each other, Lacoue and Kittler, and they were both inveterate smokers. In fact, Friedrich stopped coming to the United States because he could not leave off the cigarettes for the duration of a transatlantic flight.

As an over-the-top *angoissée*, then, I need more affirmation than the average writing Dasein, and Gd knows they need affirmation, those *Erdmännchen*, the meerkat variety of writerly narcissists. My needs come from a different place, a different constellation of distress—that of thoroughgoing depletion, the impoverished stasis of the abandoned. But is that not standard issue, the sound off of the plaint, repeating, if slightly shifting, the preposterous assertion of every narcissist who presumes to follow the travel plan of historacular insinuation? These considerations, I would hope, are not essentially guided by the flaring anxieties of narcissistic calamity or maneuvered solely by the threat of destinal shutdown.

To moderate Freud's case study and my allegedly American approach, Lacoue opened a file that subsequently became important and structuring for me: the doubt he expressed led eventually to the study of America as philosopheme, as a tropological tipping point in all kinds of texts—including the most Germanically immured—and referential networks. In modern philosophical works, the nearly unconscious resentment and need for "America" in a thinking of technological epochality became by a flip, a matter of primary order—a gesture common to dialing down an attack or fending off traumatic incursion. Henceforth, launched by a defining moment of insult, Lacoue's complaint about my essay *à venir*, I was bound by his sendoff and hitched a ride on Kafka's boat to Amerika. I reapproached the land of a particular kind of rhetoricity, but not without first listening to what Mary Shelley says about the disaster of America, due to its not having been discovered gradually enough, according to a less traumatic timeline. The ghost story *Frankenstein* lists the American breaker as one of the prime aberrations with which to contend. The fast-track overtaking of North America by European invaders presented a recipe for inassimilable violence, unleashing a looming monstrosity ever on the rebound. She should know.

On a far lesser scale, my endangered essay, newly Americanized, reviewed its options. Humbled and all but cast off, it lay low for quite a long while. He may have redirected my intention, nearly snuffing out an audacious resolve to figure out, in the wake of Lacan and Shakespeare, what it means to hit bottom. The motif of bottoming out, in conjunction with anal leasing operations in psychoanalysis, is linked to specific language usage with which Hamlet and fellow world-class punsters are routinely associated (Shakespeare, Lacan, et al.). This type of language launches and resets registers of meaning, implicates the one or many bodies that absorb or somatize around specific linguistic hits. Enter

Shakespeare's uncharacter, Bottom, whose relation to the obsessional neurotic anal descent charges the capacity for punning. Paronomasia—the rhetorical term for punning, playing with words, adding levels of double-entendre and such—remains a problematic aspect of language's ability to slip up and slime entire regions of being, though some forms of punning activity have been elevated for their semantic prowess. When Heidegger famously says "wir leben indem wir leiben," something happens in the House of Being ("we live by bodying," not particularly paronomastic in the crossover to English, Spanish, Italian or French). On the other hand, punning audacity also makes one suspect, prey to charges of broad unseriousness and a hankering for jargon. Adorno seized on this apparent weakness in the thinker's diction when taking on Heidegger's supposed jargon of authenticity. The thinker became a mere tinkerer, even while making a play for high-stakes authenticity, ontologically cast.

Out of the range of textual signifying chains—in the vicinity of cherished alliances and friendship, for instance—it remains advisable to follow the imperative never to point a loaded pun at a friend. I may have been the fastest pun in the West, but that did not mean my work could be wrapped up with the brand, "typiquement Américain." In order to get out of this hole, I decided that the best of them would fit the condescending description. Were not also Pynchon, Bessie Smith, and the Statue of Liberty also typically American, and what about certain genres of film and comic stances that the French adore? How different was I from Jerry Lewis?—they have loved him well. Let us not count out the more sober variety of franchises inclusive of Poe, and Dylan, Emily Dickinson, and the rest of them. Whether or not I made the cut, proleptically speaking (a grrrl can dream), I was in good company. In the final analysis, what was my gripe? How long is this wound supposed to last?

Anyway, viewed from another perspective I could wear the putdown as an accomplishment, an immigrant's mark of distinction. Wouldn't my parents, who pretended so hard to be American, bemoan my bad reaction—"*Oy, Avi!* HAVE YOU LOST YOUR MIND? WHAT AN INGRATE"—to what was after all a compliment, you *Dummköpfchen*, wouldn't they be correspondingly *proud* that I, Avitalchen, was declared—in French, no less, and they should know—typically American? After all their suffering and the struggle through foreboding blanks of foreign customs, yet another language to live or survive through, to carry and care about, hoping every day to lose the accent, of which I had an overabundance in the other direction, yes, I could make my way with the then-coveted Brooklyn and New Jersey accents, I aced these accents that in my family's apartment stood for the height of sophistication. I scored big time at home for speaking, my New Jersey high school teacher spat, "like a dock worker." Wasn't that good? Not the first instance of class warfare, the unending humiliation in the classroom. At least I was speaking English by this time, truly American English, and not showing up, as I did in Washington Heights, in Hebrew, without subtitles. Apart from my flawless Brooklyn accent, matching that of Joe Pesci, my childhood was a study in humiliation. Lacoue says he knows all about humiliation, its world-encroaching grip. In his 2000 address to an African congress on philosophy and colonialism, he expresses his sorrow over the humiliating outrages that subjugated peoples must endure. He knows about historical humiliation, he avers; yet, he will speak frankly ("Je vais pourtant essayer de parler avec franchise").[4] I recognize the ethical tonalities of his courage—he will not mince words, conceding outrage to the beat of philosophical tough love. Isn't this, in miniaturized portions, what he served me and other, more thick-skinned, black-, brown-, or white-skinned friends? He understood historical humiliation in a manner equal to the degree that a European could understand such a thing. He understood, moreover, that it was not his place to "over"-identify with or lavish compassion on the persecuted peoples of our poorly shared world. He was careful not to sign a projectile launched from a typically European bad conscience. In this regard, he was a good Arendtian, going easy on the noxious phantasms of compassion. In my case, he'd let loose and didn't seem to mind throwing me overboard with a quick shove of outsourced humiliation. Maybe he didn't mean to attack me, and if he did, it was only by some identificatory lapse, putting me forth as someone to be pushed around. *Wait.* I'm not sure he was that pathetic. Forget the purported identification. Plus, I was only a girl in those days, struggling for recognition in largely hostile territories.

As judgment of a yet unwritten text, his aggressive dismissal—or was it not rather a tender remark, now that I think of it, and Claire said as much at the Lacoue-Labarthe conference in Baltimore just the other day?—may have been aimed at the wrong target, like so many complaints and cluster bombs of curses that terrorize in a displaced region of address. For the most part, soft and understanding, patient if firm, some people behave like disenfranchised bullies, blue or white collar, who, according to different pitches of frustration and bravado, come home, complaining to a substitute, preferring not to face the aggravating cause, possibly the boss. Maybe I was the recipient of a deflected complaint, postponed and reassigned? I may not have been subbing as wife-function in the scenario, so I cannot take this speculative reverie much further. Something in any case was off, and it broke my stride. In those days, unexpectedly busted and stalled, I kept repeating to myself, in mimetic rivalry with Marlon Brando, "I coulda been a contender."

One reason that Lacoue-Labarthe's remark continues to sting is that I could not tell what kind of a discursive permit he was carrying. This hesitation regarding locution and intention, in terms of the difficulty, precisely, to determine the *type* of remark he was making, motivates in part the current need to stay close to *Phrase*, make good on my promise to the introjected friend to figure this one out and stay with the complexity he ascribes to language's ability to throw you. He had slapped me with a phrase. I often go after what stings and provokes, unable to let go. The status of the phrase is not easy to gauge and, as Fynsk points out, involves an elusive thought of renunciation.[5] In German, renunciation, more or less invented for literary speech by Goethe, is *Entsagung*, a kind of de- or unSaying, a disjunctive relinquishing of the ability (or wish) to say. Questions of phrase and phrasing persist in French thinking about language and doing or, more to the point, about the failure to do or endure, its *Entsagung*.

I've put in time with Lyotard's phrasal regimens, the ethics of *enchaînement* or phrasal linkage—the requirement he places on us to find a link, even in silence or disabled signage, to seek and speak language "after" Auschwitz, without entertaining the illusion that one had picked up and "moved on." So much in the domain of phrasing has vanished or run the course of its own perishability. One can consider the end put by Jean-Christophe Bailly in his works to certain kinds of phrases—the way he reflects on the disappearance in our era of the chant, for instance, the silencing of *Gesang*, the trill of poetry, what he has to say about the poetic fadeout (which is not the same as its erasure or full stop, on the contrary: poetry appears to flourish in the encounter with its voided address). I have pursued the exquisite strategies of Pierre Alféri's work on the phrase and the way he tracks, more recently, the shrinkage of text to the time of a cigarette break. In Lacoue's *Phrase*, an appeal both philosophical and poetic, the text labors in its own way under the threat of extinction, laying low as the attenuated phrase of imminent phase-out. Trying to face down the taunt of its emptied if oppressive addressee, the work devotes a great deal of thought to the status of the *plainte*, however. It wavers among discursive feints, roaming around the uncertain identities to which they are prone, in a probe of their diverse cognitive proving grounds, the way they offer "la pure adresse vide." Somewhere between "prière et discours" the phrase haplessly falters, unable to achieve the quality span of a dialogue.[6]

Though it reaches out to touch, phrase unavoidably recoils, collapsing in on itself. An "assombrissement interminable" (an interminable dulling or darkening, gloominess), it finds itself skimming "les pires césures de notre existence" (the worst caesurae of our existence), beseeching without callback. At one point the "I" of the lyrical philosophy claims that if it/she/he were to say what it has to say, this would amount to something not easily endured ("si je disais ce que j'ai à dire, ce ne serait pas très supportable").[7] The philosophical-poetic plaint moves in the direction of a retreat, retracing its steps in order, precisely, to *not* say what has to be said—the particular form of its Saying. The tactical freeze of the plaintive urge gives pause, covering the grounds of not or unSaying. The haunting refrain echoing from elsewhere, maybe from your friends, or from a community of the defeated or as a shrug of those who muster a strain of affirmation, "I can't complain" returns, in this instance, sounding a complaint that withholds or desists, will not spell itself out, but retracts the very phrase with which its meaning is charged and whose saying must be prevented. "I can't complain" proves more exposing somehow than its ostensible opposite—for it is not clear who or what, how one or the other *can* complain. In saying I can't, I stifle a complaint halfway emitted. I am still in relation to the complaint. Something different happens, however, when the complaint has a say, seeks to arrive. By contrast to the stance of desistance—"I can't complain"—the complaint in fact *protects* the addressee, however emptied, from the traumatic incursion of the unsayable insight, cuts into the dialogic fiction; it is proffered *as if* there were someone to hear the address, someone artificially put together enough to receive, prepared on some level to sign for receipt. Yet, the complaint, at once vented and frozen in *Phrase*, orients itself toward that which cannot receive or hear or take on such a call, permanently aborting its mission. To communicate itself, it must refrain from communicating, from endorsing the myth of a landed communication, and is always close to the renunciation of language.

The complaint, no matter how familiar, carries no workable content. Or, rather, it does not ask for something to cease—be it a quality of harm, a hurtful charge, the event of wrongdoing; on the other hand, it cannot express its nullifying state of sorrow. It might be tempted to ask, without being a question or pleading, "que cesse une peine," for pain to stop; nor would it revert merely to the saying of a "désolation." If the complaint does ask for something, the question, the request or plea, remains "strictément informulable" (strictly speaking, unformulable). Complaint thus is not at all about telling, observing, plumping a demand or rounding out a declarative sentence. The assumption that it would be prone to description or assertion, that it *could say* the troubling undertow, incurs a travesty, according to the perspective offered by Lacoue-Labarthe. His poetic rendering tenses up around an essential standoff, which makes saying what a complaint must but cannot say that much more unaccountable: "Ne pas dire: c'est une ignominie / Mais dans ce dénuement, dans cette elocution": Let me take a stab at paraphrasing and translating this drop phrase.[8]

Ignominy. Withholding a final punctuation mark, or the punctuation of finality, Poem 5—the fifth part of *Phrase*—leaves things at that, hanging in the suspension of a delivery that does not reach any finish line. It is very possible that the refusal to run the phrase to the end of a thought constitutes the very ignominy under which it groans, locked in a self-accusing display of insufficiency. The thought-poem could be saying (or not saying) that not to say is a disgrace—in other words, that one is bound to say, ethically prompted to tell, or inexplicably driven to throw language to the winds by taking positing risks that comprise any saying and its inevitable dispersal. "It is disgraceful *not* to say." But, turning off-kilter, the phrase could also be issuing an injunction that tells you *not to say*, that it would be an ignominy to say, revealing part of the humiliation of being. If you were to say, moving out of the premises of "I can't say," it would be under peril—of extinction, distortion, error. The constitutively incomplete phrasing creates added uncertainty around withholding acts of not saying. The Hölderlinian *aber*, the *mais* or "but" that breaks the stride of the verse disturbs the negative glamour of disgrace, disrupting the verdict of "ignominie"; yet, without upturning it, tries to urge a countercurrent. The line swerves to approach a condition of destitution (*dénuement*), the utter deprivation to which language is tied—and breaks off in the stirring locution that must refrain from saying. Refraining, it nonetheless objects to the ban on saying precisely because it issues from privative zones of destitution: the line follows the law of a calling that culminates with the cancellation of any call. If injunction there is, it would revert to this type of statement: one must put out the call yet accept its failure to deliver. Staying with its reluctance to yield any recognizable or stabilizing semantics—not to say the consolation of a punctuation mark—one must commit to two nearly canceling gestures, and dwell in the "nearly." We're nearly done.

What does the removal of the punctuation mark, its phantomization, say— or not say? How does reading deal with the urging of a spectral mark that was supposed to be there, assure some sort of nominal closure, complete the thought or offer some inkling of direction, some directive coming from the top, or even squeaking from the bottom? Closed off from its own closure, the near phrase leaves things open. It also repeats the structure of *Entsagung*, the unsaying that paces and restrains *Phrase*. Without end, a phrase cannot point to a beginning, whether situated ahead or behind it. Unpunctuated, there will have been no "end-of-story, finished, period, *Punkt*." Nor has there ever been, in the first place, a story—a theme developed by Lacoue's friend and reader, Alféri. No story to tell or remake, no backstory or forward-tending story to console: this is why we tend to tell ourselves stories, arranging the world according to so many metaphysically tinged, mythically bolstered tales, indulging the narrative temptation to no end. We turn to stories in the destitution of telling. Lacoue-Labarthe calls this an aborted pronunciation, the haunted hue

CHAPTER 4

of telling, *littérature* ("cette prononciation avortée, cette hantise, je l'appelle décidement littérature").[9]

Literature, as phrase—as *Phrase*—is practically always the same: it renders the phrase according to differently modulated moments tuned either according to the plaint, jubilation, despair, energy, or fatigue ("selon la plainte, la jubilation, le désarroi, l'énergie, la fatigue").[10] The lineup of literary keys or transgenres may seem driven by decisiveness—perhaps even surprising us in terms of its inclusive span, the choices made here. Other modulations appear to be turned away from the non-telling/telling propensity of literature that persistently presents itself, when deigning to present itself, with the rebellious defiance of a nabbed criminal: "I ain't talking!" Literature stems from the complaint. The literary adventure is tuned in the first place to the complaint as it travels, according to idiomatic registers of saying, through its purported countercurrent, jubilation, then moves to dwell in disarray before moving on to a nearly Aristotelean opening of energy, when it doesn't finish itself off first and foremost with fatigue.

I find the inclusion of fatigue particularly compelling, not only for its somewhat aberrant showing on the list of literary instigators but for its poignant tracking of that which, for the most part, remains unthematizable, on the edge of phenomenality, a quality that barely has breathing room in the spectrum outlining modern accounts of literature. A form of negation, fatigue lacks the propulsion to dialectize or move on. Fatigue, Lacoue says elsewhere, is the failure of experience. It relieves something like consciousness of knowing what it's doing. Cognitive certitude droops, fades out, leaving literature to rest on other grounds, another logic of telling. For our purposes, I should be satisfied to note that *la plainte* heads off the enumeration Lacoue offers for the essential prompts of the literary inabsolute, the changing moods and modulations, the swings of *Stimmungen* and stances that affect literary saying, extending the lifeline of the unsayable and the impossibly hounded nature of literary imparting. Yet fatigue, whether in the form of the exhaustion of metaphysics or extinction of the gods, or the wearing down of the conditions that allow for dialogue, tells us something about the other end, or, rather, the beginning of the spectrum—that which, borne of a certain level of hopelessness, never tires of repeating itself, even when running on empty. Fatigue, the sigh and exasperation of saying, runs out of complaint but may also define the very thing it gives up on a priori. Beyond its inescapable alliance with fatigue as winded start-up engine, the complaint however also *affects* fatigue, wears down the alive or dead interlocutor, maybe has shooed the gods away in the first place. How many complaints can they handle per diem? No wonder they have fled their

A Pass of Friendship

posts! On the ground level of things and their unstoppable consequences, the complainer leaves one spent—de-energized, "sick and tired," numb, snapping up whatever aura is left of life. Those who have filed complaints with administrators, insurance companies, lovers, and other common institutions, know that these impervious correspondents have to be worn down before they relent, surrender to your clamor—or cut loose, leaving the bereaved complainer in the rut of repetition compulsion. *Ach!*

To set the phrase, Lacoue-Labarthe releases "l'armature grammaticale" in order to attain to what affects us as "pure syntaxe, pure parataxe."[11] The deletion of a punctuation mark asks that we consider with greater attentiveness the mark that initiates phrase. For if any phrase is poised "en attente indéfiniment, / de sa chute et de sa fermerture," indefinitely awaiting its own fall and closure, then this small unit of saying has been preceded by a colon—a mark, according to Heidegger, that calls out, even as it awaits deferred closure.[12] In Lacoue-Labarthe, the colon has separated two instances of a quasi-imperative imperative, what consists in modalities of not saying, on one side, and what declares an ignominy, a humiliation, on the other side of the phrase. "Ne pas dire: c'est une ignominie." The border patrol along the colon, keeping apart what is connected, begins with an injunctive not to say; or, establishing the rule of what has not been said, should not be said, it awaits crossing over into being-said. The imperative, such as it is, wavers in its performance between possible assertion and description, undecidably pit between a form of "do not say" and "not to say." The sliding status of the "not" is followed by a firm declaration stating "this is a disgrace." Given the logic of the text, and its internal incidents of condemnation, the disgrace takes hold of the entire text, referring to a syntax of unrelieved double-crossing: it says that not to have said, the non-saying, inadmissible, is still a form of saying. The phrase, humiliated, shakes down the possibilities of its existence as phrase. It is not so much involved with coming out of ignominy into the light of having been pushed to say what was withheld; it appears, rather, to contend with the very humiliation that remains its fate, ignominy without redemption. It is never acceptable not to say; the humiliating defeat of the phrase that thinks it's saying what can and must be said, however, remains deluded. But how do a quasi-imperative and the power punch of condemnation gain force?

Dearth of Cause. The complaint cries over its voided character, "ce pur transport vide." As empty transport, it dwells in the calamity of not knowing what it is that presses us down. Part 6 begins in the middle of a searing nowhere. Here, in nowhere, coming out of nowhere, one is spoken at and pummeled, given over to unidentifiable destruction:

grande, terrible, admettre que ce qui nous parle
et nous terasse, nous abat, nous ruine
dans un tel silence est inconnu, reste

(car cela ne dit rien)
sans aucun rapport à ce qui nous semble

tenir à nous.[13]

The undisclosable silence of that which beats us down, and, at the same time *speaks*, is unknown—yet this in itself, the utterance parenthetically offers, says nothing, thus speaking while holding silence, clattering in silence, repeating the way plaintive language butts up against the inertia of its own saying. Not only are we thrown down by an undiscoverable silence that does not preclude speech, but it seems also to go on relentlessly without any relation to us. We take a pounding not even intended for us or for whatever appears to regard us. Caught in the backslide of "destinerring," Derrida's disrupted itinerary spelled out in *La Carte postale*, we nonetheless take the hit of a complaint without origin or destination—the takedown does not even have us in its remorseless sights, the sideswipes and slapdowns not being particularly onto you. This persecution-without-aim may indicate a predicament even worse than the systems and correctional facilities set up by Gd or Santa or Superego gunning for you without respite, tallying up your naughty infractions and issuing the dreadfully precise, and so, paralyzing summons. Neither guilty nor innocent, you are marked for anonymous reprisal.

The text pitches a precarious indecision. On the one hand, it continually tracks distress, the incessant arrival of separation.[14] The event of separation, the categorical turning of and from the gods, the attendant crush of *Not*, the German word for distress, function as key anchors in Lacoue's vocabulary of dread. One would do well to underscore the importance of Lacoue-Labarthe's thinking of distress, the emphatic Hölderlinian tonalities to which he reverts and his critical recourse to Heidegger's thinking of impoverishment (*Armut*) that stops short of itself in blind logjam. On the other hand, and I believe this to designate a newly drawn line in terms of the articulations of his oeuvre, the object of distress that appears in and as *Phrase* is in itself often stripped down, depicted as lamentable. The lamentable frames the text and gives focus to the struggle with its own emergence and sustainability. The text laments what is lamentable about its strained ability to lament, to launch a complaint that, by necessity, rests on insufficiency, dearth of cause and drained-off meaning. He may be playing the same hand all along the textual frontier, for this moment of distress doesn't even warrant the consolation of a literary pickup.

A Pass of Friendship

The provisionally placed other hand, then, avows that the text is engaged in the un-exalted, the "not grand moments" to which the "I" must succumb but that do not relate to me, standing without "rapport à moi-même," throwing me "vis-à-vis de quoi je suis à jamais sans rapport" and in face of what "ne m'arrive déjà plus" (without self-relation, facing what I am forever lacking relation with, and already no longer happens to me).[15] The non-address of pain multiplies its near-misses, fails to prop up a subject, as a subject of pain or discernible lack—something around which to organize and reboot, for pity's sake. The demeaning moments that prove complaint worthy turn their backs on Kafka's destinal clampdown, showing themselves not to be particularly determined or headed for you. Where Kafka's hick from the country learns the door was "nur für dich bestimmt," meant only for you, little Lacoue is bowed by the burdened understanding that nothing is meant for you, or—following a perfectly Kafkan syntax—even if it were meant for you, and had been yours to own and disown, it has run out the clock and no longer is so. You are on your own with a pain that cannot be owned, theologically recuperated and justified, laundered by means of refundable Christian love. Pain is unjustifiable. *Punkt*; period; end of story. The urge to justify pain, as Nancy indicates in *L'intrus*, is part of a highly successful Christian tactical maneuver.[16] Yet, pain is *unjustifiable*, he cries out in protest. Lacoue is right there with him and alone with his pain. On your own with irrecuperable suffering, you are simply thrown. No appeal is divinely inspired or aspirated. The reactivity machine switches on the mark of detestation. Unrelatable to me, the phrase, its plaintive tact, emerges somewhere "entre la haine, l'hébétude ou la honte" (among hatred, stupor, or shame).[17] This is how he situates the "forme informe" of the non-rapport, that which squints at me, taking my breath, asphyxiating me.

Written in 1979, the wheezing lines set down in part 6, a nearly philosophical constriction, foreshadow Philippe's expiration, the last breathless draws to be taken in the near final stages of his life to which I became witness. Of course, this being Philippe, no matter how diminished and infirm, he starts bossing me around the minute we're alone, when his wife, Claire Nancy, goes out for groceries. Lacoue asked me to turn off the oxygen and light up a cigarette for him. I was baffled, at a loss. He shouts, weakly yet with the authority of someone who could punch out your lights, "C'mon, just do it, girl!" Shaking, I do as ordered. I ransack the house to find Claire's pack, hidden in the bathroom, and prep the effing cigarette. Hacking and coughing severely, he inhales.

Phrase covers a lot of ground and even more groundlessness. It cannot hold a secret, for there is none there. Instead, it indicates a secretive demeanor, a cover-up of its own groundless plunge. Prompted by a steady leveling or debilitation, *Phrase* belongs to the slow drag of twilight and hovers in realms of

CHAPTER 4

the half-dead, the undead, or already dead with one shaky foot in life. Bounced among the holding cells that start off as complaint, "ce secret sans secret" (the secret without secret), has entered the scene accompanied by the facticity or shared mood, at least, named in hatred, stupor, or shame: "entre la haine, l'hébétude ou la honte."[18]

To what do these motivators, such as they are, attach? Without being certain whether or not each of the enlisted tones and mood downers belongs to a proper name that has made claims on the peculiar qualities standing for the work (Bataille, Hölderlin, Kafka, maybe Flaubert—the writers who made these into world-class literary terms and tone-setters), one understands that these instigators, coming from the zones of feebleminded or dazed diminishment, drive the plaintive cry. Lacoue turns us toward the horizon of "notre infirmité native" (our native infirmity) when (or where) "[n]ous sommes déjà mort" (we are already dead).[19] The encounter with deadly enfeeblement prepares the complaint's engagement with diminished life, an existence poorly accommodated. The philosophical poem's vision may be prompted in part by the deaths that preceded themselves in Hölderlin and Nietzsche, down for the count in anticipation of their demise, or by the way one is returned time and again to the suffocating "domaine des morts" (domain of the dead) where the experience of a return, that "du vide en nous," an inner emptiness, prevails as a halt and suspension "d'où vient / la peur" (from where fear is foisted).[20] This is what the lyrical "I" has awaited: "c'est ce que j'attendais; . . . j'en redoutais la venue" (what I awaited . . . of which I dreaded the arrival), in the mode of Hölderlinian presentiment, an intense non-present mode of receptive stillness inherited, with a supplement of dread, from Rousseau's fifth *Rêverie*. Under a quotation from Hölderlin ("Not as I want, but as you command me to do") the section of the book, titled "Phrase IV," opens an oblique light with a matinal tread, before part 6 recedes into the night of pained non-understanding, the affliction of fatigue: "Nous, désolés, nous dans la douleur / et dans le dénuement. Ne comprenant pas. Affligés. / Après quoi reste la fatigue, et la nuit vient" (We, aggrieved, we in pain / and in the grips of destitution. Not understanding. Afflicted. / After which remains fatigue, and night comes).[21] The night snuffs out cognition under the renewed press of pain.

Before rolling down to the advent of this night, the thought-poem has been elsewhere. Streamed by radiant ease, it lets itself experience a reprieve, the relieving caesura of simplicity, in the form of summer's light—a tonality of being that requires little space and, parenthetically, "(et donc de force, ou d'attention) / et surtout ne nous obligent en rien," has refrained from requiring any "force or attention," releasing the thematized couple from all obligation and doing.[22] Generous reprieve, discreetly linked to the granting of ethical furlough. These

A Pass of Friendship

passages, poignant yet light, relaxing the pressures of a certain vigilant readiness described in other sections, allow for a kind of ontological sigh to let out, a release that signals the benevolent retraction of the bite marked by the relentless self-surveillance of ethical watchfulness. The tensing-up related to ethical alertness dissipates, allowing for something else to happen, or rather, not to happen, but here there is no grandiose distinction to be drawn between that which does tend to come about and that which desists from happening. The benevolent flicker of relaxed attention, allied as it is to Rousseau's *far niente*, where in the *Rêveries* all doing is relinquished in favor of a different order of awareness, moves the text to one of its core discoveries. Provisional yet imperial—submitted to the laws of temporality—the light-filled opening discovers "une disposition favorable / du temps," the possibility for another type of relation to time, a relenting temporality that consists essentially and solely in its favorable disposition.

There is something about time, without mystifying itself or falling or dragging down onto "inauthentic" ground, that incurs a favorable inducement, rests upon a giving dormancy, when it carries within its soft-spoken disclosures "une grande réserve de mémoire inemployée," a terrific reserve of idled memory—one could see this as "unemployed" or "undeployed" memory, "quelque chose de tranché aussi bien, en suspens, / il ne nous appartient pas d'en accomplir / la conséquence."[23] Something lifts out of the flow of time without requiring completion, or any kind of shaping intervention, teleological tug. Given over to forgetfulness, unused memory idles, but even the abolition of memory would mean too much effort, calling on the strains of intentional doing, structuring, and home deliveries of meaning.

Like the Hölderlinian god, the latent store of memory is "near but difficult to grasp" ("Nah ist, und schwer zu fassen / der Gott," *Patmos*). Memory, mother of the muses—Hölderlin's adoption of Mnemosyne—imposes her limits, for she does not allow us to draw out the consequence of the reserve that remains nearby. Untapped, inaccessible, memory hangs back. Deserting mind or beckoning, she refuses the call of any appeal to presencing. "D'où, c'est inevitable, la détresse:" (wherefore, the inevitable—distress:). The section naming the source of distress ends on a colon, the callout to another page that announces "we submit, without breathing a word" (*nous subissons, sans souffler mot*).[24] Distress, a kind of inevitable blowback, streams out from an enfeebled hold on depotentiated memory, the stagnation of which leaves one chagrined and restive. Memory can no longer be put to work, eluding the work in standstill reticence. Wordless, breathless, stuck within the walls of a ruthless incapacitation, one has struggled with a favor, offered by temporal granting, that cannot be put to use, employed, if at all retrieved. The favorable granting is not as such withheld, but rendered rigorously useless—no use value, no surplus value, not even a hint of a "sub-" or an "undervalue" that could render it part of a magical syntax of gifting or the aneconomical surge. Nothing can be done or turned with this gift that insinuates its nearness but will not arrive or accomplish its accordance of donation.

Waived yet announced, to some degree awaited, the giftless granting induces a just kind of imploration, "un chant, / un mode ténu, chaque fois, mais juste, de l'imploration."[25] Before turning away—Lacoue follows Hölderlin's categorical turning away, the way the gods have turned away, the way we must turn away in the destinal rhythm of separation, and in a sense, this is what anchors and releases the complaint at once, the requirement, indisputably set, that we separate, that separation must occur, that any spark of Parousia pulls away, recedes—the thought-poem pivots on this important theme that recurs in Hölderlin's great hymns on turning and mourning, on remembrance and solemnity, when separation becomes law. Lacoue practically had this law tattooed on his body and weighted on whatever remnant of soul he incorporated. In terms of his ownmost history and the anthropological markers he allowed to stand for his autobiographemes, he could not help but deplore separation and simply could not abide breakoffs of any kind—a fancy way, but rooted in his thinking, or ex-pressed in his thought, his understanding of theater, music, poetry, and now literature (elsewhere he makes a point of recalling that Hölderlin wrote a novel, that the great poet understood the urgency of this form, and practiced it, when stabilizing his speculative dialectics and testing the literary absolute forged in correspondence with schoolmates Hegel and Schelling, separating off from the poetic word)—all this, a fancy way of saying he could not stand to be alone. I make this remark not, I hope, by indelicate explication, to call him out on a private and contingent tendency, but because this man or rather Dasein, or maybe this undead or effect of the phantom, a Hamletian offshoot that says and knows the law ("we are already dead," he writes here), suffered atrociously when asked by circumstance or material decree to stay by himself, to be alone. How many times did I have to park him at someone's house for a few hours at a time when I had to go teach in Berkeley? How many times did he take the next plane out when put in a hotel room, bereft of immediate, if not fused, companionship, in anticipation of a lecture?

Undeployed memory, flanked by distress, comes at us from the very core of being. In an important essay that revs up at about the same time as *Phrase*, in 1979, Lacoue offers an alternative tradition to the history of philosophical unfolding, which relies heavily on what is retained, driven back in the form of the gift, the donation of being. "Tradition et Verité, à partir de la philosophie" was published in 2010 and includes a remarkable commentary on Heidegger's "es gibt Sein," a temperate scale-back from the astonished discovery punctuated by Parmenides as *esti gar einai*, "Yes, indeed, there is being!"[26] In the speculative process proper to the philosophical tradition, values such as inscribe the true, the absolute, the will are rigorously tethered to an economy governed by determined moves of negation and reappropriation. Recourse taken to tradition has very often been motivated by the desire to keep these values intact, a service offered to maintain the domination of truth, calculability, production, and subsequent allies of related concepts and operations. The stir of the "es gibt" allows for another turn in thought—a decisive breakthrough—and the approach of an aneconomical tradition. I skip over the development of the argument sketched in the essay in order to make the point that bears on memory's reserve in *Phrase*. This hurts, the aborted exegetical mission, a commentary supplanted by abbreviated paraphrase, condensed and thus distorted. I complain: I do not like to cut down drastically on philosophical explication, but I have not been granted an aneconomical allotment in which to deliver the theoretical gift.

In "PHRASE VIII (La Signification des Larmes [The Significance of Tears])," led by "*Stabat mater dolorosa lacrimosa*," the section opens with the image of a figure brought to her knees, clutched in pain. Then a quote: "En grand déchirement s'accomplit la séparation" (In terrific sundering separation completes itself): if anything must be accomplished, or perfected, it is separation, an act or terrible passivity that, in order to match its abyssal promise, must tear you apart, turning you over to the experience of "fureur / et la dépossession" (furor and dispossession). Lacoue offers an image of affliction, the fixed pose of one whose hands are spread forward, bowing, forehead leaning down, on her knees, "agenouillée, douloureuse"—the precision of perfect clarity, fixed by the recognition "qu'il faut subir," that one must submit.[27] Bowed by fate, one must submit, but without clearing a savings account à la Christianity or, even worse, banking on a Hegel account that pays out dividends on suffering, so one, the other one, gives you a piece of earth to inherit or a dialectical turnover to bet on.

The poet and philosopher split over a separation, the understanding of separating commitments: the *différend* between Hölderlin and Hegel draws from a dimension of separation, the internal fissuring of the Same, which Hölderlin goes to great lengths to maintain, keeping separation searing and ongoing. Clearly, if *this* were a book on speculative philosophy drawing on *Phrase*, in view of modalities of phrasing (and maybe it is), such a statement would be interrogated at great pains, with scrupulous attention to the way both Hölderlin and Hegel treat the problem of the Same, and, with a view to one of Lacoue's great topics of consequence, how they manage differing appropriations of resemblance and mimesis. For our purposes may it suffice to note how Lacoue's record of pain departs from some of the speculative outcomes signed off by his predecessors, their own readings and installations of the tragic yield, to the extent that he cannot retrieve his own tragedy or give his broken-off story a tragic lift. In other words, there is no guardrail holding back or containing and revaluing the fall of which his book is a partial record—we cannot know the full story, he does not know the full story and is barred from access to the backstory or a resolution of the conflicts it may build up. Although he allows furtive stabs at some sort of resumption of meaning or tragic recuperation of bottomless suffering, nothing in the end—to the extent that he is even granted an end, and any end, no matter how desolate, would be a happy ending at this point, precisely because it could recede into completion or the echo of a story told and nicely folded, with or without the bow, a punctuation mark or satisfactory wrap—resembles the bestowal of tragic dignity.

On Abandonment. Lacoue resolutely yields to catastrophe, which in his lexicon trumps tragedy, barring the tragic rebooting of sense, a survival kit of futurity, a sense of paying forward that even Hamlet's story as a matter of history still gets when Fortinbras stops the unstoppable *fort/da* of destruction and Horatio stands to tell the story, spinning it into a tragic blockbuster of meaningful eventfulness. From start to finish, with only furtive flickers of reprieve, Lacoue will have been brought to his knees, streaming tears rather than story. With nothing and no one to raise him up (though there were plenty of volunteers), the catastrophic turn has the last word, without having the security of being the last of anything that might hold or make sense, "étant la clarté meme, reconnaissant qu'il faut subir" (being clarity itself, recognizing that we must submit).[28]

Without seeking a means of redemption—"ô combien triste et affligée" (oh how I was sad and afflicted)—the dispossessed troubadour gives form to his "imploration" with the one irrepressible question that emerges as a quote resuscitated. The thought-poem gives back a sentence to the song that relays the complaint, securing, namely, the beseeching word recurring in every plaintive outcry, whether or not properly spelled out or rendered coherently: "'Pourquoi devons-nous être abandonnés?'" (Why must we be abandoned?).[29] Poignant, immemorially affecting, the cry of abandonment signals a troubled dilemma. Such a cry risks overturning the vessel, drowning out the subtle rawness of its despair by seizing on pathos. This is a risk that Lacoue takes a number of times in the work but reels it in with pain blockers. In this case the imploring song, argues the poetically tuned speaker, does not require us to turn away; "encore moins désirer que cela / cesse: car ce serait pour nous sans raison" (even less

A Pass of Friendship

desire that this / cease: since for us it would be without reason). There is no point, no reason, to wish for the cessation of this state of affairs—he at no point says merely that we are abandoned, in the present, but instead reasons with the unreasonable, launching a hypothetical consideration: that if such is the case ("Mais s'il en est ainsi"), then I do not believe that one must ward this off or turn away—a non-Hölderlinian point of deliberation at this juncture, a downshift from the categorical turn, and the assumption of a non-Christian sense of pain in the face of abandonment. Against all odds, the experience of abandonment is what keeps us here, if only at half-speed. *We are destined to our own abandonment.* This destiny is compatible with and attests to an evisceration of the destinal call.

The consequences of Lacoue-Labarthe's shift to another logic of abandonment are considerable, impinging on the thought of history in relation to historiality, *Geschichte* and *Historie*. Abandonment no longer hitches a ride with destiny, but is abandoned by its claims. Among other consequences, it marks down any expectation for the destiny and promise of Germania, part of the mythologizations put out through Heidegger's abduction of Hölderlin. The abandonment of destiny and the destiny of abandonment come very close to the destruction of destiny, a breakoff that *is* our destiny, keeps us going: going nowhere, going down (*veillissant*, aging, deteriorating). The fateful horizon, together with all horizon, empties itself out, nearing the precipice of fate, its acknowledged death knell. Henceforth, it is our destiny to be without a destiny, to break a historical appointment, or relinquish the temptation, in this or other examples of its kind, of national self-glorification, the vocabulary of recovered greatness.

Here I seem to be getting ahead of myself—or is it not the case that I have been left behind, abandoned by the prompts of destinal motivation and mystified acceleration: "d'ou la détresse?" foisted on me by distress. It may seem that we are at a loss, falling out of touch with a world that is abandoning, left to the random promptings of a fateless prod. This is not entirely so, but certainly almost entirely so, when you lean into the emptiness of what has been lifted.

The predicament of finding oneself without address or destinal meeting grounds is what, strangely, holds us close to things, familiar and nearby, that surround us and whose rustling—a kind of humming facticity—is without term:

> Mais plutôt
> y penser comme à ce qui nous retient
> là, où nous sommes quand meme destinés, viellissant,
> familiers de ces choses autour de nous
> dont le bruissmement est sans terme
> dans la sombre, oblique, lente clarté du soir.[30]

> But rather
> think of it as what retains us
> there, where we are after all destined, aging,
> familiar with those things around us
> whose rustling is without term
> in the somber, oblique, slow clarity of evening.

Without the musical push-through of Nietzschean affirmation, Lacoue nonetheless manages to sound, on somber grounds, the muffled note of an affirmation that is neither entirely of life nor of death, but situated, like us, in the slowgoing clarity of evening, a weakened pulse, giving us the chance—giving us a prayer without address—of a soft demise. Let us not forget that for Goethe and the rest of them, including those latecomers who invented and witnessed the catastrophic fall of the modern German language, the German fate was bound up in the *Abendland*, the Occident, ever dimming, instated on the brink of downfall, land of a spreading evening.

This is terribly fatiguing, the rendering of remote yet assured affirmation. Due to a dimming clarity that somehow persists, holding our attention, the glimmer of affirmation keeps us tuned by a perpetual rustle, an endless humming that murmurs along, like the ongoing song that keeps to the ground of an encroachment, the regulation to which mortals must submit of being-abandoned. Lacoue brings in the plaint to circle a pain that keeps us in place, even if that place of being should let down in a Nowhere, perhaps in the oblique neighborhood of Celan's Unwhere, the *unWo*. Still, he holds back. He is not going there, though the catastrophe to which Celan holds is never far from Lacoue's reflections and historical insistence. One of his major concerns—despite all the barriers stacked up against fate and the way he's blocked the destinal call, unfriended the gods, taken up with abandonment—is that poetry has moved out of historical precincts and trivialized itself. In some backroom negotiation, poetry cut a deal with its detractors and has sold itself short, bailing on the weight of responsibility that historically toned writing imposes. Hölderlin and the Schlegels understood the delicate urgency of poetry's mission statements, the historical vigilance of *poiesis* from which Benjamin drew essential materials and of which Heidegger took advantage. Poetry has backed down from the loose appointment of a destiny without destiny, leaving in its wake a historical need for poetic sobriety, the invention of new world-formations and address. Poetry, abandoning its post of vigilance and positing, its unique capacity to respond and cast new rifts in language, has given up on itself, and us.

What interests me at this point is the way the thought-poem shifts from complaint to lament, incorporating one within the other. Lacoue, despite it all—or rather, despite nothing, betting on all and nothing—retains track marks

A Pass of Friendship

of the lament, its internal outreach program, even when no one understood better how Celan had more or less annulled lament. Having hacked into that account to redirect the poetic peal of lament to No One, leading off in his collection *Niemandsrose*, Celan holds out the rose of No One to No One, one of the masks of Philippe, a nobody introjected, crushed by a series of tellable/untellable violent episodes that the book tries to accommodate. The secretless secret to which Lacoue's thought-poem owes its impetus bears an intolerable clarity to the extent that it is said to betray a major injustice.[31] The language rides an ambiguity, despite the semantic fact that it arrives under the heading of clarity—and perhaps the intolerable character of this clarity requires that it twist in the wind of languishing ambiguity. Perhaps the language is not meant to show up in ambiguous garb, but since the notion of betrayal is so crucial to Lacoue, following Hölderlin, in forward and backward anticipation of Nietzsche's "noble traitor," one cannot simply overlook the way an announced injustice is betrayed. The thought-poem turns on the exposition of a key injustice capable, somehow, of being rendered or even laid bare, disclosed. Instead of concealment or the exploitation of secrecy, there occurs an opening posed by betrayal: the secret "trahit une injustice majeure" (betrays a major injustice). Surprisingly, the tremendous injustice betrayed comes in after the declaration, puzzling and unexpected: "Rien n'est inavouable."[32] There is no unavowable, nothing is unavowable—this assertion chafes against volumes of friendly texts, those of Jean-Luc, Blanchot, Derrida. Lacoue poses a radical pushback for the unavowable communities of writers that swirl around the secret, purposefully unable to expose though in the constant throes of self-exposure, self-betrayal. If I were on a game show asked to identify the author of these words, Lacoue-Labarthe would be the last to come to mind. Yet, precisely because it goes countercurrent to the point of having no viable currency in the neighboring textual regions from which he draws and to which he will take recourse, explicitly or covertly, the resolve of such a phrase within *Phrase* gives pause.

Enraged and provoked, this section launches against all those who have sought muteness in the face of catastrophe, who have kept silent or sought shelter in the unavowable. Granted, I have precipitated on fast-forward to call up the corresponding works on the unavowable shared by Blanchot, Nancy, and, by now, quite a few others. This historical concern with what can and cannot be said, with what must be thrown down, articulated, or confessed, may be an extended relay taken up from "Totnauberg," Celan's expression of disappointment with Heidegger's silence regarding the Catastrophe, the Shoah. But where this comes from, I cannot ascertain. Nothing guarantees such a reading, linking "Totnauberg" to *Phrase*, when so many clues have gone missing, and Lacoue does not take up the mandate to come out with it, as if that were always possible or necessary. Still, to declare that nothing is unavowable strikes a blow to all sorts of protocols to which we have become accustomed, including those that define Lacoue's own reflections on the experience of poetry. This divergence from a newly minted norm—that poetry frequents and by some discernible measure is nurtured by the *inavouable*—is thrown to the winds here, but in a way that barrels away from any certitude about the sober dispatch from which it speaks.

The defiant utterance beckons another kind of conclusion, however impudent and off-scale. Some consequential betrayals refute the hypothetical cast Nietzsche gave them of noble intention. Lower than tragedy, irrecuperable, set on the embittering human-all-too-human dial, some betrayals lower your philosophical immunity. You just can't seem to "take it philosophically" anymore or send up a lyrical lamentation to be musically sponsored by a future Monteverdi. Sometimes your lover betrays you and you have fury enough only to howl: you are left spinning your cognitive wheels, in dumb incomprehension. At the same time, it's all too clear. You've been screwed. Or, rather, as insinuated in this work, she's been screwed, behind your back, on her back, on her "front-back," whatever, in all sorts of positions that you mull over with drunken singlemindedness. The betrayal peels off layers of a once-shared field of signifiers, affects your language; you can't even say the too-sayable. Incredulous, you are taken down a few notches, left miserably to complain that things are avowable, all too avowable. You throw in the towel. Surprisingly, the writing, compromised by the most mundane letdown—who has not yelped at the mediocre inevitability of such a scene of betrayal?—the writing continues, alternating between frequencies of plaintive rage and the calming returns of remembrance.

The enigmatic passage has begun by stating its duty to end—an ending owed despite the recurring theme binding to the interminable. "Je termine, je dois terminer:" (I bring this to an end, I must stop:). The need to end, its essential propulsion, is not clearly motivated; nor does it come about as an effect of rhetorical persuasion or material finality, for the fragments continue to proliferate after the provisionally declared finish line. Regardless of such constraints, the announcement of impending termination persists, prompted by an underlying sense of duty. That sense of duty, which abounds in Lacoue's works, is not as such metaphysically driven nor necessarily shown to be justified—nor logically imposed, poetically primed. Instead, the strain toward an ending is fueled by a mood of particularity, possibly driven by strained nerves or the exhaustion marking a lifelong effort of concealing, diverting, disclosing—what? Obeying the whim of mood, a capricious prompt, and sourced in the burden carried by poetic utterance to find and name its end, the language pushes toward the mirage of a responsible ending to its lamentable paralysis. The thought-poem wants to end itself, stop its complaint, but risks drowning in affect—it has been enraged, fired up by contemptuous betrayal and must stop.

Organized around a plaintive cry, the text, whose title I would be tempted to translate as "The Severe Sentencing," tries to contain an encroaching sense of rage, uncontrollably on the take. The complaint must not tip over into hate speech, a constant temptation and vanishing point for its signatory. Poetic thinking strives instead to offer protection, securing the terrain from which the Hölderlinian gods, ever dependent on language, have fled. Yet, anger competes with the complaint, threatening to disrupt its course of relative incapacitation, as if two types of impotence were in mortal rivalry. The poetic "I" must cut itself off due to a rising swell of anger, an invasive intonation of revolt, the spectacle of which he/she/it wants in fact to spare us, or "you": "je sens monter une colère sans nom, je préférais vous en épargner le spectacle. Mais je sais bien que la violence est inevitable, il n'y a jamais d'apaisement" (I sense the rise of a nameless anger; I prefer to spare you the spectacle [of its expression]). Livid, unappeasable, the poetic stance pitches a place in the book of inevitable violence. The "inevitable" on which it wagers takes a tumble, however, when it states a turnaround: the only thing left to announce, it contends, concerns whatever advent we await—*the advent has already arrived*. Lacoue carries this temporal collar to the furthest extreme, tightening its grip around the end already attained. As wounded beings, we are already dead: "Nous sommes déjà mort, nous le savons. Même les enfants le savent, et du reste ils en pleurent. Il n'y a là aucun secret" (We are already dead, this we know. Even the children know and, what is more, they cry over this. There's no secret here).[33]

I do not know what children—whether those of the German Romantics, offspring of historical revolution going and coming, or of more empirical vintage—do and do not know concerning mortal being, and his remark makes me think that Philippe Lacoue-Labarthe ought to know better when it comes to the little ones. Does a child's lachrymose complaint play to the modernist beat of an established mortality timer? He has addressed children before in his work, teaching them philosophy, telling them not to be afraid of "big words."[34] These minoritized beings are said to sniff out death. *Children, unleashed:* they cry about playtime's last call and squirm at having to go to bed before everyone else, shut out. Maybe such abrupt expulsions, each time an ambush and an experience of injustice, draw the child to the horror of extinction, and Lacoue was right all along about the fearful taunt of relentless exposure.[35] His knowledge of children may offer a trove still to be inventoried. Not to mention that he was such a child himself, in fateful line with self-surrender and keyed to the powerless acceptance of children.

The child that Lacoue-Labarthe was—the one (or many) left off in the hollowed place of a Self—was felled, in his time, by a mother's finitizing curse. Intersecting in a dreadful way with German calamity, as its own little homegrown allegory of Nazi rule, she went after him as an envoy of historical erasure. For a long while, maybe forever, she continued to burn him up in the living hell that pulsed catastrophe in his life and works—two motifs that cannot stand up to the fatal curse, "life" and "works." By means of destructive phrasing, she dealt him out. Anger—which, Lacan reminds us, Freud never handled—prowled in the wings, as extended life span of the curse's pounce. In fact, the oversized anger "sans nom" issues from a facet of Mother that cuts into history, a modus operandi that psychoanalysts of the archetype call the Death Mother.[36]

The revolt of rage settles on having death apportioned to us, and "ces viatiques ridicules" (these ridiculous provisions) in order only "to make us vaguely forget that, in fact, we will never know it." The voice, interrupting itself, apologizes here, adding a tinge of irony released to the air of atheisms: "Mais voici que je m'emporte. Excusez-moi, je vous en prie"; pray, excuse me, please forgive me for getting carried away, for raging, for exceeding, in effect, the limits of the plaintive cry. Complaint, by comparison, stays back, flicked by low-burn dismay, energized by another generator, that of outright rage. Who has the right to rage? The poetic onslaught tries to halt and constructs a theater, a dimension of spectacle, around the effort to go silent, end its raging run. But this time the end will not be part of a theological crackdown. It will not be punctuated by "Amen," a sanctioned way of ending song and the prayer form of a plea. A stage direction: (Il se tait un long moment, se redresse un peu; He quiets down for a long while, pulls himself together). After a moment of silence the "je" of the text says, "En somme, je me refuse à dire 'Amen.' Ou: "Ce n'est rien, je l'attendais, je le veux bien" (All told, I refuse to let myself say "Amen." Or: "It's nothing, I've been expecting this, it's what I've wanted.")[37] That's it, the fragment concludes, "Voilà, c'est tout" (Alright, that's it), I hope that I have acquitted myself of my task "à peu près correctement" (more or less correctly). "Je n'en suis pas du tout sûr: c'était à la fois trop simple et trop difficile. Trop intempestif aussi. Mais on se refait pas" (La lumière s'étient., 1995–99; I'm not at all sure of having done so: it was at once too easy and too difficult. Too untimely, as well. But you can't change your nature). Trying to acquit itself, the passage falls back on doubt, faultfinding and overshooting its terminal point. Not sure of having been able to conclude, the text is prey to the endless repetition of its failure to end. Amen.

The Maternal Curse. This is not the worst of it. We should remember that *terminer* also indicates the capacity of carrying something or someone to term. It goes both ways, carrying to term, which entails both ending and birthing. When the term ends, it falls on a commencement, an ambiguous caesura warranting completion and a new start. When carried to term according to economic calculation, it is a matter of a term or date for the remittance of payment, the rendering of a debt. I owe myself the debt of ending. In the neighboring German, with which Lacoue consults, *Termin* fixes an appointment, another way of making a debt of expectation due, the restricted generosity of a fixed time. "I must end" plunges into the polysemy of all that is due, birthed, arranged in and by time, owed. We all must end what we have or have not started, but to which we maintain, often through sneaky means of disavowal, an outstanding debt. Lacoue steers *Phrase* around a terminal incision, maternally driven, fatally delivered. The traumatic slash opens the text to its termination, an ending that has preceded it. According some biographical substance to the declaration, prior to an earlier fadeout, that we are already dead, the text meets its appointed deadline on and in time, but also off the clock. The terms of a dreadful contract have been dictated by Lacoue's mother. Sparing nothing, not even the theoretical viability of his extended reflections, her terms reappear at crucial junctures of arbitration. There is thus a moment in his book that disrupts his entire thinking on poetry and the fate of prose, shaking the historical investment to which Lacoue devoted his work.

An entry, by force of its severely disruptive instigation, has pushed open an explosive section. This section, which in some ways exceeds the text trying to contain it, scrolls down to a different, less figural cast of the failure to end as ending, of not being able "to remake oneself," to rebirth oneself or even to deal in the cards of finitude's script. If the text stutters on how to end, it is, paradoxically and even perversely, because an end has been prescribed, spelled out with bitter exactitude. The section, a kind of C-section, an original caesura carved on the mother's body, is remarkable—not because it offsets the child's relation to prose and poetic saying, but also because it keeps re-marking itself like a series of unstoppable traumatic tremors punctuating the phrase. The text struggles with a dispatched death sentence that it can neither stop, link up with, and yet must, in Lyotard's phrasing, *enchaîner*, move it along, in an effort to connect with the unsayable or what defies representation.

It should no longer confound his readers if Lacoue's thinking of the unrepresentable has a default position: "Mother." Morphs of Mother emerge at different stages of his oeuvre, including as backdrop for the political scene, as stand-in for unfigurability and dearth of representation. She's the end station that no one really makes it to, though she structures a whole train of events.

CHAPTER 4

But let me focus on how Mother ends/commences the work to which we owe another look.

Recalling Rousseau, who ends it all, interminably, Lacoue rouses to tell of another expiration date, impossibly intimate, that prescribes all future expirations/inhalations. A testamentary moment that dealt him a shock will have ended it all, as certain menacing utterances are prone to do: he suddenly recounts the maternal curse cast upon him, glacially swung at him in the hours before her death. The excerpt, at once anecdotal and unreproducible, unlike the others that abound in *Phrase*, bears a precise date as a sign-off: *"(6 mars 2000)."* The section heading, following the previous dramatic fragment, is placed within parentheses: "(LA MALEDICTION)." "Phrase XVIII" is not the last of the entries, but it does constitute an exit, or rather no exit, the exit cue of cursed spite, inassimilable, untimed—an evental mark that can no longer be turned around or rescinded. Dropped into the heart of the text, it fans out to disturb the entire work without making more noise than its sudden stealth appearance in the disjointed space.

Nothing has prepared the text for the flurry of protestation that it must now entertain. Something happens to Lacoue, implicating him in a steely trap. Language comes down hard on him, keeping him down—for the rest of his life, he says. "Life" is the wrong word. The language slam, unsparing and brutal, knocks the breath out of him, irreversibly. Everything else will be but a weak retort to the irreparable blow. The work is taken down with him, becoming a contestatory pushback on an insult that however wins out, according to his own tabulations. His grievance is great, yet the means of defensive feints and antiballistic positing remain impoverished when faced with Mom's breach. As the work moves into regions of struggle with the predicament by which he has irredeemably been thrown, Lacoue runs a search on the capacity of prose to hold and defend the incapacitated, those who stand in desolated infirmity. His reflections turn to areas of language and justice that question the efficacy of protest, the justice of prose and language's ability to legislate probity, or to support the advent of a just phrasing.

Pushed hard by a verdict, the work bumps up against the finality of complaint, maternally broadcast, rendering a scene, theatrically appointed, that delivers an unforgiving refusal, or the refusal of forgiveness. In his consideration of the aporetic snags governing the scene of forgiveness, Derrida accords forgiveness a theatrical setting, an inescapably hyperbolic exposure of the granting word. Forgiveness warps a history of fault and faultfinding by turning in a word of finality, allowing performatively for its other temporal index, that of recommencement and reprieve. As enigmatic act and bestowal, as silent granting or de facto release, forgiveness introduces a warp of mes-

A Pass of Friendship

sianic domesticity into the fold of family drama. "I forgive you" reinitiates time and history, allowing the pardoned to turn a page, *the* page of default, remotivated by release from a stricturing past. The "give" in forgiveness, the *don* seamed in the *pardon*, enjoins one, finally, to take the call of futurity. The stall of the unpardoned will have ceased in part to exert historical pressure and daily squalls of blockage.

Mother rejects this option. Refusing to give time or pardon to a fragile Philippe, she holds him in freeze pose. Instead of pardon, she hurls a curse at him, accompanied by the dramatic lucidity of which madness sometimes proves capable. Not present but within remote earshot, Lacoue is handed by hearsay, dreadfully reliable, the sentence—three phrases—that she has pronounced on her three sons from her deathbed, Lacoue being the firstborn and thereupon the first-cursed in a non-dialectical run-up. It is a matter/*mater* of her phrase—what issues from her womb, her mouth. Sharing the title of this work and therefore on some level of urgency pertinent to this day, her sentence hits hard and sets off years of staggered reflection about the pounce and underworld of phrase.

Wait. "Reflection" still carries the revelatory bounce that Rousseau lent it. We cannot be certain that Lacoue felt the touch of reprieve that underlies reflection, to the extent that searing woundedness at all allows for reflection. We saw how the previous fragment sent up sudden surges of rage that must be suppressed, for they menaced the text with shutdown. What has happened here?

The dying mother sends a final *envoi*, a lasting instruction. Her sentence announces his imminent demise, prophesying, "en fausse ménade," only what a "counterfeit version" of a crazed infuriated woman, follower of Bacchus, would hurl. The domestic "mythe nazi," the maternal Führer, hands down a decree. Her curse boils down to this descriptive and therefore performative countdown, saying what Lacoue was and will have been, sealing off his autobiographical, if not life cycle: Philippe was/will be unstable, Mother thundered; an ingrate, chronically evasive, the truth of his grave deficiencies had been hidden from him by the family's exaggerated indulgence, playing along with his nonsense, treating him as if he had been normal when in fact the weight of generations hung heavy over his incapacity very simply to live. He was a lush. "Elle avait évidemment raison": Mom had gotten it right.[38] Madness, writes the receiving end of the maternal sentence, involves not only making way for "cette terrifiante lucidité" (this terrifying lucidity). Nor does a crazed pronouncement wield merely more oracular supremacy than other phrases. Rather, it tends to provoke into being the very thing that it states, actualizing its deadly content. In this regard, it is weaponized speech, exposing the accretion of meanness at the heart of constative posting. Taking to the limit the voracious capacity of speech to invade and attack its mark, it closes off any lifeline or restorative spasm in excess of its assertion.

The decline that followed upon his mother's knockdown prophesy "fut comme irréversible": from now on "it was all about apathy, absence, confusion; moronic stupor and rages, melancholy without reprieve; ruses, lies; disinterest and the readied off switch on the least bit of joy. Hollowed out body."[39] The maternal missile hit Philippe Lacoue-Labarthe when he was forty-six, in 1986 (sooner, if we calculate the buildup to this point and an entire history of destruction). It is one of those cluster bombs that multiplies and gets inside its targets with determined violence, taking out the core and leaving the shell standing upright. (He was so upright!) The poisoned Maternal spearheads a takeover of his body of work and the longstanding projects that the philosopher-poet was preparing. Pervasive and unrelenting, her curse finds its way into his fragmented contemplation of the literary, *Phrase*, a work that exceeds literature and philosophy (of which it is part), but does not stop there. Moving in and out of the Romantic thought of the fragment, the maternal slant extends equally to relation and oeuvre, occupying a place in the yield of political acumen, where she shows up as the groundless ground of patriarchy.[40] The maternal drop-off switches the terms that could be safely assimilated to the practice of fragmentary writing initiated by the Schlegels, which was never simply safe text, but did not (as far as we know) incorporate the searing event of a curse whose borders could not be fixed or soundly patrolled. The Schlegels had other *lebensphilosophischen* problems to deal with. Lacoue was angled into his demons, maternally cast, when he was not in panicked flight. She drops in all over the place, Mother, where she has no place in the history of philosophy, except, with a different pull and punch, for the famously intrusive antics of Schopenhauer's mom. His mama was brilliant, though, and was arguably the most liberated woman in Weimar.

She shows up when he handles the irrepresentable, a clip of the sublime, or a flicker in his treatment with Jean-Luc of political panic. She shows up as the spectral prompt, as the uncontainable that runs the off-scene maneuvers that overtake effects of power—all this without tracking device or mapping theoretical trajectories and political histories, occupying the forums that matter to Philippe. She lurks in the background, a malevolent spitfire. Now I think as I write this that I understand (well, not entirely) the unconscious neighborhood from which his name for me hailed. Lacoue, rhyming on "Avital," liked to call me "Abyssale." Another undecidable, but I can tell you this: his eyes would light up when he pronounced my code name, my name for and from him, a kind of unName. Exactly as he said of his mother's pronouncement, I must say of his phrase, conceding the point: "Il avait évidemment raison" (He obviously was right). Owing to this bestowal, I believe I became truly abyssal, aligning with my secret name, not entirely a curse but sometimes hard to lift out of safely. On good days, I become one of Nietzsche's inner women, affined to the abyss of truth, the player of veils—to the extent that I agree to feminizing any of the grand philosophical determinants. On bad days, my name says, if it can be permitted to say, that I am blinded by pain, crouched in a dark place of no return. *Ach!* The significance of being named by Lacoue is difficult to assess. Did he create an abyssal hollow, or can my pet name be viewed as a relatively harmless, if provocative, description? Clearly (though nothing is clear in our work or cleared for such speculative lunges), he saw something about me or about the way I wore my given name that indicated my abyssality. I cannot pretend I showed up "whole." When Lacoue-Labarthe hurled the naming injury—unless he was praising my "depth?"—I cannot refute the hypothesis that, when anointing me with my nickname (it nicked), he was not airing a grievance about our relationship. Sometimes he worried about my anxious ways of disturbing our peace, the way I would distance myself, overapplying Nietzsche's *Dis-tanz*, the way fatigue besieged me. No one matched the energy of Jean-Luc, who had the capacity for monstrous fortitude, round-the-clock readiness. . . . But let me *plier* and return to the textual instances at hand. Although tempted to go in the direction of an identificatory pass, there is no cause to rename or remake Lacoue in turn, folding him into an instance of the maternal curse to which I myself have been subjected on lifelong rounds of highly flammable textures of fire / signifier. My projective distortions are of no relevance here, even when we attain an overlap of matchy-matchy and I attached to him over the abyss of maternal insufficiency. Let us return to the drama of his mama, and leave mine for another bend in time.

Can the explosive moment deliver a hidden phrase that commands the dominant keys of *Phrase*? Or am I inventing, misapprehending alongside a section that abruptly spews? What comes up under the heading he accords to this section of "The Curse?" Philippe gives way to the curse, not only as something that has befallen him and withstands story—this is something he can tell without a stutter, if with a lifelong stagger—but as a subheading that involves his text, itself hexed or capable of throwing a spell on the rest of the work, if Jean-Christophe Bailly is right in asserting that Lacoue's entire oeuvre pivots around this crucially significant text, *Phrase*, and its implications for historical recounting. Like the Queen of the Night in the otherwise enchanted, bewitched, or fetishistically appointed *Magic Flute*, this raging maternal shows up to serve as glacial carrier of a defeating word, with the lance of malediction (OK, the Queen in Mozart is more sizzling than glacial, "Der Hölle Rache":

she summons up Hell's fury to hit hard, but these differences are part of the same polarity of wrath, fashioning the ice queen and red-hot range of the counterpart Queen). For a spell, patriarchy fizzles, shown up by an even more destructively undermining force, as Kafka himself had surmised in *Letter to Father*, where father is just a beard for mother. Don't get me started.

On the eve of her own demise, Madame Lacoue-Labarthe predicts Philippe's demise. He does not go there, not immediately—in a dreadful sense, he clearly does, but it does not receive airplay in the book—Philippe goes down as his mother in fusional overdrive. She predicts the downfall that she is the first to assume in the finalizing brunt of her withering destiny. She pulls him down with her, snuffing him out as she gives it up. Her last word and testament saps his energy for life, retrenching him to a condition of perpetual fatigue. (And, and: this is not even *my mother* we're talking about, a clip from my ownmost autobiographeme of destructive downbringing. Hell's fury set in tandem with the glacializations of condemnatory performance pieces voided Philippe much in the same way deadly takedowns ensnared me. And I didn't even have to wait for a deathbed display of revulsion to be crazyglued to pernicious predictions. Such language games, whenever they play you, cannot be called off, as Kafka knew so well! *Ach!*) What this may mean is that any malediction, whether wrapped early on or dealt in some last-minute desperation, inerasably, bears the structural urgency of a deathbed scene. Every curse is handed down from a deathbed, announcing finality, a mortal dispatch handed down as sealed testamentary absolute.

The maternal complaint will have escalated to the point of setting accusatory snares, resembling the death sentence released in Kafka's "Judgment," only there it is mostly a matter of warding off paternal thunderbolts, the smart bombs set off under patriarchal rule. OK, this is still not the proper place, but the main *Klage/Anklage*, stuffed in a textual corner of Kafka's tale, issues from the dead mother, not properly mourned while the son thrives. Not Lacoue's problem—yet, I could go into a Midrashic rewrite of both sons but, as said, this is not the proper place to track the thwarts of unmournable Mom and her accusatory rebounds through the patriarchal megaphone. There are less controversial turns to take in this riveting narrative and I, for once, desist.

In Kafka, the son takes the hit, commits suicide (or assumes the homicidal thrust of the father), throwing himself into the libidinal rush of traffic flow, vanishing in a buzz that covers over the fall that at once plummets and surges. With Lacoue, the suicide was put on a timer, doused in alcohol, parked in a medical facility, tightened by a stupor that bound him for life, such as it was, to Hölderlin and Nietzsche, the other living dead of moment. Unlike Kafka's thematization of the one judged or cursed by the double-barreled shot of parental ambush, Philippe, recipient of damning language, on the contrary, stands not the remotest chance of being released into traffic or revving up sufficiently to leap over the bridge's railing: he has been partially decimated, leaving us with the insinuation that he could entertain, in this family, no hope for a mercy killing. One is kept on to carry on, emptied out and voided, suspended in apathy, poised in decline. Philippe, stumped, is framed by his mother's announcement, posed somewhat like Nietzsche's propped-up portrait with the oversized mustache, as stage-directed by his toxic sister, Elisabeth Förster-Nietzsche.

Father stays on, effect of the phantom, haunting Lacoue as if saying and situating the scene with some authority, twenty-four years after his demise: "Te voici donc, cesse de t'aveugler" ("Well, there you have it. Stop blinding yourself.")[41] I was finally, he writes, the victim of the prohibition that they had so fervently desired. I suddenly had an intuition of the hell that I had imposed, the ravages all around me that surpassed all measure. "Il ne pouvait rester que / l'agonie, l'effacement sans protestation" (The only thing that could remain was / agony, effacement without protest). Taking a counter-Oedipal tack, repulsed by Mother, condemned by Father, yet sufficiently Oedipalized to become the victim of their desire—dead or alive, dead *and* alive—recognizing, moreover, the ruin for which he was responsible, Lacoue is urged by his father to *stop* blinding himself. Henceforth he is awake, left to twist in the agonizing wind of effacement without rebellion—or rather, in his words, without protest ("l'effacement sans protestation"). No fight left in him, no energy, he seems ready to collapse under the force of a malediction that imposes itself as law. However, something happens, possibly "internally" charged, that changes the terms of effacement without protest. The "mais" introduces a transformative manipulation that the curse could not have controlled or predicted: "Mais il arrive que la haine se transforme en pur amour" (But it happens that hatred is transformed into pure love).[42] Whether rewinding a Nietzschean twist of Christian or pessimistic love, or turning to advantage Freud's understanding of hatred born of love in cases of ambivalence and murderous rage, or maybe following the protocols of the abused and their wildly self-protective adhesions, Lacoue flips the script from hatred to pure love, which allows him to crawl out of the paralyzing standoff commissioned by the curse. The thought-poem cues up a parenthetical definition of hatred that stands for disappointment, neglect, abandonment, even betrayal: "(Haine est ici pour: déception, délaissement, abandon, trahison même)" (Hatred here means: disappointment, abandonment, betrayal itself). Each and all of these qualities, cramped within the walls of parentheses, are susceptible of sliding into pure love—not just love, but raised high by the asserted purity of love. "L'entendra qui le sait," the voice flippantly throws in—do what you want with this phrase, understand it as

CHAPTER 4

you will; anyone who knows will catch the drift. On the brink of destruction, brought to his knees by the curse, he tosses up a statement that leaves a core intact, room for an encore or living on: "Il y a de l'indestructible" (we are given a glimmer of the indestructible; there is indestructibility) the poem asserts, adding that a *decision is never entirely without consequence,* "la clarté soudainement retrouvée" (clarity suddenly found anew). If there is some indestructibility to trophy around, it can only be that destruction has been wrought; maybe something has been left standing (or crawling), but decision pushes through with a sense of consequence. The indecisive teetering of "to be or not to be," in which some of us wobble for a lifetime, momentarily suspended, gives rise to the clear-cut rendering of decisiveness that, as sheer resolve, bears consequence, bears life. Hang in there, the voice tells itself: this means, "céder, / renoncer à n'être prétendument que soi, muré" (give in, / renounce being supposedly just a self, walled in). The end of the accursed section makes its own pronouncement, at once going against the grain of any claim for something like destinality—against the language dealt by Heidegger or nation to reinforce a mythic calling—but leaning in on unstoppable calamity and historical overturning:

> Nul caractère ne fait un destin,
> Toute malediction est vulnérable.
> C'est à la catastrophe d'être nécessaire.
>   (*6 mars 2000*)

> No character makes a destiny,
> Any curse is vulnerable
> It is upon catastrophe to be necessary.

This difficult passage ends the section on the curse that holds together while splitting apart *Phrase,* as text, as paraconcept, as titular instance. Whatever the title is meant to convey, it refers, according to Jean-Christophe Bailly, neither to song or verbal statement, nor to an articulation or melody, but to a sort of buzz, "une sorte de rumeur ou de bruit de fond, une sorte de *big bang* alongui ou ralenti" (elongated or slowed down). *Phrase,* he speculates, is Lacoue's version of *Geworfenheit,* the "jeté dans l'existence" (thrownness into existence) put on the table by Heidegger and replayed by Lacoue, minus the pathos.[43] I am not absolutely sure that Heidegger backs up being-thrown with pathos, nor that the crybaby steering *Phrase* and tuning responsively to our decimated history can be totally cleared of pathos-riven crackups. Given the poisoned arrows that the telling of the non-story storied by maternal wrath absorbs, one can no doubt also see the mood of constraint engaged, the practice of Hölderlinian sobriety that accompanies each crash and caesuric upset. Lacoue follows the apportionment of measure—the pacing prescribed by Nietzsche as

A Pass of Friendship

the *juste mésure*, the rhythm that defines man but tripped up Wagner—when contending with the experience of throwness under which he stumbles. Yet, he keeps it moving by means of an ingenious technique, perhaps what can be understood as an outrageous appropriation, harvesting wind from the very force that could have knocked him out and kept him down.

Lacoue will be carried forth by catastrophe, by the overturning whose headway cannot be talked down. Without claiming for itself a triumphal edge or the full advantage of Christian transvaluation—along the lines of shit will get you the goods in the end, Gd is betting on your misery, grinding you down so you can prove heaven-worthy—the thought-poem hunkers down to reverse the predicament of which it speaks. Not in order to uplift or cancel the bad news that it carries and weighs it down—good news would be part of a Christological syntax, the good news that the end is near, for instance—but to meet the traumatic announcement head-on, to allow for collision and to encourage abyssal dwelling. Lacoue is set to absorb the damages without overcoming their serious effects—let us remember that it was he who deconstructed the thought of *Ueberwindung* in metaphysics and its compulsive naïveté. His life will have been a protest against the demolishing curse that announced his downfall with *mater*-oracular gravity.

In the section titled "Catastrophe" in *Poetry as Experience*, poetry is shown to be the interruption of the "poetic." Following Celan, Lacoue-Labarthe sees that all "real" poems, "all that are effectively poems . . . aim at nothing other than being the place where the 'poetic' collapses and becomes abyssal. The task of poetry seems to be tirelessly undoing the 'poetic,' not by 'putting an end' to figures and tropes. But by pushing them *ad absurdum*, as Lucille's 'Long live the King!' in the sharp light of death suddenly makes absurd the theatricality and grandiloquence of 'historic' discourses."[44] Like Lucille, I am pushing this too far, perhaps, but I'd like to see the malediction sprung on *Phrase*—Lacoue-Labarthe's impossible and exhausting struggle with the limits of prose—set to the "counter" in an encounter with Lucille's declaration in Celan's trek through prose, the switchover from poetry that he was forced to make in the acceptance speech that constituted the "Meridian." Marked in the feminine the voices cross swords, one declaring, at peril, life for the King, with the other, Lacoue's maman, declaring a death sentence, announcing the demise of his majesty the Ego, her pretentiously enthroned son, as she seems to inveigh—he has been indulged by the family fiction, given grounds for highest self-appraisal. Not quite symmetrical, nor the Same, but revealing of a type of pronouncement that holds up sovereignty despite its grand miscalculation, on the one hand, and

CHAPTER 4

another, equally theatrical, that calls for the demise of the blind and sovereign subject whose legitimacy the feminine spike of language now loosens.

In the face of the malediction, the plaint's point of no return, one might ask: Who has the right to condemn the other? How do the complaint and its excess in malediction reroute the question of address? When a drunk on the street throws curses at you, does this count in terms of performative fire power? Will a random snipe or ill-fitting complaint gun down the hapless target? How high is the count of the feminine-led shootout? Or must the brunt of the curse be gendered in another way to bring down the adversary? At once a sign of impotence and disclosive of deadly fire, the sniper has to be situated in such a way as to reach its target—unless the point of the curse is to let the target go, hobbling away and humbled. How can one disable a curse, spirit away its potential for destructive finality?

Goethe took it upon himself to undo a curse when he kissed a young girl-friend in defiance of his ex. The passage where Goethe narrates the break-through makes its way to Freud's case study, where this neutralization of the curse is cause for masturbatory celebration. The self-incriminating obsessional neurotic, aka the Rat Man, finds release in the passage where the great poet goes rogue. But maybe only an icon of Goethe's stature can lift a curse. That dwindles the number of those who can successfully buck the curse to zero. Lacoue understood the odds, sizing the Greeks and Goethe, so he had to go at the curse another way, disarming without presuming to weaken the effects of its fateful attack. For Freud, the stakes were different still as he traversed the minefield of killer utterances, poised to go off at any juncture of theoretical complication. The very inclusion in his case study of the curse-defying act compels allegorical attention, for Freud was himself defensively alert with regard to Goethe's paralyzing pronouncements—acts and engulfing prophesies that he could not always shake. The inaugural work of psychoanalysis, the *Interpretation of Dreams*, is agitated by the "vernichtenden Kritik" (annihilating criticism) that Goethe, paying forward, hurls at Freud's efforts.[45]

The malediction has to come from the top down, even when the source of enunciation is ailing or impoverished or defeated by forces of oppressive fortitude. Verdi's Rigoletto grapples with the loaded malediction, but his name already has him entangled in a tragic joke, occupying the acute yet subjugated position of court jester. Structurally, the boom of malediction comes from above, filtering through the studio of the Superego, diffusing from there. But where, *there*? According to "Catastrophe," the poetic word opens to "the place without place of the advent." "To put it in other terms," Lacoue offers, "the poetic act is catastrophic: an upsetting, staying upset in relation to what is an

A Pass of Friendship

upset in being, in the direction of no-thingness (the abyss)."[46] The poetic act, if it is to be construed momentarily as having a duty or task (two very different modalities of fidelity), must try to drop anchor in the upsetting, staying upset without delivering its burdened being from what is an upset—without beautifying, pacifying, understanding, rewriting. This is a tall but rigorous order, and I believe it gives an indication of the marching orders that Lacoue took when he set out to sojourn in the regions of malediction—which, as *diction*, does not necessarily inflate into a power punch of transcendent capacity. He separates the effect of the curse from its ownmost consistency as a special delivery of destinal spite. The malediction is itself vulnerable, liable to collapse on the strength of its excessive beat down. Even though entire histories, operas, epic fails, human follies, and superhuman breakdowns seem to ensue from a focused transfer of a curse, its stature, says one of the prime victims of malediction, itself remains vulnerable. Somehow you can duck or don an antiballistic shield, though this is not exactly what he means, for the thought-poem does not supply the wounded receiver with a pain-free zone or safe word. What keeps him in diminished form, a marked man, still in anticipation of death, but on this side of accelerated demise, involves the minimalist ability to meet the upset with an upset—on the condition of staying wounded, as first responder and lasting monument to a nullifying blow.

Lacoue manages to keep things on this side of recovery, but also on this side of annihilation, clutching recuperation as a lost cause, and annihilation as a close call that continues to close in on him. "In this sense, the poetic act is ecstatic. The exorbitant is the pure transcendence of being. . . . [T]he poetic act is catastrophic: an upsetting relation to what is an upset."[47] Lacoue rides the *Atemwende*, breathless and inhaling at once, barely making it; nevertheless, he is ongoing with the address of "cette protestation,"[48] drawing a quote from Euripides cited by Aristotle on the subject of "renversement"—where you have the catastrophic overturning, the upset, the verse, all living in the same neighborhood of the signifier. Near the end of the text, Aristotle riding on Euripides exhorts, "living is a death,/and death, too, is a life."[49]

Before we precipitate to the end, let me circle back to what happens directly after the bomb has dropped on its development. Can the section on malediction be contained or does it not open out to affect the text's entire endeavor, its most remote perimeters? Perhaps language traumatically fissures so that something else can arrive, the *other kind of poetry* that the text seeks. As event that is only partially defused or set aside, the malediction disturbs any sense of unfolding that would be mappable or recognizably timed. It is of course difficult to set down the temporal quality of an "afterwards" following the throw of malediction. For the curse has swallowed time, installed the infinity of death without allowing for the comfort of succession, the experience of moving forward or the mark of release. Stuck in undead time, the receiver of the curse stays on, unable to outpace the retractive beat of survival. In some regards, nothing grand survives the throwdown of malediction, just a breathless outcry—a protest without address here, an effacement without protest there. A lot turns around the gag orders placed on protestation, the faltering ability to stand up to the brutal abdication of poorly intentioned language, its malicious ability to maim. Between Nietzsche's plan to drop into the snow of Russian fatalism and just freeze or play dead—as animals have taught us—and Dostoevsky's ability to thrive on the accursed share that is apportioned to him in Siberia, one has only very little wiggle room on the existential scale of unaddressable harm. One falls mute, one rises up ecstatically, but one does not necessarily come up for seconds. This is the predicament that *Phrase* contends with, the encounter that it tries to sustain with its own restrictive limits as a type of saying, neither disturbingly regressive nor falsely emancipatory. On the level of the page, the text moves on and goes, after "(LA MALEDICTION)" to section 19 that bears the title "(PROSE)."

The text has counted off the poetry that has betrayed itself or, rather, having been placed under quotational arrest, it has denounced "poetry" as the kind of poetic gesture that has done itself in, taken itself off the table of serious cut and incursion, falling short even of the seriousness of love and a language of which something like revolutionary affect proves capable. "Poetry" actually flees the phrase, makes light of its colonizations and misses out on uprooted existence and love: "L'amour, donc, un aveuglement extra-lucide" (love, then, an extra-lucid form of blindness).[50] The text, in any case, weaves in and out of the "song of deploration," citing a blinding swerve for one who offers up a *Heiliger Dankgesang eines Genesenen / an die Gottheit* (Holy song of praise to the divine by one recovered), having been granted a *neue Kraft fühlend*, the brief stay of execution tendered by the graces: *Doch du gabst mir wieder / Kräfte mich des Abends zu finden*—Lacoue points out that strength is given despite day's end, as we enter night and lose ourselves in darkness: this would be found in "l'annonce énigmatique d'un salut" (the enigmatic announcement of a healing).[51] His language, poetically coached, at once leaves him stranded and offers a tenuous salvation, for he turns to a prayer addressed to divinity. This address does not appear to contradict the one who has claimed the emptiness of address, barred recourse to some sort of divine appeasement. Still, the prayer song of the other one, Hölderlin, holds him momentarily to the enigma of an announcement that promises healing. It may be that any announcement is couched in such a promise, is addressed with the understanding that one is tendering a Niemandsrose, still proffered, though Alice or Gd or the divine mother doesn't live here anymore: "O einer, o keiner, o Niemand, o du." This is more or less how Celan starts us out and ends us up. The voided address does not end on "Niemand" or "keiner," on "No one" or "none," but roams until it finds a "du," a *you*—enigmatic, abandoned, yet receiving the beseeching word. Lacoue takes the holy bridge to nowhere as part of the experience of "déploration," where one cannot decide between a prayer or complaint, an address or condemned site, a delivery failed or still arriving. "It's in the mail," "We're on our way": conflicting responses to a prompt of urgency called out and paused.

I think it may be of some consequence that, when wrapping the C-section of the work, "*(Malédiction)*" moves over to allow for a section naming another type of diction, the "*(Prose)*" involved in justice. Because this diction is just, it is nearly unpronounceable. But it is indestructible: "J'appelle prose la diction juste et, parce qu'elle est / juste, quasi imprononçable. Mais indestructible."[52] The clash could not be sharper between the maternal curse and language called up by prose, a diction so bound up with justice that we can hardly find our way to it, find clearance or access. Being just, in the sense of justice and rectitude—profiling of uprightness (*la droiture*)—it is hardly pronouncable, barely within the range of any speech act or scene to which we could point. Breaking away from maternal catachresis where pronouncement is promiscuous and dreadfully clear—emitting a "read-my-lips" kind of threat—the diction of justice pulls up short. Derrida once noted that we do not have before us a scene of justice that would not be violent—as imparted, for example, in King Solomon's offer to dissect a child claimed by two mothers; or, the biblical pronouncements on the order of an eye for an eye, and so forth. Whether or not it is inventoried, imaginary justice, on the receiving end of anguish, is called up: we rightly clamor for justice, we complain that it has not yet arrived, we demand its incessant appearance ("When do we want it? *Now!*"), yet justice eludes our grasp or referential pointers.

Because prose is just, it can only barely be pronounceable. Still, it indestructibly directs our inflection, scores our diction, pushing off from malediction. Loud and clear, the malediction was pronounced with the backing of hateful accelerators, meant for the most part to deck the hapless receiver. Just diction barely lands or sounds off, if it can be at all phenomenally located. Ethically intoned, allied with *justesse*, a kind of just measure, it is dictated by what is true ("la dictée du vrai"). This sounds very complicated, and I am not certain that the diction/dictation/*Dichtung* (poesy) can be justly rendered without considering that the work has barely gotten away, without fully emancipating itself, from the malediction that has preceded just diction. Throughout the netting that makes up this text, and much of his life, Lacoue-Labarthe struggles with the largely withheld advent of justice, its modalities of stubborn non-arrival. The failures of justice to break through the realms of ideal positing, or, put differently, the meager provisions of the effects of justice, made him sick.

Truth Palace: The Health Care Clinic. Lacoue, or the voice borrowed to enunciate from a phenomenal "I," broadcasts at one point from a medical facility—a kind of sanatorium or recovery ward, what the French call a "clinic"—which is described as proper, clean, white.[53] His room is bare and clear. When the spacing of language or chamber is said to be clear ("claire"), we also hear the name of Claire, who appears to be the recessive addressee of that part of the book that is a love story—weaving a story that also demands justice and *justesse*, a recount of wrongdoing or an inevitable enumeration of the species of the broken promise. As in Levinas, Nancy, and elsewhere, love becomes the place of necessity for things to be set right—or, conversely, for the commission, metonymically constellated, of injustice, as when couples squeeze out a third party or play by their idiomatic rules or force one to listen to baby talk, stupid blabbering, repetitive bars of their idiotic duets . . . but here I have skidded off the text. We were in the French clinic. The page after the malediction where, closed off, near the catatonic cohorts, Philippe whiles away, dwelling in the nearly unpronounceable precincts of disrepair. Before letting us know that this section or ward involves a medical clinic, he states that prose is what should not under any circumstances involve a lie or provoke humiliation or induce distress without recourse. But this is not sufficient: justness is the dictation of what is true.[54] These assertions seem foreboding, highly complex and troubling to me. Even so, this state of affairs does not crowd out my hermeneutic compulsion, but is, on the contrary, *inviting*, calling down trouble and analysis. Psyched, I tell myself that I could become the chief exegete of the opacity of the "true" he sets to work but, after an initial go at it, my own enfeebled sense of justness holds me back. Examining different speculative facets of the case, I don't know how to revert to the crawl space of "what is true." Nor can I estimate the reverberance of the true in a health care facility, where patients, routinely overmedicated and controlled, slump into another reflective zone. But who's hallucinating now?! I suppose the way to proceed here would involve jamming on "dictation," receiving the implicit poeticity of the true, but then I would be responsible to the dilemma of the lie he wants to expunge from the record, the renunciation of rhetoric and inevitable off-the-point embellishment, desecration, disturbance of prose. The sudden catch of a rhetorical pink slip confounds my inner hermeneut. The takeaway, provisionally, must be tied up in the acute aversion to humiliation, to irreparable distress—a threatened collapse to which prose must answer. For my part and historical cuts, I don't see how humiliation can be avoided.

Lacoue, supine or sitting up, in his own way motionless, writes in this section about *droiture*, uprightedness, slanting his text toward rectitude. The other *pensionnaires*, his fellow patients, the boarders, chatter along, but he barely addresses them. There are many whose gazes remain fixed, absent, infinitely pained, who do not pronounce a word, unless they're clamoring for a cigarette or three francs to get coffee (this is a pre-Euro French clinic). "Ceux-la, si proche, sont déjà morts. Leur élocution à peine audible / est la véridiction. C'est pour apprendre ce balbutiement / que j'ai choisi de venir ici, contre moi, / au bord de la menace et de la destruction, / dans cette infâme solitude" (Those [patients], so near, are already dead. Their elocution hardly audible / is veridiction. It is in order to learn to burble [this stammering] that I chose to come here, against myself / on the verge of menace and destruction / in this vile solitude).[55]

Look, I don't know what to tell you. In some ways, this material is untouchable. One is pulled into a vortex of suffering that doesn't let up, growing quiet in places, even as it emits signs of plaintive distress. I am tempted to tow this section toward my own work, yet I don't want to pull a Badiou, and I couldn't succeed, no matter how hard I tried to reappropriate the heart-thudding yowls to my many workouts in the regions of despair that I could call my own, if only fleetingly. Familiar motifs pack the scene: the clinic, Wordsworth's "Idiot Boy," the slump of cognition and the shakedowns of blubbering idiots, the most poetic of breakdowns—somehow the temptation to go there and sit with him or, as in Kafka's *Country Doctor*, after seeing his wound, to lie down with him, seems both warranted and obscene, and I sense my internal police force cordoning off a sector, putting up a cable with a "No Trespassing" sign bobbing on it. Or not. Maybe I am meant to go in there and let him suffer me.

Alain Badiou says that the mention of truth brings this work into its philosophical element. Yes and no. Yes, to the extent that they ended up in a slump, in the stupor signed by Hölderlin or Nietzsche or Lenz or Schreber, and so many other boarders who were committed to phrasing and the death of just prose. To that extent yes, and no. Truth in the asylum may be the philosophical endnote, but it may also be the irony of truth and its vertiginous downgrade. I am not convinced we all have to go there (in case we are not yet there, in case we know how to get to the "there" that's purportedly there). This is the institution of learning that Lacoue had chosen for himself, he says, that of just diction, a wing of the clinic's truth-telling gusts of language, barely comprehensible, burbling spats of truth on a return trip to the murmur of which he has written wakefully. I cannot help wanting to bolt, to break out of this confinement that seems unbearably tight.

To brighten my mood as I read this, I remember an episode when, in retrospective sobriety, I showed insufferable chutzpah and broke into the very clinic of which he writes. Lacoue was said to be out of commission, in silent vigilance over his breakdown. He was to be left alone in his despair. I was in Berkeley, finishing a book manuscript and could not find where Heidegger had said something that I needed to footnote. I had the brilliant idea that *I would call Philippe* to find what I needed. Even though he supposedly could not speak or cognize, or maybe he would be unable to realize it was me, I bet to myself that he would give me the information I required. I obtained the number from Claire, a little surprised that she did not interrogate me on my intentions or turn me down, or hesitate to give me the information I sought. I dialed myself into the clinic. He was summoned to the phone. I made no excuses, but picked up as though we are still in Berkeley or Strasbourg, in conversation. Without missing a beat, he tells me where Heidegger had written the quote I gave him. Then he returned to his place, resumed his mute vigil in the white room. Click.

I am literate enough to know that extreme moments can yield a truth, particularly in the realm of poetic intensity, at the limits of referential clamor. If Hamlet is prone to name himself as he jumps into a grave, "I am Hamlet, the Dane," then Lacoue can state, from the clinic, "I call prose the just diction"; he can even state a truth when all bets are off, something of an enormity insinuates itself, or leaves us stranded—a state of abandonment that in itself opens up spaces for that glimmer of truthful pointing. Nonetheless, the passage makes me nervous, unless the residence is meant to move deeper into the aftermath of the maternal curse and return him to the clinic where birth/death become restlessly entwined and burbling has the last word. Yet, the clinic as holding pen for the infirm Lacoue seems somehow overly dramatic—even if it happened in terms of what can happen to us with historical insolence, that is, empirically, and continues to happen to our memory of Philippe. What kind of a scene has Lacoue constructed at the very instant he wants to sideline rhetorical manipulation? Perhaps we are given a clue in a work that sets up what Jean-Luc considers their variances. Nancy describes their difference over the meaning and directions of staging the points of placement in *Scène*.[56] I will limit my remarks here to a single indication that can be pursued elsewhere. This book between the two philosopher friends, a published correspondence, involves a supplementary fold, another complication in the reading they propose of Aristotle's *Poetics*, which has a cameo in *Phrase*. Nancy opens that exchange by pitting his understanding of Aristotelian spectacle against Philippe's installation of scenes of solitary reading. Paradoxically, Nancy, asserts, it is Philippe who is involved in theater production, yet keeps this activity out of range of his philosophical and rhetorical practice. I would argue that the clinic issues from a commitment to dramaturgy, as set and frame of upset, the location to which he passes for a conflicted encounter of non-reciprocal discursive drives. To what extent does a medical facility take in the complaint of language, admit poetic dread or an extreme mimetology of prescriptive language usage, not to say the deflation of subjective myth and authoritarian holdovers? The great themes of Philippe's oeuvre appear to run their course in a poetic house of corrections, a sanatorium. The very scene in which he asks for the removal of scene, its attendant rhetorical apparatus, is implicated in staging, setting up props even as they are scrubbed, left clean and bare. The ruse of the true on which he calls comes, in part, from such a setup . . . So. Where were we? asks the scholar.

Perhaps I am apprehensive because truth in this passage shows so little characteristic *desistence*, a non-dialectical negation that Derrida detected in the work of Lacoue-Labarthe. It could also be the case that the spectacle of his suffering upsets me inordinately. Whatever the case may be—I lose exegetical command of my vessel here—I cannot account for my own resistance and hope that the full disclosure I have given of a friendship demonstrates the limits of the experience of excessive amity. Among other things—and this is a grievance of friendship—one loses the ability to read, to approach without some element of pathos or identification and, watching this happen, one makes other wrong turns; at the same time, one is hopping with excitement over each text that appears or is at the very least announced, keenly awaited. In my case I bare my appropriating claws, ready to write it up, commit to a thoroughgoing reading, despite any and all phenomenological hurdles. I trust that my candor will cover me, at least for a while. I believe I can explain how amity disturbs any hope for a serenity of reading, but, let's face it, nearly everything disturbs me. Understanding this much, I nevertheless heed a call, for every text appears to ask for one's friendship—except those of Nietzsche and some cranky followers who tell you to bugger off. I'm not sure they mean it, but it's an important line to toe, a distance to respect. Alain handles it differently, keeping friendship and the strength of clean-cut intervention more or less intact. I see why Badiou puts up such a tenacious shield and defensive strategy when breaking down the passages at hand. The mastery he shows comes at a price, though, as he obtains his power position in part by knocking aside the walls of the clinic and dimming the lights on the medicated subjects that it shelters.

Well, I, of all readers, should not complain that something has suddenly become too difficult, numbing and portentous for my delicate, if overtrained sensors. Perhaps I can concede a point or two, for I see that Lacoue manages the scene without pathos; yet, he does not indicate the ironic anxiety, a now-familiar ploy to which I have grown accustomed: that of Thomas Bernhard when skirting lunatic asylums. Bernhard planned his literary round-trips from cemetery to asylum, from medical facility to writing desk. And why should the philosopher follow suit? What could Lacoue have done with Bernhard's often sniveling yet controlled complaints about his health and sister-belted stalls? Despite Bernhard's rundown states, he still was sustainable in his way—he appeared to have energy that Philippe constitutively lacked, counting himself out at least from the time of the curse. Let me just state, without pretense of grasping fully the stakes and prompts of the institutional mise-en-scène— and for all I know the bold assertion represents, if anything, an act of sheer courage, for we also know how seriously Lacoue appreciated "Dichtermut," Hölderlin's poem on the poet's courage—that passages such as this one are, as he has promised and complained, intolerable. Yet here, within the blank walls of a medical clinic, is where he drops into the question of prose and justice, on the edge of cognition, hanging between life and death, refashioning a modern twilight: truth and infirmity beam out from this existential hovel.

Following the malediction he will have issued statements in the opening parts of this very section, framed by a translation of T. S. Eliot, announcing that prose should never lie or provoke absolute humiliation or cause undue distress. In a way that Nietzsche taught us to read, we note that the definition urged relies on what prose should *not* and never do. Nietzsche makes the "nots" repeat and invert the Ten Commandments, establishing law, and reach beyond merely good ethical propositions. In material terms of the book's sequencing, prose pulls away from maternal recklessness, but to such an extent that it would be stripped of powered-up rhetoric and fictional forays: it must not commit perjury, nor humiliate, and certainly not distress. It sounds the call for a strenuous kind of ethical vigilance—so ethical that it is overseen by the dead, who observe a strict and viable relation to the truth. This is where Eliot, to hold the fort, comes in, having understood that the dead can now, in death, tell us what they had no word for when alive.[57] Lacoue calls this watchful relation to truth *diction*, and I would put it on the other side of malediction (understanding that we cannot simply take sides when bouncing against such extreme limits or have this squabble at the boundary of intelligibility).

The irony of assertion entails truthful saying that comes from the dead, who break their silence, when they pass out of life. This could befit Lacoue today, but cannot pertain to his mother on her deathbed, who mouthed off prematurely, rounding out the humiliation and distress that knew no recourse or appeal. "Autrement dit: il faut à la prose d'énoncer une vérité / que les morts, s'ils sont justes, nous permettraient de soutenir" (In other words: prose must say a truth / that the dead, if they are just, would permit us to support). This instance of dead-serious truth-telling is never assured. In the first place, it must be dosed out in measures that mortals can support. If the truth borne by the dead is not sufficiently distilled, the dead can paralyze their interlocutors in their saying, as by the example of King Hamlet. For the rest of them, the dead, by virtue of saying nothing, in the end hold only a little piece of authority. Still, they command supreme authority: this structure of justice and command touches the paradox of authority, its mystical foundation, which in this case is rendered by the core assignment of prose. The quote from Eliot reaches parabolic dimensions, for the departed can say nothing in their living form, and they say nothing now—but theirs represents the authority to authorize the saying when it comes to exposing a truth component of prose.

Given the parabolic aporias stipulating who or what can say the truth, at which end of what line—or rope—the relation to what prose must bring about should not be relaxed, but tightened, and we must do our impossible, as it were, to try to come to terms with the mise-en-scène that Lacoue proposes for the recalcitrant unfolding of truthfulness under clinical hold and death rattle. According to Badiou, the mere assertion of truth makes this section the philosophical core of the work. Yet, this section—following, or still stuck in, the C-section that at once births and death-binds it—is also the most theatrical, meticulously staged, if also hesitatingly ushered to the edge of intelligibility and doused in searing insight, whether or not prosthetically supported by meds, telephone calls, writing pads.

Lacoue is martyred to his truth, a scene of writing poised among the historical columns of great asylum seekers of note and letters, where walls are knocked down, others erected, and something unsayable is immured while patiently tapping out behind the secret codes of the confined. This is where Philippe Lacoue-Labarthe learns to burble—a great philosophical forum? Maybe. He's stripped down to minimalist continuation, persisting "contre moi"—leaning against himself, opposing or versus himself, rhyming with the Nietzschean signature—at the limit of destruction, he writes, pinned to this vile solitude, among the tables of the cafeteria, the trees in the park, not set down in order to regroup or renounce eloquence, but in order to say as precisely as possible ("au plus près") the very thing, or being, or disposition that I must let go of, renounce. He sends up a colon—:—calling out to that which must henceforth be renounced, namely, or callingly, "this bitter falsification, this evasive discourse, the residual bits (or this surplus [ou cet excédent]) of 'poetry' / that have spoiled (détérioré) our most just prose."[58]

Just Prose. "Poetry" has wrecked our prose, our justice—setting up a rap sheet, despite the searing complaint, that hands power to poetry, even in its corrupt overuse or rhetorical capacity for destruction. But this is where he refuses to widen the lens and adds, parenthetically, that he means "our" prose, not that of centuries, colon—:—, I am addressing you, as you know ("[c'est à toi que je m'adresse, tu le sais]").[59] Maybe a lover's discourse could lead the way, abandon the false flourishes or mock abysses that counterfeit "poetry," that of pompous complaint and injurious feint. Maybe in the minor key of Bataille and related other tonalities of a distinguished cohort, the figure comprising lovers can push back against the reign of injustice. Badiou supports the hypothesis of amorous dispute taking the lead in how to demand and say justice from the other, at least, I suppose as a start-off point and model for something like social justice and its nearly impossible edges.

The Interruptive Complaint of Alain B. Besides Goethe, who ditched his mother at a very young age (which is why we have a scintillating correspondence between postal mother and son), we can count another powerhouse who claims success in removing Mother's residual traces of early interference. Able to fend off the disturbing effects of his own mother's disapproval ratings, Alain Badiou regrets that Lacoue, for his part, was such a wuss on the matter of his *mater*. Badiou explains that his thought on the "Il arrive que" (it happens that) manages to evade, and, in fact, does not at all encounter the substantial complications that constrain Philippe: one should be able to see things, even the most disruptive incursions, as a matter of a gift without ulterior motive or *arrière plan*.[60] Cleaning up and returning the whole explosive mess in *Phrase* as a surplus insight to the ground rules and regs of his own work, Badiou writes, "Il est ce qui, chez moi sous le nom d'événement, autorisant par grâce pure la pensée, n'a pas à être pensé, mais seulement accepté, suivi, déployé dans ses conséquences" (It's this way. In my [work] the name of event, authorizing thought by means of pure grace, does not have to be [an object of] thought, but only accepted, followed, laid out in terms of its consequences).[61] So, more or less, roughly: there are things in my work that come about as events that should not become incessant objects of thought, but, authorizing thinking by a stroke of pure grace, ought rather to be accepted, pursued, developed. Wait! It gets more insistent, more chilling. It's like we have Hermann Kafka on the line—I'm not kidding, he's really swooping down on his buddy from the authoritarian perch. Not only does he dig in by reappropriating the section to his own work on the event, saying, more or less, "Just deal with it," there's nothing to think about here (a powerful instruction from a thinker: I suppose that, like Claudius, he collapses thinking with brooding, or, like New Agers, reflection with "overthinking," or, like teenagers, concern with obsessing, or, never mind . . .).

It gets better. Alain delivers a concession that could itself blow up the scene of writing. It turns out that *his* mother hated him, too! Well, maybe she was just resentful, disappointed in finding herself pregnant and, as time passed, was not pleased with what he had become (a philosopher). "Je sais pourtant que ma mere n'a pas non plus aimé que je naisse, ni vraiment que je deviennent qui je suis" (I however know that my mother also did not love that I was born, nor really that I become who I am).[62] If this were about him (which he asserts it is, transferring the whole account to *his* work and birth, reappropriating the inappropriable, suppressing all the stutters and breakdowns to which Philippe was vulnerable), I would want to interrogate the use of "vraiment" at this moment of his commentary to see how truth claims work in Badiou and the primal syntax of philosophical-maternal rejection. His mom didn't really (*truly*) like what he became, either, he writes. Allow me to skip over to where he asserts the difference between his handling of the maternal curse and Lacoue's Sisyphusian backslides (what Rickels calls Sissy-phus). Throwing himself into spheres that separate off from her, successfully compartmentalizing and accepting the perpetual joy of innumerable worlds, Badiou triumphantly has known to break out of the range of maternal follow-up. "Je me suis ainsi détourné de toute alliance entre le naître fatal et la mourir indifferent" (I thus turned away from any link or alliance between a fatal birth and an indifferent dying).[63] Now we arrive at one of the pet peeves of the materialists/*materialists* but truly "immaternalists," as he coins, that link my f(r)iends Žižek and Badiou: their flight from finitude, the maternal snare. I have always wondered about the intensity of their *repugnance* for the finite, the way they growled at its very mention, as if the phenomenological-existentialist-deconstructive and (sometimes) media-technological recourse to the thought of finitude were at all times, that is infinitely, radioactive—or, at best, a game that could be called off. Now I see that the veto on finitude belongs to a struggle with the evil-Knieval mother, and the alleged containability of the gust winds of her curse. Good luck with that!

Well, Badiou claims to have had good luck with it, and this very difference in overcoming/succumbing to the maternal hurl, her vomit, her birthing, her foul language and excitable speech, is what defines the crux of his *différend* with Lacoue, their essential dispute. Otherwise, he really likes the guy, Lacoue, his buddy, Badiou emphasizes. Alain Badiou knew how to shake it off: I was able to leave behind any hitch between a fatal birth and indifferent death. "J'ai laissé le fini loin de la vie et l'infini loin de la mort" (I left the finite far behind life and the infinite far from death, which meant that "my phrase could not be the same as Lacoue's.") Lacoue, thrown by the curse, had his death always in front of him, and thus became *enslaved by it*. The responses to the curse, fundamentally different, allow Alain to pull ahead, for life: Lacoue responded to the maternal curse not so much by means of fiction but by attaching to the enigma—the enigma that renders his birth invalid by means of maternal judgment and by which the corruption of all prose transits.[64]

Badiou pushes their inaccordance one step further to explain their standoff concerning Wagner. Philippe in *Musica ficta* could not stomach the type of consolation that Wagner offers but saw it as myth, an opportunistic negation of the inconsolable. "I, on the contrary, enveloped myself in the harmonic ambivalence of Wagner, for I could see what Lacoue was unable to see: the accomplishment of separation. Wagner, moreover, musically evokes (*enchante musicalement*) the nostalgia of the mother with his '*Mutter, mutter*' on the background of cello and base clarinet."[65] Lacoue remains inconsolable, but Badiou has known to move on and separate off from childhood's backdraft, with a little help from Wagner.

It gets better. Wagner continues to be crucial in the philosophical playoffs begun since Nietzsche, after which Heidegger went up against him. "Wagner is the music of poetry with air quotes, its prose corrupted by injustice, the lost phrase." Badiou returns to himself. "Pour moi, évidemment, c'est tout autre chose" (For me, it's altogether another matter). His drift: Parsifal is the proposition of a new Ceremony, releasing us from childhood or birth. Parsifal is the one who renounces, in the name of the Idea, the desire that his mother love and embrace him, even if she were to appear as the most beautiful among women to have crossed the world in the certainty of her sovereignty. Wagner thus is the musician of the adult who has known to sideline forever the curse ("qui a su écarter pour toujours la malédiction"; [who knew to set aside the curse forever]).[66] He is the very promise of prose. He is the phrase . . . Wagner thus continues to serve as the test site for thought, ever since he was a proving ground in France, beginning with Baudelaire. Let us leave off now, understanding that the *différend* between Lacoue-Labarthe and Badiou, otherwise in perpetual consortium, cuts across the meaning of a maternal curse and its broadcast system affixed to Wagner. *Ach, ach!* It's a gripping dialogue, at times a duet—at other times a full-blown orchestra that would require a few more bars.

They both circuit justice through love. Let me be frank here. *Ach!* Being trained in icy Germanic zones—even when taking the deviant off-track signed "Jena," the site of experimental and dangerous proposals of the Romantics, who experimented with life, *Lebensphilosophie*, and each other—I struggle with the estrangement of a lover's vocabulary of wounded justice, though I appreciate Lacoue's complaint about its limits: one can only expect so much from the exigency of justice—so much and too much, so much, not enough, still not enough, but much too much. For he also states that prose, in this district, where love drives the stakes, is corrupted by the desire for what is definitive, requiring the undeterred assertion of an irrevocable commitment. Love makes language bypass the knowledge of its own unreliability to engage loyalty oaths on the one hand, and unleash unpinnable vengeance on the other, lashing out without the constraints of a referential checkpoint. The flexion of a lover's dispute, aggressive and despotic, nonetheless has its good points to the extent that it bespeaks life's vivacity, touching a region of saying that inspires prose. Still, love, a point of pride for Philippe, seems to regress the thought on prose and justice that has motivated these sections. This complaint may have more to do with my own hang-ups than with his unrivalled tenacity of reflection.

He reaches for poetry to tranquilize the onslaught of blind rage, a lover's dowry. He dumps Hölderlin. Whether his new arrangement represents a categorical turn, an error or release, I cannot say. But it indicates a significant step back, as when Werther leaves Homer for Ossian. A line recruited from Rimbaud has the virtue of inducing an unprecedented calmness, on the side of life, changing things up to the tune of love and eternity. According to Badiou this departure indicates the point of turnaround. In some ways, a welcome climate change in the overheated text, the introduction of Rimbaud establishes new valorizations that line up with the poet's tranquility, the serene version of being-toward-death—though "death" is precisely what Badiou sees as moved out of the philosopher's pinched range.

"Elle est retrouvée"—eternity rediscovered, ocean-riding into the sunset, her partnered bliss. There it is, or will be, intemporally: a track that brings the lover's voice up to a glimpse of eternity, announcing the resting point of calm. For Badiou, this calm is exactly what one feels in the midst of political storms, artistic commotions, under the brusque lightning of mathematics, as well, "évidemment," as in the intensity of the declaration of love: "un calme surhumain étrangement composé de la violence de ce qui vient" (a calm strangely composed of the violence of that which comes). Badiou wants to conclude on the evocation of "eternity," that which lets Lacoue see, finally, that the experience of prose as *véridiction* is not limited to death. This interpretation allows him to rewrite Rimbaud's famous verse—"Elle est arrive, quoi? L'éternité," which no longer is "la mer allée avec le soleil," but something more precious, "the certitude that love is compatible with poetry and thus that love exists in this world, under the species of prose." "Thus I contradict our friend, the great philosopher Lacoue, on a capital point: whatever he said at times, he did find prose" (*il a trouvé la prose*).[67] Broad and assured, Badious's commentary brings love into compatibility with poetry—as certitude—which means that love, of and in our world, part of our being-in-the-world, claims us in the mode

CHAPTER 4

and as a species—he might have said "type"—of prose. In this regard, prose would near our sense of the prosaic, a way of saying and living in the world. One could add, but who would dare, "Wir leben indem wir leiben," we live while we body, extending the lifeline of loved life, lived love, as an experience of prose. According to Badiou, our philosopher-poet, Philippe, did find prose. His wallowing in complaint proved nearly pointless, a runaway contingency.

I am not going pull up the files where Derrida shows Lacan and psycho-analysis finding what they never wanted to lose, putting in place a compulsive plot to fend off loss and find the proper place of a purportedly lost object. Our friend, Lacoue, according to Badiou, was erroneously contending with a loss that didn't have to be mourned, much less plaintively registered. Badiou picks up the assignment that Lacoue-Labarthe has left off for us. For his part, Lacoue lamented the merely possible existence of prose, thereby conferring a task upon us to keep looking, and finding, everywhere where it occurs, no matter how rare the instances or places, under a species so foreign as that of the phrase.[68] This would be Lacoue's testament, to have us find what he had ticketed as lost. That sums up our task henceforth, perhaps—but by no evident means—imprinted by Benjamin, who understood task as what has to be given up while pursued, whose pursuit depends on our ability to let go.

Here is where Badiou and his friend Lacoue draw the line, marking a lasting dispute: to contest Lacoue's strikingly negative stance, Badiou wrote not one but two philosophical manifestos, he emphasizes, that are meant to protest and agitate *for* philosophy. He has already published *Manifeste pour la philosophie* and announces in "À la recherche de la prose perdue" that "I am a repeat offender for, not hesitating to parody André Breton, I shall publish in a few weeks a *Second Manifesto for Philosophy*."[69] The point of contestation? Lacoue went off on philosophy with unrelenting brutality in *La Fiction du politique* (1987), where he declared "La philosophie est finie" (philosophy is over and/or philosophy is finite). He raises the stakes of a finalizing instance, inevitably disabling dialectical retrieval and robust transfer systems—killing the lights for someone like Badiou, close to the core of dialectical operations. Philosophy is done, but it gets worse. One cannot *want* philosophy back nor want anything in its place anymore. Moreover, do not even *think* of engaging desire when fac-ing the forlorn crustiness of philosophical abandonment. This "bye-bye-love" theme in Lacoue's work does not suit Alain Badiou who, despite it all, has his own bevy of desiring machines and thus bemoans the lack stubbornly left by Lacoue: "il ne faut plus être en désir de philosophie" (no longer should one be in a state of desiring philosophy).[70]

How does Lacoue-Labarthe resolve his dilemma of rejecting philosophy, or, rather, of dismissing out of hand the desire for the philosophical and continue to philosophize? He makes a strong and theorized appeal to modesty, which commands acts of philosophizing without hope. This riles up Badiou, the course Lacoue follows, doubling down on relentless loss and its continuation in philosophical reticence. The beautiful essay on modesty did not sit well with the philosopher king. He, for his part, makes it a question of taste, divergent taste: the ensemble formed by the end, tradition—an obstinateness incapable of affirmation and the retreat of any desire—could not be to my liking ("ne pouvait être de mon gout"). I therefore wrote entirely to the contrary: philosophy continues as before, it (she, *la philosophie*: they are kind of fighting over the body of a woman) is capable of new and fundamental theses, and constructs a proper desire. Badiou declares himself *for* philosophy. "J'ai, contre Lacoue, manifesté et declaré pour la philosophie" (I agitated and issued declarations, against Lacoue, on behalf of philosophy).[71] The point of rupture between the frenemies widens. Lacoue hits hard against his contemporaries, denouncing them for their journalistic Socratism and anthropological approximations, which have nothing to do with the work of thinking.[72] Badiou allows that he shares the "taste," when necessary, for destructive and violent style. Yet, even when the invective clearly is aimed at Bernard-Henri Lévy, Badiou sees himself shoved into the target zone: "Let us say even, beyond the notorious impostors in his sights, that I was perhaps the only one to support so clearly, if not with equal violence, the [position] that Lacoue condemned for its vacuity." *Boom, boom.* What is worse, Lacoue goes after "mon maître" Sartre with unacceptable vehemence, demonstrating a steely contempt that allows him to pick on Sartre as a twice-over counterfeit epigone who loudly arrogated to his cause the title of "philosophy." "Eh bien là, non et non," cries out Badiou.[73] No way! Much in the way that Philippe didn't know what Levinas was getting at with the preposterous title "Otherwise than Being"—being *is* otherwise, other than itself, richly unmanageable and self-voiding—Badiou has no idea why Lacoue would be obsessed with ending it all, or, settling another score, why he would brutalize the philosopher-progenitor, Sartre. Not cool!

Happily, there is, symmetrically, another philosophy that consists in the obstinateness of not renouncing thought, even as the relation to thinking is pursued under a devastated, loser name of "philosophy." I would say this, says Badiou, to Lacoue's formulation that we haven't the least idea of "thinking" beyond "philosophy": from "the inscrutable beyond of its end, its death, philosophy still judges what's at stake with thinking." Just as only the dead (who have not known what to say) have the power to judge prose, so philosophy—finished, impracticable, impossible—"should still and always be that according to which thought attempts to find its prose." And here is what "I have finally come to understand. Under the name of prose we have the cloth of the phrase in the encounter of love and poetry, in the fusion of poetry and philosophizing—a fusion that takes place only when prescribed by a place beyond place, namely, from and by death. The operation of Lacoue convokes a beyond of philosophizing—prose as poem of thought—that, for the moment, is valid only if philosophy occupies in this game the place of death." This insight, bold and decisive, just about accounts for the crux of the *différend* between the two philosophers, one forwarding beyond, the other, in contestatory standoff, raising a voice from the living: "My resistance, without mercy, is precisely (*justement*) to maintain philosophy outside this place and to posit that there is no such beyond, for the simple reason that we, on the contrary, at the beginning of philosophizing, that is, that philosophy in the element of the definitive retreat of the divine has barely begun, and thus we are the pre-Socratics, Lacoue as well as I."[74] Together with Derrida, Badiou destabilizes the "beyond," be it of the pleasure principle or philosophy, in order to stand up for the living and reorder the temporality of rising philosophical astonishments. Taking off in the retreat of the divine, philosophizing has barely begun. Even so, I am not certain that Lacoue's sober assessments of a philosophical letdown, perhaps a necessary humiliation, amounts to a deathwatch, or secures the habitat of a beyond, crowding out the living, but I can see the benefits of such a topography and the time zones it arranges for thinking.

Badiou's task before the oeuvre of Lacoue consists in bringing to light the returned futural flash of pre-Socratism. Badiou finds some leverage in the work, the somber work, that *Phrase* itself offers, where a glimpse into a true diction has been given in terms of love. Hence the work supports other bases for philosophizing that diverge from mere acceptance of finitude or dwelling in the vicinity of death. This divergence from its own death-trapped tailspins "effectively offers an entirely different narration" (*en effet une toute autre narration*).[75]

Let me circle back to eternity, the word on which he wants to conclude— "'Eternité', cest le mot sur lequel je veux conclure." I'll leave aside whether one can conclude on or with eternity, even when held in place by quotation marks, pinning together a spread of eternity without finitude, the sunlit spree. Meow. Scratch, scratch. Badiou discovers another voice inhabiting the work, which comes up for him like a miracle of enticing description, incorporated in the depressed body of the work, signaling as part of a process of a truth believed to be on the side of happiness and power. "Oui, pour Lacoue," we have the affect of prose, for me the affect of all subjectivization in a procedure of truth: we no longer have "fear or harm" (*ni peur ni mal*).[76] I don't know. Can one really power through to a place or atopos without fear or harm/evil? Badiou seems to want the power, its colloquy with truth, settled in a relation without malignancy. I feel he ought to know better, but I understand the pull,

A Pass of Friendship

the draw of what has to be considered a series of false stabilities. Still, one can concede the point that there's something in Philippe that wants this, too, but he can under no circumstances let himself have this, or give himself access to such a "procedure of truth" and its lure of metaphysical comfort. Lacoue, in the end, rigorously stays put in the realm of discomfort, raking its field as an almost ethical opening to—everything. And nothing. He at no point skirts the fear of nothingness.

In section 20 of *Phrase*, Lacoue's language nonetheless catches a glimpse of eternity, touches down on calmness. The addressed beloved of greenish-blue eyes comes into view, eyes glinting in a way that makes her appear superhuman, or other than human: "your gestures, your stride, of which only animals are capable." She confers on the work another track, as Badiou rightly notes, bringing around the loving voice of intelligence and recognition, the "don consenti, / de l'éternité entrevue, touchée" (the granted gift, / of eternity glimpsed, touched).[77] We know that Badiou likes playing for keeps, and there's something here that he wants to hang onto, bring into prominence, make stick for him and Lacoue, as if they wanted to walk off into the sunset—an explicit theme, poetically upheld, at the end of the commentary. Eternity rises up as concluding word, which offers a broad-based assist. The whimpering edges of the plaintive song, the tyrannical draw of finitude, can now be disposed of. Owing to the way *Phrase* switches things up for this glimmering moment, the experience of prose as veridiction no longer seems constrained by death. The mere glimpse of eternity suffices to overthrow the melancholic cry that, until this syncope of time, has seemed to dominate the mood of the text. "The experience can certainly invite the touch of eternity, here and now, by a fidelity whose reward indeed is an unknown calm."[78] However fleeting or insubstantial its touching down on us, eternity can graze the speaker, suspending the plaint of finitude yet inviting pre-Socratic beginnings.

The trope of calm that Philippe will have known, according to the intervening other voice, the other experience of prose, rewrites and exceeds in some ways the celebrity verse of Rimbaud. Found. Yet in Rimbaud, what is sought or arrives unexpectedly is found on the condition of departing: Eternity is figured as the sea, but not only the sea, gone with the sun, leaving with the sun, or cleaving to the Sun King, the emblazoned mark in poetic diction for time. For eternity is not found, but *re-found*, already in repetition and loss, a non-originary occurrence, which is to say, that eternity, if found, hardly arrives but, captured momentarily, comes around in time, as time, in hindsight, on the cusp of disappearance, clocking out definitively, leaving with the hint of a promised return, like the sun, with the sun, if the sun does not leave her behind in one of the agonized turns toward return. If the sun sets, it is also because it is setting time.

Ach! If I had Derridean expanses, if I had the touch of eternity on my aching shoulders, I would now open the dossier on the calm that Badiou hopes is not deathlike, does not lead right back to beyond the pleasure principle or Kant's perpetual peace, the cemetery that the old philosopher (Kant) cannot and will not evade. I would then go for the jugular of what cuts into the text as a death-denial-like drive in Badiou—a strange insistence among those launched by Hegelian materialisms, underscored by the way they in effect hit the pause button on dialectics, the way they suppress the overtime work of negation on certain corners of being, but, hey-hey-Hegel, who are we to complain about the reign of eternity and the approaching dissolution of fear? . . . I think that now would be the time (but we are concluding on eternity, so never would be the time, or right time, or true instance of my death, still: *now* would have been the time) to haul in Heidegger's thought of serenification and resign all the peace entreaties made by the hall-of-famers, the grand complainers on our lists, those who have signaled and continue to punch in by registering their complaints, without clocking recuperative calm sought at critical times, in time, by philosophy, or assuming (the power, etc.) effectively to soothe or dial(ectic) it down.

The line recruited from Rimbaud has another virtue, that of taking a particular turn, marking an allegorical irony, not only because the event of an eternity found again rides on the back of paradise lost—though, granted and given, maybe the quasi-mystical couple of sea and sun, as they depart, nonetheless appease, eternalize on the Nietzschean scale of "Alle Lust will Ewigkeit, tiefe, tiefe Ewigkeit—" the experience of desire may *want* eternity, but it's not gonna get it, with or without the kickoff of the Eternal Return. Let me return to the threesome consisting of Lacoue-Labarthe, Rimbaud, and Badiou, to follow the way our philosophers organize libidinally around poetry. Whether unwilled or meticulously planned out, yet seemingly inadvertent, Badiou is returned to the very narration he has more or less discarded when he chooses this verse, redacting Rimbaud, realigning *Phrase* with the phrasing of eternity. In my character as Diotima, I am going to run with the unmarked brilliance of the ending he offers Lacoue, a moment in his commentary that breaks its own stride when calling in, with radiant acuity, the return of the repressed.

Eternity recharged, clearing out as she arrives, pulling up stakes homonymically, serves to recall the maternal in the bridged intonation of *la mer/la mère* (the sea/Mother). The very verse meant to reaffirm a newly found calm—in a work that menaces at each stage of its articulation to plummet—hits a snag.

Pulled back by Badiou to its traumatic moment of distress from which Badiou has claimed, for his part, to have separated off, it pulls a fast one: Eternity is found, only to be disrupted by the uncontrolled returns and departures of Mother, grasping onto the sun/son. Where Badiou has evacuated the femalédiction, made ample space for the "immaternal"-eternal returns that could henceforth pacify our friend, Lacoue, the rhetoric of the stay outsmarts his good wishes with a malicious play of finitude, pitting its relentless *fort-da* against the imaginary bliss of eternity. When referring to Philippe's troubled waters, Badiou calls him "our friend," urging his hapless chum to get over himself, to become another kind of son who won't settle or set.

At the end of *Phrase* 19 ("PROSE"), Lacoue sends up a flare of return, almost on the order of hope. A diction could come back to us, the last stanza offers, a kind that turns down the decibels of the curse: "nulle raison / d'en désespérer" (no reason / to despair of this return), if I make the effort no longer to rely on the fury of words, and if we are capable of respecting the unpronounceable—"et si nous sommes capables de respecter l'imprononçable."[79] The curse fatally competes with the unpronounceable, with what vibrates with the unsaid.

In "*Katharsis et Mathèsis*," Lacoue evokes Bataille, who was profoundly touched, he writes, by "la 'mère tragédie'" ("mother tragedy," and behind her, he continues parenthetically, sacrificial experience in general) called "la pratique de la joie devant la mort" (the practice of joy in the face of death).[80] Perhaps it is not altogether far-fetched to integrate this tonality into the great plaint of Lacoue-Labarthe, and let it live and resonate together with the Greek experience, to which he devotes multifaceted activities of translation and writing, of *ekplèxis*: shock, stupor and *phobos*: fear and terror. It is as if the Greek grasp of the lamentable in life were only now beginning to dawn on us, provoking a plaintive howl through the centuries that bind us. Lacoue's acute sense of terror, modern yet part of an essential ancient vocabulary, is shared by very few. Part of a recurring rebound from Aristotle's writings on politics and poetics, this inheritance of terror clutches and visits us all, however.

The extreme experience of "fear and terror," of "shock and stupor," the implications of which so many commentators try explicitly to throw or ease down, and still others simply ignore, continues no doubt to practice its covert shakedowns in the worlds we still share and are shattered by.

Hannah Arendt Swallows the Lessing Prize

> Real are the dead whom you have forgotten. . . .
> They are living ghosts.
> —Hannah Arendt, "The Aftermath of Nazi Rule"

The Drama of a Citation. I don't like the narcissistic hot spot of complaining. Jubilation is more to my taste and feeds my sense of human dignity, what's left of it. Granted, jubilation is a hard one to hold, though we can rejoice in whatever occasions the enthusiastic spree of sudden leaps and bounds, no matter how short-lived the existential jump for joy. Does the breakout dance of jubilation not cut itself short out of a lucid sense of limitation?

A close relative of flushed euphoria, *enthusiasm*—as Nietzsche knew, Kant had suspected and Lyotard glimpsed—can easily trip into stupidity. Enthusiastic acclaim for any cause or thing can easily run its course foolishly. Of course, jubilant enthusiasm, or whatever does not offer up a profile of reserve—an exemplary Jamesian quality, indicating intelligence—threatens to break the mold of dignity. What about the stance of complaining, does it not indicate from the start a sizable dose of neurotic standstill—a form, indeed, of stupefaction and *stupidity*; or, is it rather a meme of intelligence, striking a defiant pose of resistance to the supposed "what is" of world? Let me turn to a place where the one is embedded in the other, jubilant acknowledgment hosting complaint, in a tense standoff set by Hannah Arendt. For, when honored by the German city of Hamburg, Hannah responded to the festive acknowledgment of her stature, as work and person, as historical marker, with a solicitous thinking of the complainer's woe. Stupefied and troubled, she found herself, as recipient of an official citation, ensnared in the granting of a distinction that could not evade the aggressive qualities and edges of performative imposition.

Addressing the foreign/homeland audience through the traumatic filter of complaint in poetic language, she moves toward the social dedication to rejoicing, enrolling the great Enlightenment thinker, Gotthold Ephraim Lessing, to front for the double exigency of exultation and complaint. In the end, Hannah left everyone floored. I will start here by reviewing the case of the inassimilable prize, noting the historical investment of a densely freighted ode to joy onto which Arendt attaches her argument. The prize-bestowal crucially depends on the recipient's capacity to pump and spread joy, to knock off the corrupting temptation of debilitating sadness, a historical inevitability and interpretive stake of depressive consequence.

Cutting close to the bone of the *Klage*, Lessing however also placed a premium on a socializing kind of joyfulness that makes room for the creation of complicities and bonds among its celebrants. Turned for its expression toward a community of fellow beings, joy generates modalities of nearness, throwing bridges across the abyss of human relations. In Arendt's view, unsuppressed joy primes political bonds. Much as Kant will draw on shared aspects of experience promoted by the beautiful form—particularly when he explores the need for communicability—Lessing establishes the communitarian accent of generous affect. His theoretical work accounts for an affirmative turning away from oneself toward the exigency of social bonding, responsive to prompts of rejoicing. The address of joy accrues to and even *constitutes* the friend. In a sense, friendship for Lessing conducts joy to the forefront of binding discourse, marking the experience of a viable shareability that is pulled into place by a political tow. Joy in friendship—the signature affect of amicable closeness and political acuity—acts as the superglue that has kept one world-bound. For Arendt, "gladness, not sadness, is talkative" (*Gesprächig ist die Freude, nicht das Leid*), and "truly human dialogue differs from mere talk or even discussion in that it is entirely permeated by pleasure in the other person and what he says. It is tuned to gladness, we might say."[1] I want to grant this point to Arendt, even though I have visited zones of adept loquacity when falling across the sorrow of the bereft or destitute. Clearly, greatest sorrow goes silent at times, and I will not push a theory of phrasal regimens to include silence in and on the way of language. Nonetheless, I cannot imagine that Arendt would hold these affective levers very far apart for long, since one turns into and to the other at regular intervals of existential off-centeredness.

Hannah had every reason to scrap modulations of muteness from her registry, for she is mistrustful of those who went silent in the night of need, retreating to the relative safety of an "inner emigration." Thus, Germans who practiced some form of muteness, barely squeaking out protest, fell short of the creditable bar: "while they may well produce sound, they do not produce speech and certainly not dialogue."[2] Dialogue tutors political practicability; it's the way of showing that you count yourself in. Too many contemporaries have faded out and ducked into muted refuge. I am not saying that the conditions and stipulations for dialogue were available or to be seized; *she* is making it a breaking point, and I get it.

The flair for taking pleasure in the other seems to matter to her argument, establishing a path to the acknowledgment of her dilemma—where is the pleasure in throwing a cable to her donors, the appointed prize-bestowers, those who think they can appraise her accomplishment or understand her sensitive predicament in the face of catastrophic erasure? I am not "overexaggerating" the stakes, as my students might say. Arising neither from whim nor subjective contingency, the ability to take pleasure in others also holds an expansive quality. It allows us to take in a politics based on joy accorded and requisitioned by a fellow citizen or friend. For this and other reasons, Arendt orients us away from suffering, if only to keep our shared world going. Joy is not only world affirming, but world giving, and its adoption is almost befitting an obligation of ethical and political proportions. If one is bound up in acts and affects of world giving, then the happy place from which world surges cannot be prior to the donation of joy, but must be mustered, driven up from latency or nonexistence. According to a Lessing-like syntax of being, no one should have to shoulder this "must." Yet, for Arendt, world must happen—or, more precisely, world must have happened, yet requires continual renewal, especially in times of radical disjointure. The absorption or, more likely, production of joy ligatures us to one another's inhabitable worlds while also providing the basis for freedom: *movement*.

Freedom of movement and joyful indulgence in others lay the groundwork for a rethinking of politics and openhearted social release. Could one imagine applying such an interpretation today to the obstinate cold front of social phobias and legal restrictions, the language saturated with so-called aliens, whether legal or illegal? The opening of borders begins with minute euphoric incursions, pushing back on what Nietzsche described as the encroachments of a monstrously cold state. Thus ritual ceremonies marking accomplishment of any scale—the event of anniversary, benchmark, dissertation defense, best office worker, or holiday—bring communities together in celebration, warming a place for *Mitsein*.

Placing the emphasis on gladness in ceremony, the recipient no doubt raises the stakes, ironizing the concession made to a call she feels she must take. Resolved, after considerable hesitation and prodding, to accept her prize, Hannah Arendt appears to come prepared with a theoretical understanding of the act (or tweak of passivity) that beckons her. Following her philosophically backed precepts, she is at the ready, reporting for duty in the toned anticipation of friendship, showing a willingness to initiate and answer to the prompt of dialogue. Intending perhaps to take a stab at friendship in unallowable precincts, she steps up according to the imperative that writes her ticket. At one point of her more or less commissioned speech she quotes Lessing's Nathan, who moves onto the scene with an imposing sense of desperation and righteousness: "*We must, must be friends*" (original emphasis).[3] There is no way around this injunction, it seems, if speech is at all to be sounded or delivered. Friendship edges into an imperious necessity, precisely where it has been socially doomed or historically foreclosed.

There was a time, she reminds us, when it would have been preposterous for the German and the Jew to cleave in friendship. "I come in friendship": this phrase, resonating Roman nobility, well describes Arendt's projected approach, with gladness no doubt posed as a regulatory ideal; whether or not sustainable, it somehow was cast as the lead affect. The feeling tone for which she advocates entails pleasure in the other, perhaps held in reserve as memory trace or promise, if not bracketed out at this point of the encounter. Yet, for this ceremony to stay coherent with her sense of things, gladness must hold some kind of measurable sway. Her source book is Lessing; even so, one must wonder whether he would have forced gladness upon her, and the proneness to political friendship. In Lessing's work, the injunction of friendship runs up against his famous Enlightenment-based statement, "Kein Mensch muß müssen"—an economical and grammatically adept way of saying that nobody can be forced to do anything—that "nobody must 'must'" or "has to have to," freeing up any and all from constraints. The slogan-leaning utterance is difficult to render without taking recourse to the noncoercive grammaticality, for once, of the German language. In both statements by Lessing, the "must" is doubled, in one case to offer emphasis, in the other case to cancel out "müssen."[4] To the degree that the doubling of "must" destabilizes the phrase in which it is encrusted as moral imperative, it may understand itself already to knock the friendship, the "must happen" of friendship, to the second power, and out of the ring.

To come in friendship: this is a tall order. Arendt sets things up in such a way as to enforce the unenforceable with an iron fist—or, perhaps more to the point, with the jab of bitter irony, whether or not she desires or controls the scene of address. Setting up the parameters of showing up for oneself, for another, and on behalf of those who can no longer stand for themselves, she sets herself up. How can gladness be instituted, practiced as world-friendly duty? What bearing does it have on the scenography of the *Preis-Rede*? What are the conceptual threads that hold up her acceptance of a distinction, fraught with

CHAPTER 5

knotted impediments?[5] In the first place, of course, though psychoanalysis may contradict such an assumption, gladness cannot be a result of some coercive *mainmise* or supervisory stranglehold.[6] It cannot be legislated. Like grace, its range of occurrence seems to fall outside the rule of law or the beat of social regulation. Still, Superego governs the controls when it comes to enjoyment, and pleasure in the other seems to underlie Arendt's politics in the matter of the prize and its satellite contingencies. She is certainly driven by superegoical considerations to show up for it, prepared to shoulder the encumbering bestowal with grace and purposefulness. She *must* accept the prize, befriend and dialogue with the conveners of ambiguous bestowal. The precondition for "humanity," she argues, placing "humanity" in quotation marks—a first sullen destabilizer—consists in this openness to others, a disposition or *question*, she says, that simultaneously raises the question of selflessness. "It seems evident that sharing joy is absolutely superior in this respect to sharing suffering. Gladness, not sadness, is talkative." Sharing joy is *absolutely* superior, she asserts, raising the stakes of phrasing. Yet, how much cheer can she bring to this table? Her partner should be the contested, chronically angered and unmanaged Lessing as reliable carrier of social joyfulness: *really?* How does the concept or question of selflessness come into play here? Accepting a prize now, under circumstances that she will not hesitate to describe, involves giving up something, a piece of floated self or corner of being, even as recovered joy steers the event of an implicit investiture.

The constraints inhibiting Hannah Arendt have something to do with a historically disrupted delivery. She is charged, by the legacy and phantom of Lessing, with delivering the "gift of friendship"—a counter-endowment of sorts, an undeliverable granting, with no viable trustee at the reception desk, ready to sign for it: *really* sign for it, *versteht sich*, and not just sign off on her according to some sinister calculation of reimbursement or restitutional deposition. Beyond all sorts of incalculables, the claim of selflessness also serves to immunize the recipient from the compassion of the donors, for there is always a suspicion that the conferral can come about merely as a mercy prize, a way of shutting a door. Let us see how this works for her.

Before stepping up to receive the honors, Hannah Arendt must wade through "the cheerful unconcern of the pariah" and the thudding irreality of those whose lives are bowed by worldlessness. Incorporating these states without entirely overcoming their implications, she makes some remarkable claims in this section of her acceptance speech, evincing moments that in part unhinge the notion of gladness advanced by her to bolster political reasoning. The pariah that haunts the scene delivers strange supplies of warmth and cheer, a version of gladness that however fails the political litmus test. Revolutions

Arendt Swallows the Lessing Prize

and pariahs tend to go overboard with deluded anticipations of intimate exchange. For, in the dark light of "enthusiastic excess" there emerge feelings of warmth and fraternity, a "warmth of human relationships which may strike those who have had some experience with such groups as an almost physical phenomenon." In this case the cuddly pariahs get so close that they squeeze out world ("it is as if under the pressure of persecution the persecuted have moved so closely together that the interspace which we have called world [and which of course existed between them before the persecution, keeping them at a distance from one another] has simply disappeared." This is not a bad thing, she hastens to add, in part because persecuted people do feel a joy "in the simple fact of being alive, rather suggesting that life comes fully into its own only among those who are, in worldly terms, the insulted and injured."[7] Such joy comes at a price, however, deregulating its allotted "charm and intensity." The insight about the joy of living as a pariah, its attendant rhetoric of "there, thereness," an estranging coat of consolation, leaves me speechless, but let us go on. One can still write through tunnels of speechlessness.

The problem with the charms of pariah living "is also due to the fact that the pariahs of this world enjoy the great privilege of being unburdened by care for the world."[8] The pariahs of the world get away with worldlessness. Are they then of the world? I prefer not to quibble with a wayward rhetoric of privilege, though I do want to underscore the price of sticking close to the world from which the one counted out, the pariah, "enjoys" expulsion. It is as if the New York phrase, "include me out" were a viable motto here, except that the pariah could never get behind—or ahead of—such phrasing of choice. Arendt chooses to bypass any splinter of language usage that would account for violent exclusion; citing the pariah as "unburdened" of care may serve only to show that rhetorical operations, including those governing her own phrasing, can also be responsible for wrongdoing. Nonetheless, despite these telling stumbles and rhetorical backslides, Hannah has a point to score that makes political sense and is worth reviewing, if with a drop of worldless sorrow at this point.

According to Arendt, the distressed state of the persecuted—those beaten down, insulted and injured in modern historical times—has allowed for a nearly overdrive identification with the distressed, adding the notion of *fraternité* to flank liberty and equality in the language introduced by the French Revolution. If I may be allowed a spoiler alert, Arendt rehearses the rhetorical supplement involving *fraternity*, a political categorem still going strong, in order to contrast it with Lessing's reflections on *friendship*. Fraternity and friendship enter a contest of serious political consequence for Arendt. The introduction of the notion of fraternity, argues Arendt, has had its "natural place among the repressed and persecuted, the exploited and humiliated, whom the eighteenth century called the unfortunates, *les malheureux*, and the nineteenth century the wretched, *les misérables*." She ascribes the political upgrade of the persecuted to the reinvention of *compassion*, which allowed both Rousseau and Lessing to designate common ground among "all men," and became the rallying cry and "central motive of the revolutionary Robespierre." Compassion called up insurrection and "[e]ver since, compassion has remained inseparably and unmistakably part of the history of European revolutions."[9]

Arendt understands compassion as "unquestionably a natural, creature affect which involuntarily touches every normal person at the sight of suffering, however alien the sufferer may be." As such, it serves as an ideal basis for "a feeling that reaching out to all mankind would establish a society in which men might really become brothers." One's alerts always go off when a philosopher says "unquestionably," edging into apodictic territory and perhaps hedging some conceptual bets. There is a great deal of literature on compassion and revolutionary fervor, but what interests me here is the way Arendt adopts an unquestioning stance in order to place compassion at the bottom of a politically stacked food chain, making compassion primitive, natural, a matter of an involuntary lurch of feeling.[10] When philosophers talk that way, the ostensibly approved value of a motif or category is on the chopping block, ready to be overcome or somehow sublated, dealt out of discursive ranks. So it should come as no surprise that Arendt brings up brotherhood to cut it down, for, in her view, "solidarity with the unfortunate and the miserable—an effort tantamount to penetrating the very domain of brotherhood," just doesn't cut it. Forms of political fraternity prove insufficient, for "this kind of humanitarianism," she writes, "whose purest form is a privilege of the pariah, is not transmissible and cannot be easily acquired by those who do not belong among the pariahs."[11] Compassion acts as predatory replacement for justice, a wrong turn in the universe of revolutionary affect. To prevent such usurpation, one cannot dive into the place reserved for the pariahs of, or not of, the world.

Neither compassion nor actual suffering is enough, asserts Arendt. In fact, she sees compassion as having instigated mostly wrongheaded actions and general mischief when introduced into modern revolutions "by attempts to improve the lot of the unfortunate rather than to establish justice for all." In order to make the point stick, a nearly Nietzschean point in terms of the toxicity of pity—pity placing as neighboring affect, arguably, to compassion—Arendt shows how the mature political experience of the ancient world teaches us about the unreliability of compassion as political instigator or durable form of sociality. Both modern times and antiquity regard compassion "as something totally natural, as inescapable to man as, say, fear." This is where antiquity trumps the modern sensibility, for it saw compassion as no more laudable than fear, as something that can befall us "without our being able to fend it off."[12]

Once again, the rhetoric gives pause, for fear is introduced in and as a byway. Introducing fear by means of "say," as though it were one of many possible examples, Arendt in fact promotes fear as a lever that serves to destabilize compassion. "Because they so clearly recognized the affective nature of compassion," she argues, as something that cannot be fended off, "the ancients regarded the most compassionate person as no more entitled to be called the best than the most fearful." She emphasizes that both emotions, "because they are purely passive, make action impossible. This is the reason Aristotle treated compassion and fear together." At the same time, she does not see these "emotions" or "affects" (they work interchangeably) as reducible to each other. What she retains is that neither fear nor compassion makes the grade as concerns preparedness for political action. Shaking off the merits of compassion, she seems to find it humiliating and "shabby" in the end. Referring to *Tusculanae Disputationes* 3.21, Arendt recalls how Cicero surprisingly notes that the Stoics saw compassion and envy in the same terms. The concern here is that those who are pained by someone's misfortune are "'also pained by another's prosperity.'" Cicero wonders why we pity another rather than give assistance to one in need. Arendt understands the paucity of pity as motor force in relation to suffering and the sufferer: "In other words, should human beings be so shabby that they are incapable of acting humanly unless spurred and as it were compelled by their own pain when they see others suffer?"[13] Arendt skips a beat in order to arrive at this point, for Cicero does not appear to mark the specular impulse toward compassion, a matter of bringing it back to one's own pain, but what matters is that we see where she is going with it—and possibly, more pressingly, where she is not going with the logic that she recruits to advance her argument.

There is almost something on the order of a traumatic cut-off point when Arendt shifts from the insufficient social railings provided by compassion to the affirmation of shared joy, an affect "absolutely superior in this respect to sharing suffering." The sharing of suffering, so thinly grounded, provokes calamity and comes from a toxic field of identificatory impulses. It can easily tip over to envy as the basis for relatedness. Or, compassion proves simply to be an economical way of refraining from lending a helping hand and building up appropriate governing structures, ethically appointed, such as would befit "justice for all." Coming close to the statements of her contemporary phenomenologists, Arendt warns of the mush and chaotic prompts of ungroundable affect, emotions without a sealant to hold them to the implicit promise of reparation—here we move into the even remoter territory of yet another thinker-analyst, Melanie Klein, who makes envy a crucial signpost for socially

CHAPTER 5

bridging or halting "the question of openness to others, which in fact is the precondition for 'humanity' in every sense of that word."[14]

Still, after dwelling quite a bit on the topos, Arendt makes the convincing antithesis to compassion not envy but *cruelty*. She points out that envy "is an affect no less than compassion, for it is a perversion, a feeling of pleasure where pain would naturally be felt." However, both pleasure and pain, part of the same experience of affect, "like everything instinctual," tend to muteness, bypassing, if not foreclosing, the entreaties of speech and dialogue essential to Arendt's sense of political upbringing and worthiness. For these reasons, she states, "the humanitarianism of brotherhood" will just not measure up, and "scarcely befits those who do not belong among the insulted and injured and can share in it only through their compassion." Moreover, the "warmth of the pariah peoples cannot rightfully extend to those whose different position in the world imposes on them a responsibility for the world and does not allow them to share the cheerful unconcern of the pariah." The danger of the situation, framing the condition in which the warmth of the pariah peoples prevails, is at least twofold. Warmth, a substitute for light, emerges in dark times of "weird irreality" in human relationships, developing in absolute worldlessness, when all are detached from the world common to all people. Something like "human nature" (in quotation marks placed by Arendt) takes over from a world in common, leading in with feelings common to all, such as the capacity for compassion and those that tie to brotherhood of all men. Such feelings, according to Arendt, are mere substitutes of a psychological order, "localized in the realm of invisibility," replacing or covering for the loss of the common, visible world. Such replacements, focusing "human nature" and the feeling of "fraternity that accompany it, manifest themselves only in darkness and hence cannot be identified in the world." Even more to the point, "in conditions of visibility they dissolve into nothingness like phantoms." Relying on the metaphysical metaphorology of light and darkness in order to dispatch psychology, Hannah Arendt then makes this uncompromising statement: "The humanity of the insulted and injured has never yet survived the hour of liberation by so much as a minute." These feelings, destined to phantomal disappearance once the heat of persecution is off, carry significance only to the degree that they make "insult and injury endurable."[15] In political terms, however, they are "absolutely irrelevant": "Human nature" and fraternity remain politically inconsequential—*absolutely irrelevant*. On one hand, the affects stemming from compassion poll as excessively democratic, common to all, easily pervertible, close relatives of cruelty. On the other hand, they are phantasmal and ghostlike, run on politically evanescent fumes, cannot be counted on. Am I wrong to demand a recount—or is there something irrefutable about the *need* she spells

Arendt Swallows the Lessing Prize

out, namely, that of protecting social bonding from entrapment by compassion and its wayward extensions, flips, predatory victories?

All this business about compassion and its savage offspring serves as one big preparatory remark, incisive and historically wrenching, for exploring the possibility itself of accepting the commendation. At the end of her speech the audience remained silent, withholding the approbation that would seal the deal unambiguously. Bound by the prize in which she was double-billed with Lessing, she did not receive from the bestowing other a "yes, yes," the double mark of distinction, Nietzschean and on the return, that would ratify the conferral. She had burdened herself with the nonnegotiable, the ethical incentive to show up, but at the same time, opening herself to world—against every possible grain and many odds—she canceled the policy by means of what she delivered as the so-called acceptance speech. (As Derrida shows, apropos of Nietzsche, you have to sign twice to make the eternal return stick, have it accepted: *yes, yes* and, adding Nietzsche's exclamation marks, "*Yes, yes!*")[16] What is there to accept? How could she guarantee her compliance with the superior imperative of social gladness? Who even has the right to confer recognition, whether sought or abominated, embraced or repelled? Are we friends? *We must, we must be friends.* Still, are we friends?

Part 3 of the speech tunes questions relevant to the "proper attitude in 'dark times'" that are "of course especially familiar to the generation and the group to which I belong." Here Arendt zeroes in on specific implications of prize acceptance, grounded in political purposefulness—underscoring, that is, what remains adherent to the opening and contact with world. In fact, receiving honors belongs to the experience of world-acceptance and attunement: "If concord with the world, which is part and parcel of receiving honors, has never been an easy matter, it is even less so for us. Certainly honors were no part of our birthright, and it would not be surprising if we were no longer capable of the openness and trustfulness that are needed simply to accept gratefully what the world offers in good faith."[17]

Given the plight of the persecuted group to which she does not conceal her affiliation, no one expects or aspires to receiving "the stamp of public approval." Even when they did manage to schedule some semblance of public speaking engagements, the persecuted and insulted members of these groups "tended only to address their friends or to speak to those unknown, scattered readers and listeners with whom everyone who speaks and writes at all cannot help feeling joined in some rather obscure brotherhood." Here Arendt turns in brotherhood—already devalorized as ephemeral euphoria of connection and political irrelevance—seeing in it an unpinnable sense of relatedness accorded to the disseminative outposts of the readership or those who might be listening in. Such speakers "felt very little responsibility toward the world," bringing in language from which some minimum of humanity might be gleaned "in a world grown inhuman." One was speaking against the grain "as far as possible resisting the weird irreality of this worldlessness—each after his own fashion and some few by seeking the limits of their ability to understand even the inhumanity and the intellectual and political monstrosities of a time out of joint."[18]

Armed with Hamletian disjointure, Arendt begins to rewrite *Nathan der Weise* (*Nathan the Wise*) answering the principal dramatic question—"Who are you?"—by means of the only answer that "took into account the reality of persecution." *Who are you? A Jew.* "I cannot gloss over the fact that for many years I considered the only adequate reply to the question, Who are you? to be: A Jew." By contrast the statement with which Nathan "(in effect, though not in actual wording)" countered the command: "Step closer, Jew" falls dismally short. Arendt counters, "—the statement: I am a man—I would have considered nothing but a grotesque and dangerous evasion of reality." She remains on course, tough as nails, clearing another misunderstanding that may ensue from her coming out, not as some pumped-up insignia of universal mankind, but as Jew. "When I use the word 'Jew' I do not mean to suggest any special kind of human being, as though the Jewish fate were either representative of or a model for the fate of mankind." In times of defamation and directed persecution (such times have not ceased to phantomize and strike), one has to stand up to the destruction made in the name of an identity, but without arrogating to oneself the privilege of exploiting or revaluating the identity in extreme question and under threat. There is no dialectical flexibility in the answer to a doubling down of the question that any prize conferral implicitly asks, "Who are you? What are you?" What—or who—responsibly can be offered in response to the interrogation of partly repressed identity papers? To reply that one is merely a human being, like everyone else who claims to be singular-plural, can no longer suffice. Yet, to cling to a formerly disavowed adherence may collapse into an act of bad faith. Stepping up as a discredited envoy of a despised group, she abandons any lever that would turn the crushed outcast into a glorious remnant, a transcendentally remortgaged identity. She cannot allow herself to fall "into the trap set by Hitler," like those who "had succumbed to the spirit of Hitlerism in their own way." She must thus "bluntly reveal the personal background of my reflections" without angling for any kind of flip-side profit margin when interrogated—once again—about her identity, a forced alias. She sees no out but possibly only to model a rejection: Hannah Arendt refuses to take a faux high road optioned by those Germans who followed the call of "inner emigration," suspending by means of inward retreat a confirmable connection to the political cruelty of the day. One may feel "wonderfully superior" for having quietly turned one's back, shut one's wide-open eyes, "but their superiority is then truly no longer of this world; it is the superiority of a more or less well-equipped cloud-cuckoo-land."[19] The way I see it, she is smoking mad, picking up Lessing's polemical style and throwing it down! For her part, Arendt pushes back on the notion that a revealed identity holds exemplarity, can be generalized or upgraded by dint of its sacred emaciation and bare-threaded social survival. Instead, she rigorously holds to the position of dislodging any imposed or struck identity, whether levied by state fiat or insinuated by hostile decree and incessant slap-down. Her phrase "I am a Jew" is not partially or wholly substantializable, nor a key to any city or citizenship ready to pour on the compassion or confer a dubious distinction of purported brotherhood. Poof!

But friendship is another matter—even, my friends, if there is no friend in times of darkness. Lessing understood that "there can be no happiness or good fortune for anyone unless a friend shares the joy of it." In this regard Lessing departs from Rousseau and the modern understanding of friendship as an address of sheltering association, "solely as a phenomenon of intimacy, in which friends open their hearts to each other unmolested by the world and its demands." The modern cast of friendship recoils from worldliness, repairing to the secret chambers of palliative counsel. Rousseau, not Lessing, is the best advocate of this view, writes Arendt, which conforms "so well to the basic attitude of the modern individual, who in his alienation from the world can truly reveal himself only in privacy and in the intimacy of face-to-face encounters."[20] Suspending the threads of connectiveness, the friend in modernity becomes a prod or an excuse for beating a retreat—something that Rousseau famously enacted when switching from revolution to the quieter thrall of rêverie.[21] Friendship, in this view, politically primes solitude—inviting a meeting, as Nietzsche and Blanchot enjoy saying, of two or more solitudes. Arendt adds, "[t]hus it is hard for us to understand the political relevance of friendship." Modern estrangement from a shareable world ushers the friend, if there is one, into private spaces of social defeat, where a certain dosage of misanthropy sets the tone. Classical antiquity stipulates otherwise, and in Lessing's pickup game the essential attitude is, accordingly, more resolute about stepping forward, leaning into the world, creating and practicing a discourse of friendship: the Greeks and Lessing prove to be, to a high degree, world receptive, inclusive, and ready to share. "The Greeks called this humanness which is achieved in the discourse of friendship *philanthropia*, 'love of man,' since it manifests itself in a readiness to share the world with other man."[22]

If Hannah Arendt rises ambiguously to accept her reward in the draft of these terms—analyzing, through Lessing and Rousseau, the tenets driving apart classical and modern notions of friendship—this is largely because she must walk away with a prize that is ethically booby-trapped, at once standing as an offer of political friendship and, as supra-political citation, masks a fraud.

The Lessing Prize, conferred by the Free City of Hamburg, unleashes a historical grievance. Nearly coercing some act of forgiveness on the part of the for-now Jewish recipient, it displays the covert aggression of any prize bestowal, something that threatens to take ownership of the one so ceremoniously distinguished or inducted into the branding club, group, or collectivity. Paradoxically cast, the bestowal requires some gesture of humility, a suitable syntax of thankfulness from the one selected for *Auszeichnung*: one is singled out, *recognized* by the very group or force by which one has been largely repelled, or, in this case, historically disputed, violently placed under erasure. One's hand is forced, double or triple bound. Hannah's first instinct would have been to walk away, to take with her the hounded legacy of Gotthold Ephraim Lessing, in whose name the prize is bestowed, and run. Yet a double-focused reading keeps her in place, tentatively resolving an anguished dilemma. One prompt is guided by *philanthropia*; the other concerns Lessing, his place as signator of a contested oeuvre and purveyor, not so much of truth, but of a chronic polemical attitude toward any purported truth. He ran counter to the very Enlightenment principles with which he is associated. Philanthropy involves the "Greek readiness to share the world with other men," a stance that Arendt opposes to that of the misanthrope who "finds no one with whom he cares to share the world." The misanthrope "regards nobody as worthy of rejoicing with him in the world and nature and the cosmos." Greek philanthropy, she shows, underwent many changes in the process of becoming Roman *humanitas*. The form of humaneness that we inherit from the Romans, sober and cool "rather than sentimental," teaches us, she writes, that "humanity is exemplified not in fraternity but in friendship; that friendship is not intimately personal but makes political demands and preserves the reference to the world." It may seem perplexing to find quite kindred features in Lessing's drama, *Nathan the Wise*, "which, modern as it is, might with some justice be called the classical drama of friendship."[23] Let me stay with some of these terms and leave the world alone—not by means of an aggravated form of inner emigration, but in terms of how the very concept of a recognizable "world" has been steadily abandoning and exhausting its promise. Arendt at no point takes apart the world or taints the rumored purity of *mundus* in order to give account of its shattering, in order to think something or someone else. She also refrains from breaking down "man."

Avital Helps Hannah Accept the Lessing Prize. What will it have meant for a friend to mankind, a thinker or writer, a social activist, to be awarded with a celebrative sign, a prize—something that may or may not indicate a prior contest or competition in which one has been unwittingly enrolled?

When urged to join a panel of scholars to offer some reflections on the barely emergent theme or thought of the literary and philosophical award, I was frankly dumbfounded. Even though I had devoted quite some pages to Freud's highly invested and, therefore, vexed acceptance of the Goethe-Prize, I had never before considered the status and stakes of the fact itself—or facticity—of an award, perhaps a secular downgrade from the poetic-drunken days of more transcendent supports and bestowals, not to forget the orders and honors distributed at whim by feudal lords. On the other, far less lofty hand, historically or culturally manufactured—apart from the chronicled inventories of honors and distinctions linked to military and athletic cultures—I have often wondered about those scoundrels closer to home who receive awards or go after grants with some sort of institutionally sanctioned E-ZPass. A rhetorical flair for double dealing, the rendering of a credible promissory note, and a well-shuffled horde of recommenders can acquire a packet of prestige for the unremarkable contender.

As one can see, from the perspective of a self-declared or chronic reject, the question of such a prize can cue up resentment, for how can it be that so-and-so, *and* so-and-so, were awarded the grand prix of x-achievement when I, like Benjamin's stripped-down allegory, walk away empty-handed?! Yet, melancholy and allegorical voiding seem to name one of the essential stakes of these acts of granting and the call they put out for a watchful acceptance speech. One recalls the struggle Celan (and scores of others) had to engage in before stepping up to receive the announced prize. In the case of Celan, he had to convert to prose and map the *Meridian*, his famous speech that asks "Wer bist du?"—*Who are you?* One of the imperious gestures of the prize consists in telling you who you are, what you are, how you're faring, maybe even where you belong. It presumes accessible membership and confers all sorts of dialectical chaos around the notion of recognition.

I assigned myself to Hannah Arendt when a colleague, Uli Baer, offhandedly suggested that I look at her reflections on the *Klage*—the topic that had commanded my attention for two or more years, particularly in view of the playoffs initiated by Goethe's *Werther*, where the asserted difference, starting on letter one, between complaint and lament becomes a matter of life and death. "Was ist der Mensch, daß er klagen darf?" (What is it about humans, that they can lament?) sets the tonal stakes against which Werther's fateful reconciliation via the complaint (*Beschwerde*), with its earthy heaviness—the *schwer* in *Beschwerde* weighs in here—stays on the side of life and vital economies. Werther can answer to the call of the complaint, but the *Klage* does him in—a subject that fills another dossier, but one that marks and frames Arendt's acceptance, not-so-acceptance speech when awarded the Lessing Prize. "Wer bist du?"

If I've already fast-tracked an allegorical structure that may hold together and, at the same time, void Arendt's syntax of acceptance, this in part is because we are confronted from the beginning by a conceptual snag, a knot of stalls and ethical starts that make this speech impossible for Arendt to assume, always referring back to the other, who is the future but also the covert destination of the prize made in his name and conferred upon Arendt, who must take and *give the prize back*, if it is at all to be "accepted," in and to the name of Lessing. The prize is destined to her in and by the name, Lessing, but he can only illegitimately issue an award to the extent that the Germans denied him recognition: they could never award him a prize, having failed to understand or prize Lessing's radicalism, which is now bestowed upon her, in his name, as if to avoid his lastingly destructive accomplishment. Equally jarring, Lessing did not "believe" in truth, he polemicized and offended, he insisted on befriending the most inimical aliens and held his ground as he was faltering, powered up on rage. Lessing's temper disclosed world. "Aber der Zorn, und vor allem der Lessingsche Zorn, stellt die Welt bloß" (Anger, above all Lessing's anger, reveals world, 10). Moreover, "Lessing hat mit der Welt, in der er lebte, seinen Frieden nie gemacht" (Lessing never made peace with the world in which he lived, 9).[24] Unappeasable, Lessing stalks the scene. His name is that of bestowal, which can never revert to him but must be paid back to his estate like a haunting debt that one in fact can never repay. Nevertheless, Hannah adopts Lessing to make a pitch for *Selbstdenken* without a self, his "famous independent thinking for oneself" in darkest, morally downtrodden times, when one stands and falls on one's own, but not even on one's so-called own, because all that pretend-independence has been taken away.

Literature sometimes proves capable of breaking the fall, and this is where William Faulkner shades in, a writer who shows that "nothing is 'mastered'" in the sequences that has the tragic hero "resuffering the past" (23), throttled by indignation and just anger, fueled and revved up by the mega-rival of Lessing and the rest of the guys, with the exception, maybe, of Schiller and Nietzsche, who resolutely honored Goethe: "as Goethe has said" (24; in the dedication to *Faust*):

Der Schmerz wird neu, es wiederholt die Klage
Des Lebens labyrinthisch irren Lauf." (21)

Pain returns again, lament repeats
Life's labyrinthine, erring/insane course.

I would love to get into the labyrinthine itinerary that has Goethe (rather than Lessing) nail the action that "establishes its meaning and that permanent significance which then enters into history." Goethe appears on the scene when another kind of action insinuates itself into the politically and world-binding argument, that of poetic being. Poetic saying signals an intrinsic activity and need for "relating what has happened"—an act that, shaping history, however "solves no problems and assuages no suffering; it does not master anything once and for all." The "mastering" of the past is relegated to a tentative stance: it cowers behind quotation marks. Instead of establishing mastery, poetry cites itself citing and reiterating a once forgotten pain capable only of reappearing, searing, writing itself out in repetition. "The tragic impact of this repetition in lamentation," writes Arendt, "affects one of the key elements of all action," entering history. Historical safekeeping must be placed in the custody of poetic repetition, trusting the poetic act that names its own relation to repetition, repeating itself at the end of an action, for "the meaning of a committed act is revealed only when the action itself has come to an end and become a story susceptible to narration. Insofar as any 'mastering' of the past is possible, it consists in relating what has happened."[25] Poetry breaks into the caesura, picking up the slack of a pause that resists closing woundedness in a gesture that is not identical to closure. Arendt believes that an action comes to an end, readied for narration.

The literary theorist in me will leave her in peace on this point, hoping only to indicate the reverberations of nonending and the possibility that narration, in its own ways, makes and betrays history, rhetorically kidnapping some of its referential cognates. But I refrain from quibbling, and my complaint does not amount to a hill of beings or a halt in her solid argument and diacritical subversions.

The poetic recap—an originary mark—is, then, the only means by which to master the past. Arendt is rigorous on this point, for she keeps "mastery" at bay with quotation marks. It may be the only way to master the past, but not for us. (We just "master" the past.) As per usual, Goethe scrambles the master codes. The dedication does not supply content or the slightest narrative clue about what might have instigated the named affliction. It runs only with the thought of repetition as cohort to pain. Without backdrop or forward-looking indication, Goethe appears, on the contrary, to withhold story. Blurring meaning or graspable significance, the dedication talks to ghosts, allows friendship and love to capsize on unconscious waves, rides on the lament/complaint's capacity to shroud narrativity or downplay story. Hannah Arendt brings in Goethe to assure testimony where he refuses attestation, while allowing for the form of *Klage* to assume the place of sheer repetitive affliction. He disturbs

CHAPTER 5

her running, if diminishing, economies of acceptance, undermining the cause for which he's made to stand, including the most hypothetically restricted recuperations of history and cognition.

Even so, undeterred by the unmastered past, the master poet approaches the scene of political inscription, indicating, if not explicitly stating—but his signature, I would say, suffices to make this happen, to exemplify and enact—that "we are constantly preparing the way for 'poetry,' in the broadest sense, as a human potentiality." The insight into preparatory phrasing—an essential relation to and of poetry—indicates where the crucial motif of survival enters the discursive scene. For the "telling over of what took place comes to a halt for the time being and a formed narrative, one more item, is added to the world's stock." Flanked by quotation marks, "poetry" in this context bears a different valence than "mastery," bowed and marked down by the same (but not identical) quotation marks. "Poetry," by contrast, expands under the accompanying marks, making it a quality of historical being for which *we always prepare*; whether or not we recognize "poetry," it is our way in, a flex of survival pulled by the death drive. Ceding to traumatic rendering and repetition, "the narrative has been given its place in the world, where it will survive us."[26] Poetry builds toward what will stay on.

Where have I heard that before? Even though Goethe has supplanted Lessing to score the point of narrative exigency and traumatic repetition, the wisdom Arendt locates to poetic being comes, one would have to say, from Hölderlin, poet of a certain cut of instauration and survival. He stated, "Was bleibet aber / stiften die Dichter"[27] (roughly: "what remains, what survives / is grounded by the poets")—a poetic phrase become by now almost too famous, but one that Arendt quietly cues in terms of historical, though not of historial, granting, which we find in Heidegger's reflections on founding acts. Moving unmasterable experience into poetic phrasing connects the unbearable to the borne world, marking our finitude by means of the poeticity that lives, or rather, limps on. I am suggesting that there is a covert scene, supportive of another, if silent track that seals in the name of Hölderlin and the relentless appropriations of his poetic saying made by the mentor, Heidegger. By dropping the curtain on these players, Arendt is also saying what she is not saying in her acceptance / rejection speech, namely, in part, that we no longer recruit poetry to the cause of destinal instauration of nation or community, but count on it to name and *survive*, if on the crutches of quotation marks, the traumatic destruction of such endangering mystifications and ideological loopholes for which poetry allows but cannot, in the end, after the end, sign. Neither Lessing nor Goethe belongs particularly to part of the team of Heideggerian primal poets. In fact, Heidegger's choices, including those that land him on Hölderlin and Trakl, were remarkably off the wall—at least, off the traditional Listservs of secured critical value. At the time Heidegger selected them for his mission statements, Hölderlin and Trakl were not the critical blockbusters—and ghostbusters—that they have since become. But that is another story, or un-story, requiring another run at him, complicating the Heideggerian legacy even further.

Arendt deposes the baggage consisting of destiny, destination, nation, Volk in order to place her world-binding wager. Her literary bodyguards bet on worldliness, consistently showing nothing but scorn for the puny yet destructive pretensions of the language-ballooning myths of national destiny. Tropes of survival require another platform.

On the face of it, then, Goethe pinch-hits for Lessing at a moment of crucial elaboration, when themes of traumatic grief and historical-poetic saying converge. Here and elsewhere in German letters, Goethe acts as guarantor for *sur-vie*, an arc of sur- or "supervival," the strength of non-ressentimental living-on for which Nietzsche and Blanchot have credited him. Let us, however, leave this largely Derridean and Benjaminian reflection aside for now. Signing and living on, Goethe crushes his contemporaries or anyone that gets in the way—the upstarts or those crawling, consociates dead or alive, any present or future rivals. In terms of his contemporaries, Goethe tended to knock them off the table, blithely carrying on while the neighboring poets knew only shipwreck. Blanchot surmises that the great poet will never be forgiven his ability to step over corpses—well, Blanchot is less crude about getting this point across: the great poet, Goethe, will never be forgiven for surviving while the others fell apart. I have tried to track his stock of power pills and their side effects all the way up to Freud and Benjamin, who by remote control were also shaken to the core, felled at critical moments by the strength of this signifier, the monumentality of a German language-bearer without institutional rival, then or now. Goethe's vampirizations and tremendous appetite for devouring the other writers behind and ahead of the rounds he continues to make is not part, alas, of my beat today. Let me just indicate that Arendt takes recourse to the particularly strong yet enigmatic *Klage* at the starting gate of *Faust* for the purpose of naming the unmasterable aporia that has her accepting a prize from the committee at Hamburg, in the German language, treating Lessing "as though he were a contemporary," riddled by doubters, resituated in "the first half of the twentieth century with it political catastrophes, its moral disasters, and its astonishing development of the arts and sciences."[28]

The *Klage* bears its own form of generativity, underscoring the plaintive position of disillusionment from which she must take courage. There were other plaintiffs lined up behind her, who tripped over their own vocabularies of unmasterability and pinched survival. For her part, Arendt travels between

Weimar and Oxford, Mississippi, with only a stopover in Hamburg. Faulkner himself made poignant inroads in his own acceptance speech in 1949 for the Nobel Prize. One should read both these speeches together, bifocally, to see how Arendt bounces and feeds off the writer from the South and the range of the chiasmic complications of her identification with William Faulkner. Such a reading, which would take us far afield in the context of our current analysis, would have to pick up threads of Arendt's own missteps regarding her adopted homeland's forms of racism and discredited strategies of segregation. Her engagement with Faulkner would instruct us on the way her views mirror back the unmasterable German past—meaning, how she understands, in a relay ongoing between Germany and the Deep South, that which cannot pass or be surpassed according simple geochronological schedules, but keeps returning and displacing, dynamically locating the historical haunts in Faulkner's disrupted narrations of the South. Despite the way he makes us weep and shudder, Faulkner calls up less of a shock than Goethe. The inclusion of Faulkner represents for Arendt a "less painful example" of what, by means of Goethe, she must tell us.[29] It is not clear, though, that Arendt herself is not prevented at each juncture from completing her narrative.

. . . *Wait.* I thought I could step to the side, even walk away, but Goethe's uncanny pull reels me in, again. Faulkner has prepared the ground for Goethe's breakthrough appearance in the Arendt speech, offsetting Lessing's prominence in the text. How did Goethe's strange dedication drop into, and onto, the Lessing text? Arendt has called on Goethe, rather than Lessing, to back the action that bears permanent significance in history. Does the switchover run interference with the point Arendt is urging, or does this maneuver serve to protect her tenuous pairing with Lessing? Has she quoted the right verse, or does the turn to Goethe not efface the language that names the stakes she intends to articulate? In the development of her argument, Goethe arrives as the possibility of reconciling ourselves to a past that we "can no more master . . . than undo." The conciliatory form is the lament, she writes, but without quoting a lament. In order to tune us to the description of pain embedded in Goethe's dedicatory verses, she begins with the process of recognition inherent to tragedy, a form in which the "tragic hero becomes knowledgeable by re-experiencing what has been done in the way of suffering, and in this *pathos*, in resuffering the past, the network of individual acts is transformed into an event, a significant whole." The dramatic climax of tragedy, she offers, "occurs when the actor turns into a sufferer, therein lies its peripeteia."[30]

The resuffering of the past befalls those wading through "even non-tragic plots [that] become genuine events only when they are experienced a second time in the form of suffering by memory operating retrospectively and perceptively." Such memory can speak "only when indignation and just anger, which impel us to action, have been silenced—and that needs time."[31] She might have said, when Lessing has been silenced. For his is the name of anger and intervention, while the lament, to which she associates Goethe, is allied to recollection, the ability to sink into remembrance, to think about things in a movement of acceptance and integration, maybe even allowing for the acceptance of a prize encased in the name of just anger—evoking thus the Lessing insignia, the frozen cry of restless insurrection, the freeze frame of his renowned *Laocöon* legacy. Hannah must choose between these proper names when she decides on the disturbed scene of resuffering. Still, there have been three rings to choose from—a theme of impossible choosing that pervades the *Nathan* drama framing Arendt's drama.

The *Zueignung* meant to open *Faust*, also closes it down with "Zu," mystifying as it establishes the premises of a world-historical drama of overreach and demonic temptation. Goethe could have used a more regulated term for dedication, *Widmung*, for instance, but chooses to play off the indications released by the cluster signification of *eigen* and *Neigung* ("Fühl ich mein Herz noch jenem Wahn geneigt?," l. 4; Do I feel my heart still inclined to earlier delusion?). Part of, yet removed from, the body of the text, prior to the famous "Vorspiel auf dem Theater" that in the past I have abusively, that is, *literally* translated as "foreplay in the theater," the open/close dedicatory flysheet conjures phantoms and disjunctive crashes of friendship, love, lament.[32] Pressed by approaching phantoms, the voice is confronted with "Bilder froher Tage, / und manche liebe Schatten" (depictions of glad days / and many sweet shadows) that however provoke anguish.[33] Like a faded saga, first love and friendship come to light once more (ll. 9–12). *Verklungen* (in "gleich einen alten, halbverklungnen Saga," l. 11) refers to the fade-out of sound, connecting with *Klage's* remoter spheres. Where the recall of first loves and friendship seems to prompt happy memories, the dedicatory phase in fact opts to put up an anacoluthic swerve, pulling a fast one on an affect that remains thematically unbridged. Bringing forth the love and friendship of yore, it refrains entirely from indulging gladness, but jumps instead straightaway into the hell of pain's persistent ache, inventing or experiencing for the first time *in remembrance* the ravaging pangs of friendship. Reviving elements of an intimate attachment befallen by catastrophic disturbance, the plaintive narrative, the *Zueignung*, marks and remarks on laceration without recovery, isolating a pang that returns or inflicts a shudder of suppressed affliction.

Repetition initiates what I would call a kind of *panguage* that refuses to assuage or allow for a nostalgic containment or accessorization of affect. Life pangs emerge with and through originary friendship in consort with a first love, an apparently indissociable fit. Do the renascent pain and original cut of suffering comprise two different events, or are they meant to disclose each other reciprocally, as fractured narration brings to light a hidden scene of utmost suffering? The dedication does not tell us. The dramatic poem opener goes on, riding on remnants reorganized, seeing the friendly audience or mob marked off as perished, "zerstorben ist das freundliche Gedränge, verklungen, ach, der erste Widerklang!"(roughly: the friendly throng has perished, off-key, alas, the first dissonant clash!). Friendship's finitude, the perishability of love, the thud of ending move beyond the limits of a remembered event to travel into realms of work and audience, staining the hope of any possible embrace, whether on the level of work or intimacy. It is not clear that one can count on a resurrection of lost love or retrieve disappeared friendship except in the mode of pained repetitive *Klang/Klage*, conjuring the warp-noise of complaint, the rhythmic beat of lament. The applause has died down.

As if repelling the intrusion of the maternal breast and mother tongue in the work of the other lady, Melanie Klein, who had to switch the native tongue from German to English, Hannah's first impulse was to refuse the prize. She agonized over which language to take in. She must do some reparative work in order to accept and internalize the ostensibly good object being offered to her. Although the bad breast of German destruction prevails, and it remains difficult to take in the prize, Hannah has to swallow the compliment, and hold it down. In this regard she is not Nietzschean, most emetic of philosophers, who threw up such distinctions to reverse dialectics, nor does she come very close to Thomas Bernhard, who railed, derailed, took the booty and booby prize, and resumed the tirade, railing to the end. Such reactions, indicators of differing gradations of negative and positive transferences onto acts of honoring, make one wonder where indeed such a prize may "land"—which orifice receives it according to symbolic mapping and imaginary charters. How will the receiving mouth fill itself with the given gift, the mother tongue that, in this case, has lashed at her with severe consistency and unprecedented cruelty, dispensing a blinding overdose of aggression? Or what kind of shuttle system exists, following well-known psychoanalytic schedules, between mouth and anus? What kind of a compromise formation does the assumption of the prize entail—in this sense, according to more ordinary calculations, what kind of disturbing sellout turns her into a world-deluded perp and agent of betrayal? How will she negotiate "the legitimate hatred that makes you ugly nevertheless, the well-founded wrath that makes the voice grow hoarse"?[34] "*Wer bist du?*" asks the conferral.

On the other, double-bound hand, isn't Arendt somehow obligated, by a compelling logic, to get over herself, step up, appropriate the prize, if only to return it to the first one to have received an eviction notice, Lessing, and his *Nathan der Weise*? I am tempted here to jam on the homonymy, *Waise* (orphan), referring to those brutally orphaned by the very cities and citations that now put muscle on the counter-signatory force of their names to clean up their historical acts and, in the manner outlined by Arendt, to make amends for the noted failure to rise to appropriate action.

This bestowal on the name of Arendt, in the name of the Muslim- and Jew-loving Lessing, would require one to jump into an abyssal series of calculations that continues to weigh on us today. *Nathan im Waisenhaus des Seins* shows up in the orphanage of being, ungrounded, language-strapped. "Tritt näher, Jude!" "Ich bin ein Mensch" goes the dramatic dialogue: Step closer, Jew! I am human. From her shattered perspective, this response no longer suffices. When asked to step closer, to step up, become public and in some sense world bound, one cannot be content merely to plead, "I am human." Forced on this point by a history of humiliation, one has to say—no matter how assimilated, remote, or foreign to one's so-called sense of self—that I am a Jew: I step up as a Jew to the extent that this call, the name, *Jude*, has been subjected to absolute destruction. Yes, something in Hannah would rather run in the other direction, refuse the call, decline the conferral. Instead, pulling herself together, she hitches a ride on allegory, creates a binding world, and serves herself an imperative.

Among other extraordinarily sharp and well-dealt points, she will have considered the stakes of political refusal, the inward turn, even when guided by justified rage, turning oneself f-ugly. One has the wish to repel the bestowing Germans. "Beat it!" one snaps. You don't deserve to award me value and reopen a theater of honoring, because this presumption comes from an eviscerated and blank space, annulled by whatever the *opposite* of bestowal is—the destruction of personhood, an annihilation of the figures consigned to polyfocal Judeities, measurements of the untapped rhythm of Jewish heartbeats. All sorts of sinister calculations impose themselves here, even in the fairly calm columns of figuring out who or what in the end the beneficiaries of general commendations are.

In a Kantian sense, one can ask, Who gets to proffer the prize, along the lines of who has the *right* to offer hospitality?—must you not in the first place (and the question of place is important here) own the property from which you extend hospitable generosity? Thus, what kind of institutional prestige guzzler sets the stage for such granting? How does the bestowal of a prize jack up the value of the bestower? Can one imagine a prize that breaks the economy and does not revert to the shares of the one judging?[35] Who is Germany, or its primed synecdoche, the "Free City of Hamburg," that it may judge the suitableness and declare the legitimacy of the awardee? The granting can

CHAPTER 5

by no means be neutralized, performatively contained or seem entirely innocent—be taken for granted. Besides which, *really*, have they effectively jacked into critique and judgment to the extent that the They, Heidegger's vapid "das Man," can ascribe value and recognize dignity of accomplishment? A Jewish thinker is to be thanked in the name of the *Waise*, Nathan? But, like the statue in *Don Giovanni*, Hannah Arendt steps up to accept the prize—maybe she steps up from and for the dead, unmemorialized, the still unlamented.

She steps up because, driven by political acumen and halted by historical trauma, she cannot do otherwise. The scene of granting a prize to a designated recipient, the acceptance and affirmation thereof, is world bound, creates a world for the first time and anew. Arendt skips a beat when stating that the prize recalls for us the thankfulness owed to the world (she does not view the prize itself as a flex of thankfulness, in this instance, for her work and being). Let me switch to German when it comes to the matter of her guilt and undischarged debt. Exchanging *Weise* for *Weise*, wise for way, she strikes the way in which the distinction admonishes us: "Aber die Ehrung mahnt uns nicht nur auf besondere, unüberhörbare Weise and die Dankbarkeit, die wir der Welt schulden; sie ist darüberhinaus in einem sehr hohen Maße weltverpflichtend." As sign of support and prototype of attestation, as clinch, the prize obligates you to world, "weil sie uns, da wir sie ja auch immer ablehnen können, in unserer Stellung zur Welt nicht nur bestärkt, sondern uns auch auf sie festlegt." World and persons are not the same thing to the extent that world "liegt zwischen den Menschen" (roughly: is spaced between and among people). Persons have no adhesion or viability without a world that at once separates and links them. While "Rückzug aus der Welt" (retreat from the world) has been an option for some, including the genius, it is not, at this point of troubled and foreclosive shutdown, an option for the politically trained thinker. Such a retreat involves *Weltverlust*, world-loss, endangering the very world that discloses itself, if as phantasmal flickering, in the bestowal of the gift: "was verloren geht, ist der spezifische und meist unersetzliche Zwischenraum, der sich gerade zwischen diesem Menschen und seinen Mitmenschen gebildet hätte." The wish to secure an intervallic space of Mitsein furnishes strong motivation for Arendt to show up for the Hamburger Senat and claim her prize. She sets her intention on engaging the world that has become an object of greatest concern—"größten Sorge unter offenbarsten Erschütterung in nahezu allen Ländern der Erde." The world has lost "die Leuchtkraft, die ursprünglich zu ihrem eigensten Wesen gehört."[36] By traversing the toxic sites of an abandoning history, Arendt stands up for world, even where it fails to light up and has given way to "Zwischenraum," a between space. The promised allegory, to which I cannot do justice at this or any time, involves those who don't or can't show up to line up world, its remains, who cannot depose for justice. Arendt, tossed into the arena by the ambivalence of surrogacy, finds herself responding to a call in the most adverse circumstances and in the face of derisory insults, where awarding a distinction doubles for awarding *Gerechtigkeit*, justice. The award poses as allegory for justice. But can justice be rendered? In the name of whom or what? As a generality or does it attach only to you, the designated recipient—committing an injustice in the guise of acquitting itself justly? Can it be conferred or even as such *imagined*?

You, you've made it, you rock recognition, you've hit it out of the park! But what a desultory park, as Celan described, what a world-class *unWo*, the poet's unWhere. Hannah knows all this, broadcasts its lessons and articulations in all her languages. She carries another burden, that of one who cannot allow herself, or award herself the luxurious suspension of any "inner emigration." Her relation, even if nonrelation, to the *as if* of world requires her to walk up to the podium and engage the *Gespräch* (conversation), no matter how unreciprocated or, precisely, *staged* its conditions and unfolding drama—for the prize, despite it all, in its form as "sur-prize" is a way of "Sprechen mit anderen" (speaking with others), engaging speech, thus spanning while securing the recollection of world.[37] The poet Hölderlin made *Gespräch* a condition for being-together, for being capacitated in the sense that one can at all *hear* from the other. If one finds oneself in conversation this is because one listens intently for the "panguage" of another listening being who, heeding a call—whether traceable or not—chooses to respond.

She takes on the vitality of *Gespräch*—the urgency of conversation set in a voided breadth in this speech—but without thematizing the virtual shutdown into which the German language went for many of its most passionate speakers, the strangely toxic fumes it unceasingly released into the air of postwar Europe. The question remains: what language was Hannah Arendt dreaming when the political imperative of *Gespräch* had her swallow the Lessing-prize? In her slo-mo accession to the podium, she recollects how SOME WERE NEVER ABLE TO RETURN TO THE GERMAN LANGUAGE. German will have become the language of *Klage* and the *Anklage*—the registered complaint and pointed accusation, a poison-language of non-address—a language to be faced evermore by the historical plaintiff. It is as if the German language, as binding experience of speech and worldless saying, has sounded an unreceivable complaint.

6

The Right Not to Complain
On Johnson's Reparative Process

Black Lives Matter

On the Mat. Not that I want to complain or overshare, but when I was younger I practically had to bribe people to publish my oddball work. That was before the fateful encounter with Bill Regier. He sought me out at a bustling convention of the Modern Language Association in the early '80s, offering to publish my next book. Taken off guard by the first generous person I met in the precincts of our profession, I told him flat out that he was mistaken: I was nothing but trouble; the book just published had prepared my expulsion from my chosen field, Germanistik. He said, more or less, no worries—he and his team were battle-ready. Fields change. His steadfastness gave me something like hope, a discernible prospect. Still, such an offer, earnest and finally innocent, should not be exploited. I was unruly compared to my contemporaries, I reflected, not to speak of the precursors. Dr. Regier was at the time director of the University of Nebraska Press, a serious publishing house; very possibly a bit of an outlaw branch, they had brought out Blanchot, Derrida, Ann Smock, as well as some renegades that I devoured. I had been on the phone with Larry, in the lobby of a Hilton or Sheraton, whatever, a hotel, narrating a humiliating meeting I had taken at the convention, where one had to hustle up any scrap of attention. You have no idea how discordant things were for me, and bleak, on occasions of professional self-presentation. I even courted trouble because I wasn't wearing a skirt. In those days pants were totally verboten for the ladies at our conference, so when a security guard blocked my entrance—I couldn't attend my own talk—I ran across the street to buy a skirt at the department store, Macy's, or whatever. This time the skirt was too short, revealing my knees, and I had to run across the street again, tasked with finding more "appropriate attire." Investing in a career on a graduate student's puny stipend was no breeze. No institutional support was set aside for the mildly deviant, professors averted their gazes. I couldn't even break into the dress code! I had been on the phone, narrating. Bill waited patiently while I ranted to my prime interlocutor about our profession, its built-in degradations and pious misogyny. Bill invited me to sit down and discuss our future. I felt, for the first time, taken seriously, protected—and that I wouldn't have to cut impossible deals in order to get published. As if writing weren't difficult enough, I had constantly to scramble, beg, betray the work in its nascent stages to get my stuff even *considered* for publication. You have to be careful what you wish for, and other relevant clichés: Nowadays I am often made to feel duty-bound when asked to produce texts for occasions that are admittedly entirely legitimate, in terms of tone and intention moving and justly ceremonious; yet, to the extent that—nowadays—when they reel me in with no apparent room for negotiation, these assignments can become constraining. There's never any time for a break in the second-string hell I've created of overexertion and chronically disturbed sleep. Not that I'm complaining.

Others in my field have it worse. Graduate students and adjuncts continue to struggle, even when they don't always have to wear skirts. Sleepless and anxious, they still have to bribe and seduce people to publish a few pages that could determine all sorts of professional and existential outcomes like landing a job or securing tenure, if that goalpost still stands. My own struggles may have changed in kind, but not in terms of serving up despairing intensities. A few years ago, under enormous strain, I wanted finally to pack it in, but decided instead to cool my jets for a spell by going on an inward journey—not that I believe, then or now, in such fixed locations or observe strict boundaries purportedly keeping apart inside and outside. Sometimes I play along and take the express train to the world of "as if." In this case it was *as if* interiority beckoned, *as if* I could bail from external pressures, *as if* I could relax—maybe release some toxins, maybe go so far as to relinquish some phantoms and gently shoo away other persistent agitators ready to pounce and capable of breaking my stride. I booked out of NYC, en route to meditative calm.

It was probably a coincidence, nothing more than the furtive meeting of two dissociated events. The phone rang as I was suiting up to go on a yoga retreat. Judith giving me the heads up. I would be contacted soon about contributing to a volume meant to honor Barbara Johnson. I can't, I can't: I'm overwhelmed, psychically flooded, don't want to postpone the book to which I'm enslaved. Can't lose my thread, too fragile. Won't abide the separation from the consistently interrupted work, not even for Barbara, cherished and admired. She asked that you contribute to the volume. Pause. I don't see that you have much of a choice here, says the sympathetic voice on the other end. The deadline is soon. My heart sinks.

What gives with these constricted deadlines? I have to go. There's no way I'm going to mention the retreat when I write on her, I say to myself; it may compromise my reportedly kick-ass image and kill my street cred. Or something. I shouldn't be taking work with me on retreat, this impromptu dutifulness defeats the whole purpose and prospect of letting go. *Ach!* Another double bind, just what I needed. If I write on her now, I don't want to reveal my weakness, my need for silence and solitude. Anyway, don't worry, I said to myself, who cares? It's probably not even much of a revelation: you've already swiped in as a yogic type, spiked with dharmic anxieties, the ten thousand and one doubts, remember, the koan as test site, and the failed synchronies of tai chi, it's OK, at this point, I'm sure. No biggie. What gives with this phantasm of a reputation still to be saved, I wonder. Who seriously worries about yogic discretion? Or their so-called reputation? Long ago, in Berkeley, Denis Hollier had counseled me not to worry on this account. My reputation, irremediably wrecked, left me free to do what I wanted.

Anyway, the temptation to tie the two into a reflection will not be strong, for to my knowledge, there is nothing strongly Asian or silencing in her work. At the time she was still with us, making choices, reading, judging, suffering, writing to the end, sitting through her days without so much as a complaint, I was concerned that she'd read my contribution and wonder what I'd been smoking when I took to writing about her. Barbara wouldn't like it. So forget about it.

The refrain went like this: I want to please her, I don't know if I can, well maybe I can't—or maybe I can if she doesn't read it, but just knows that something was traveling toward her from me, from something "in" or around me, even from an extinguished space of contemplation. Still, as I packed the mat and my comfortably dreary outfits, I tossed two of her books, including the still unread *Persons and Things*, in the suitcase and thought, I will sneak your work into the space of silence and meditation for unsanctioned forays. This was not what I had in mind. *Ach!* I shouldn't have anything in mind. Maybe I'll just bring a couple of her texts, and what about "Nothing Succeeds Like Failure," let them accumulate energy or whatever, and not even crack them open. *Namaste.*

As it happened, the very fact of bringing Barbara Johnson with me into the space of focused centering made her appear. I would find myself dropping into her work, chanting a phrase from her or covertly rowing toward one of her shores, making her my road less traveled or letting her fire up the archetypes, to invoke the language of the seminar on Jung and Yoga in which I had enrolled. It was appalling for me to contemplate hanging in Jungian spaces, prodded by my shadow, anxious over a possible betrayal of Freud, but I wanted to have the chance to study with Marion Woodman, renowned Jungian analyst, and Stephen Cope, the house philosopher at the ashram.

The good thing about taking Barbara Johnson's work with me was that a lot of it was on psychoanalysis and would morph into my Freud-shield, my secret ally in an often wild terrain of flourishing intuition, a practice that at times abandoned itself to an underbrush of dance and imagery—something that I could only weakly absorb. Since my illness I have kept an open mind about healing practices and the rhetoric of *samvega*. For what it's worth, *samvega* designates a moment of terrific disillusionment with world, disclosing the distress of being. It seats you in your shadow, somewhere in the vicinity of Heideggerian *Sorge*. The refusal to encounter the insistence of certain archetypes, the avoidance of essential energies, said Marion, is responsible for autoimmune reactivity, the body's distress signals. Jungian analysis considers that, what you can't carry psychically, the body will take over. We store our psychoses in the body. You need to bring the body to consciousness, otherwise she'll carry the psychosis and break you down. Unconsciously stuffed, chronically neglected, disturbed, body's grievance will carry compromise to all sorts of transits and internal addresses, including the vital organs. The Death Mother wins out, drumming energy that turns against and overrules life by bringing on autoimmune breakdown and addictions.

Marion Woodman reads Jung bifocally with poetry, putting Emily Dickinson at the helm, often in the tense company of Ted Hughes and Sylvia Plath. There is no getting away from Shakespeare—a staple of insight that great analysts tend to share, beginning with my main man, Freud. Like many top-notch analysts, poets, or scholars, Woodman works with her own list of grievances. She deplores the destruction of Earth, patriarchal war zones (she distinguishes patriarchy from masculine qualities, locating the masculine both in men and women), the autoimmune attacks on body and psyche that she finds to be as prevalent among earthlings as among her private patients. She seeks a repository of virgin energy to bring forth a new masculine, but the motif of becoming-virgin is getting us off to another start, I say to myself. I knew that Barbara had been ill, and I wondered if she followed alternative paths of healing. I, for my part, have tried everything; that is what California has given me, I tell myself, a different staircase, another spiral and swirl, when trying to resignify the body's undecipherable howl. I surrender, I bow, I caterwaul in compassion with the drowning cat that I sometimes am. Then, sometimes, the unexpected release: I get to pounce again. I'm sprung from the dragging burden of an undeflectable companion, my illness, my complaint. I pull myself out of quicksand or lie silently on the floor, suddenly, where energy bubbles out.

When I can't make it and exhaustion dictates the returns of the day, I let go, if under protest. But then I really give up, writing out around me a vocabulary of acceptance. This is by no means easy for a superegoically held hostage. I have learned to "give myself permission," distracting the internal naysayers, sending Superego on a long walk. Permission granted. To listen to music, to read as a grazer, to watch TV, to stroll with the punches. I wonder how Barbara engaged her illness, it seems so indiscreet of me even to wonder, so I push aside my thoughts—my puppy-mind thoughts, they also call it "monkey-mind thoughts" when you're really racing and all over the place—and I go into silence, yielding to concentration and focus, and then think, Barbara has always been really disciplined, very focused.

One morning in corpse pose, while emptying my mind, I started tallying, unconsciously, the relatively few encounters we have had, my fear and admiration of her, my relation to intellectual women, to keepers of the fire. It is no secret that I am a kind of father's daughter, and this is what gives Jung a pass in these terms, at least, namely, his understanding that powerful work can be instantiated by Emily Dickinson as traversals through the father. My father thing aggravates some people, especially since I weave in and out of paternal placeholders with shuddering ambivalence. One day I'm all about father, the next day I go on record officially as a father slayer. Slavoj Žižek doesn't like my uncomplaining wrap around Derrida, the unwavering transference, he's said so a number of times, and again in his film. Tough titties. Once I told Jacques that Žižek slammed me for *not* betraying him or giving him up in the form of one long discursive whistle-blowing grievance—this was after my lecture on Nietzsche's "noble traitor." We both had a laugh over the taunt, for reasons that are obvious, I suppose. Now I remember Larry once saying that if Slavoj didn't work through the slow burn of negative transference, he, Slavoj, would harden himself into the position that Jung to this day is stuck in with regard to Freud, the resentful, spinning, disavowing disciple, because Derrida in the beginning took in and supported Žižek, who more or less "cashed him in" for Lacan. I think he may have come around lately, and he's put in some hours on different aspects of Derrida's oeuvre. Still, in the earlier days, I got some slack for my über-loyalty to my teacher. We discussed it briefly, launched by Žižek's remarks. The laugh that we shared, the burst of laughter—who knows what it meant to each of us. Perhaps the laughter at Slavoj's criticism of my compliance, my kind of "oversubordination," the dutiful daughter overkill, crept into spaces where things were not so obvious or determinable. Like, how does Žižek know that I have *not* betrayed Derrida, and where is one securely to locate the limits of loyalty, especially after Nietzsche's historial, as Heidegger

The Right Not to Complain

says, betrayal/love of Wagner? OK, this gets complicated, and I notice there are a lot of boyz in the mix when it comes to breaking off filiation.

Years ago, one fall semester, when he was teaching at NYU, Barbara called me in order to get Jacques's phone number. He was too tired, he had asserted a week earlier, to go speak at Harvard. I was commissioned to give her the news, which I accomplished via e-mail. On the phone to Jacques, she cried, he relented and said, "Yes." It's not clear to whom he said yes, or whom she was supplicating, because her burst of tears over the telephone was meant, she later confided to me, for the ghost of de Man, and was not part of the intentional negotiations with Derrida. I thought that this avowal might disturb Jacques—what is he to her, metonymic meatloaf, a mere substitution? But he smiled, said he had understood that transferential necessity, and was touched. So he said yes to her as, I guess, Paul de Man, or de Man said yes to Barbara Johnson from Derrida: yes, they would come in their, his, singularity. We were all split, and maybe that's where I want to go with this, to visit with some split-off parts.

Although they are miles apart on the hit charts, something about Barbara Johnson recalls to me my outrageous friend Kathy Acker, who initiated, I believe, a kind of *spliterature*, split and splitting with an energy force that at once courts and holds ambivalence in a strong clutch of reflection.[1] It is amazing to me that Barbara has accomplished so much on different terrains: having translated a crucial work of Derrida, *Dissemination*, she was an outstanding student of de Man, a consistently strong reader, and continues to mark our academic as well as social spaces in indelible ways, still to be deciphered and settled with. Traveling from Yale to Harvard at a professionally tender age, she could have pampered herself with the plums of institutionally gleaned prestige. Only she didn't. Instead, she entered more precariously chalked proving grounds, taking risks and changing the scorecard according to austere yet essential design. In her own way, and not always backed by her teachers, she started cutting up the neighborhood according to the exigencies and pressures of ethical claims, rerouting a major direction of "deconstruction" in the university, but not only in the university. She began formulating a commitment to African American literature and resolved to denounce unceasing metaphysical raids on women. Taking on the heavies of our time, her step was light.

A lot of this material came to me while on the retreat, or it came with me, waiting to be called up. When Marion Woodman discussed the significance for the unconscious of a chair as throne, linking *catheder* and cathedral, as that which gives place, she reverted to the holding enigma with which Saint Anne is associated. Setting the Virgin in Leonardo da Vinci's series, backing her up, she gradually disappears, giving way to a chair, allowing the chair to remain only as a trace of the mother of the Virgin Mother; I somewhat disruptively—puppy-mind—thought of a time, quite a while ago, when Barbara Johnson was lecturing at a meeting of the Modern Language Association but first had to put a chair on top of a desk, placing the cumbersome object so that it would face her and she could put her papers on the seat. She said to the audience that she needed this support in order to read her lecture. It was funny and poignant and earnest. If I had Derridean tracts in me, I would read that scene alone for several more pages, maybe for book-length strokes, as when he reads the position of the philosophical couple, which has Socrates seated, taking the chair, and Plato standing behind him in *La Carte postale*. If I were involved in a rigorous self-analysis, I would have to divulge that I had just given up the chair—I had built my department at NYU for nine years, laying out a plan for the future of German studies. Surrendering the chair to someone I had groomed, but who did not share my vision of necessary destructions, was not an easy thing for me to do. I had to let go, like Saint Anne. Laying her text on the seat of the chair, Barbara Johnson looked out at the audience from behind the bars of the chair, from a little boxlike constriction, or jail. Which kind of brings me to Jael and Yale.

Jael Break. Jael comes up in Johnson's work when she considers the fate of women in the Yale School, known also by its undercover name as the Male School, or, according to the Brides of Deconstruction, as the Jael School. The standout homonymy of Jael, namely Jail, is missing in signifying action but may well be implied by the guided slippage for which the article containing this series aims. In a footnote, Johnson explains:

> The story of Jael is found in Judges 4. Jael invites Sisera, the commander of the Canaanite army, into her tent, gives him a drink of milk, and then, when he has fallen asleep, drives a tent peg through his head and kills him. (I would like to thank Sima Godfrey for this pun.)[2]

Why does the writer parachute parentheses at the end of this description? Do they open things up that cannot be contained or do they brace the statement against a felt intrusion? On the face of it, there may be no rhetorical justification for the parenthetical annexation, for it follows no quotation or recognizable expository reasoning. Perhaps the parenthetical casing offers a way for the text to brace itself, for setting itself off from what has just been stated. Maybe it involves a shout-out to my sister in arms, or a maneuver that allows for shifting the blame for introducing an audacious pun. But where is the pun? Perhaps the pun is there only to the extent that language itself puns, slipping, sliding, going out of control of intended meaning. Or possibly this is a way of giving the thematically exploited feminine intrusion a lineage, even as it is embedded in enigmatic ambiguity. In the context of murderous thanklessness, Barbara Johnson offers thanks—a killing, Gd, freedom: hey, thanks. The feint of attribution, a kind of non-attribution, plants an allegory of false empowerment, I say to myself. "Perhaps I'm mistaken," I unsay to myself.

There is a lot going on in this passage and the fact that it is part of a paratextual excursion, a "cigarette narrative," as Pierre Alféri might put it, a microgram and sidebar, inevitably compels my interest.[3] In the end, a good deal is going on here, or it may be a matter of a bad deal—perhaps Barbara Johnson was dealt out in a certain way that keeps on getting replicated on the sidelines, under the text, in a miniaturized theater. But even in the shelter of a footnote, she does not allow herself to come into her own, as if such a thing were possible. Under the rubble of a massively weighted task—she has summoned her fathers and teachers and fellow inmates for some reading practice and friendly fire—she unscrolls the story of Jael. At the moment a parricidal hit has been called, Johnson relays it parenthetically to another woman, whom she thanks for the pun. The attack has been dialed down to a pun, a relatively minor intrigue for which language makes room, clearing the room, as it points a loaded pun at persons or institutions as muffled plaint. The question is, how lethal is this "pun" and why does Johnson stash it after shooting off? Or does she maneuver things differently, in order to figure herself as the daughter of the one who provided the pun, originating the assault?

Jael has just seduced and slaughtered the head honcho of the occupying enemy camp. There are a number of protocols for reading the diminishing footnote that drips or hemorrhages into a parenthetical attribution. Is this indeed a question of shifting the blame onto a hapless bystander, as Rousseau pulled off in the Marion episode? The inherent mechanism and automaticity of paronomasia would support such a hypothesis. Or, to put a stop to such lethal links, is it merely a matter of the modesty and generosity that consists in thanking another for the poignant comparison to Jael? What, regardless of rhetorical legitimacy—the whole scene concerns variously contested registers of legitimacy—is the *psychology of attribution* in a text that begins cannibalistically, expressing the hope that its author "will not have bitten off more of the hand that feeds me than I can chew?"[4] She bites, she scratches, Miss Johnson embeds herself in a crime scene, at once biblical and academic. While so doing, she advances bold conjectures concerning the parricidal daughter as well as the meekly disgruntled daughter who quietly threatens to bail.

This daughter belongs to the region, comes from a familiar literary household. She springs out of Wordsworth and Milton, where a "power reversal" occurs "between blind father and guiding daughter."[5] The relations are non-natural, for she also fills out the formal position of the poets to one another, "its pattern of reversibility between Wordsworth and Milton" in terms of father and daughter etiquette. The danger here, she writes, "is that the daughter will neither follow nor lead, but simply leave":

> For me, thy natural leader, once again
> Impatient to conduct thee, not as erst
> A tottering infant, with compliant stoop
> From flower to flower supported.[6]

The docile child has grown, assuming the place of natural leader, impatient to conduct or command the paternal metaphor and whatever holds it together. But Wordsworth puts the brakes on any such implications, reversing a woman's growth spurts. For her part, Johnson traces Wordsworth's "barring the reality of the woman as other, a way of keeping the woman in and *only* in the eyescape."

She takes on the Yale fathers in nibbles, finding recessive shares and averted motifs that point to a firm symptom: the blind excess of gender repression. She chews the hand that feeds her, posing as a parasite hosted by a great institution, as the incorporating daughter, surviving her serial billings—she takes them all on, but removes Derrida from the repertory of repressive behaviors that need to be exposed and read—and also, backing off a bit, as one who is too hungry to have fully understood. To the extent that she risks biting off more than she can chew, she risks gagging. The biting indignity here is that Barbara Johnson slips on a mask of daughter, guiding or following or threatening to book out, compliant and defiant at once, involved and excluded, in grief and grievance, a natural guide brought in, shortly after his death, as a substitute for Paul de Man on a panel where the men were asked to present their own work. She, ever the good girl, was invited, however, to stand in for and present the work of her mentor.

The chains that are rattling in male Yale jail for Jael link up with an act that captivates me, for toward the end of the essay, Johnson goes after herself, producing an act of critical auto-cannibalism, perhaps also an autoimmune response to the extent that she rips into herself with great strength and integrity, leaving herself without defense or defensiveness. In the end, a sign of self-severing: she also writes herself off—we will return to this cleaving gesture—by cutting away from the writer who signs the essay. She begins to meditate, launching a critical plaint: "In order to end with a meditation on a possible female version of the Yale School, I would like now to turn to the work of a Yale daughter. For this purpose I have chosen to focus on *The Critical Difference* by Barbara Johnson."[7]

The irony of self-doubling, at once presenting and effacing her mark, is sealed by a proper footnote to the work under investigation.

What provokes me in terms of the trajectories that she and I might parallel play on concerns an offshoot of stupidity—the largely repressed calamity of *ignorance* in relation to the fading empire of cognition. This section of her Yale essay ends on ignorance, on "'woman' as one of the things 'we do not know we do not know.'" Johnson concludes her preface with remarks about ignorance that apply ironically well to her book's own demonstration of "an ignorance that pervades Western discourse as a whole."[8] Johnson reads the heritage of ignorance, often a learned ignorance, from both sides of the stupefying divide, lining up the epistemological damage of trying to read (as) a woman. In light of a history of ignorance, its violent aftereffects, to which she reverts, I want to explore how Barbara Johnson comes off both as a cannibal and a spitball hurled against the blank wall of asserted ignorance.

As biter, she is also writer, scratching and pawing at symbolic values that remain elusive. However, she rarely poses as a victim of the institutional treats that come her way. Stealthily, on the prowl for marginal inroads, she hunts down minute traces of insurrection, plays with her object, revealing its hidden power of protest. Sometimes her focus foregrounds the latent strength of eventful masochists. Consider what she has written about the disavowed woman in Baudelaire, underscoring a certain "poetics of masochism," when she follows the record of Marceline Desbordes-Valmore in terms of a "rhythm of resistance and submission, initiative and self-effacement."[9] In a *mise en abyme* kind of way, Johnson preps the predicament of the figures that she rallies in her astonishing work, priming them on what could be called a discourse of effacement. Or maybe, in honor of her thought on the shuttle voice, one might see in her work the studied unfolding of shuttle diplomacy among entities, minoritized figures, agonized speech, snuffed voices, dialed down laments, the pout of plaint, and their powerful wardens. Johnson negotiates with the wardens, she went to Jail, I mean Jael. Let us go after her different morphs and see how she gets a pass to get out of Jael free.

Well, "free" is a buffed-up signifier that Barbara Johnson does not let slide. Taking on the aporias of Black poetry in the work and figure of Phillis Wheatley, she tracks the way in which Wheatley "wrote her way to freedom simply by letting the contradictions in her master's position speak for themselves."[10] The thought of freedom often implies, as in the *Prinz von Homburg*, writing one's own ticket in a situation that has never allowed for any practice but that of dispossession, where the weight of legal and signifying chains makes it difficult for you to slip out lightly. The double binds and knotted impasse out of which Kleist's Prinz or Johnson's Wheatley cannot extricate themselves undergird any larger thinking of freedom. Though there is some thematic justification to sanction tracking their tortured roundtrips, the paths they cut cannot be collated to the story of a bird's return to a cage whose door has been opened. Sometimes one wonders about those birds that fly right back in on a nervous victory lap, never to leave the proudly held perch again. (Yes, I see the near miss here, the stray intercept of this figural romp, an *avis* swallowing a piece of outside, but am I allowed to talk about myself *for a minute* please, my relation to the university, or does this have to be all about Barbara? OK. It has to be all about her, as if the "aboutness" could be captured, as if she were not an extension of me right now. I get it. Sure, I'll cut the narcissistic cord.) Both Phillis and Prinz organize a concept of minute salvation around the themes of delivery and Deliverance ("every human Breast . . . is impatient of oppression and pants for Delivrance" Wheatley writes in 1774, several months after she obtained her freedom).[11]

Since there is a page limit put on this plaintive tribute, and I cannot cover Derridean expanses, opening up dossiers on freedom and birds and African American letters in view of "successful manipulators and demystifiers of the narcissism inherent in white liberalism," I will be satisfied to point out that, for Johnson, "[t]he *fact* of the letter speaks for itself. Wheatley has placed in her master's hand the boomerang of compliance."[12] How feisty, I said to myself, of Barbara Johnson to review concealed ideologies of compliance, showing how the complaint is folded into its near acronym and partial antonym of compliance. How can microphenomena and near contradictory stances such as oversubordination and compliant extremism raise to a higher degree the stakes of protest? How could such pointed insight emerge from the quiet privilege of Barbara's demeanor, perhaps pulled together, at least in part, by a fabric of illusion?

Not wanting to fabricate overly smooth symmetries or scandalous analogies, I nonetheless was drawn to the place where Johnson zeroes in on the agonies of effacement. Barbara was at once outspoken and demur. What is the hidden hold that Wheatley has on her? We cannot negotiate a merger of the two writing women. Wheatley's struggle, to be sure, was differently scaled. She was a slave in the John and Susannah Wheatley household. She didn't own her name. Well, that doesn't set her apart from Barbara Johnson. One always inherits the name of another, more prior and powerful guardian. One can always be mixed up with another name tag. (When I inquired with the then chair of the CompLit Department at Berkeley about hiring Johnson, he narrowed his eyes to a closing point of malice and said, with an air of scorn, "You mean that black woman?" I was so riled at the time that I went directly to a mean and aura-sapping arch enemy in the department, an elder, and asked him how he could allow his protégé to be chair of an important department, so ignorant was he as to not know who Barbara Johnson, leading figure in the discipline of comparative literature, was, to opine ignorantly about racial difference. . . . But maybe he *did* know. Since that incident and my many muddled efforts to fight racism on the block, in camera, and on campus, I have strategically let it be known that I was identifying myself as African American, and I have heard several times that Barbara Johnson was an outstanding Black scholar. Once in a while one should stand one's ground, even if it is groundless, difficult to comprehend. Maybe I was struck and abducted by the French slogan, "Nous sommes tous des juifs allemands" [We are all German Jews], problematic though, in moments of greatest vulnerability, no doubt quite necessary. In the case of becoming a sistah, I was determined to keep all ambiguities intact, to say it loud. As anyone who knows me a little can confirm, my anguish over identity hijackings and appropriations is endless, yet the press of such anguish remains an indissociable part of the choices I make to scramble the master codes, to push back from essentialist presumptions on all scores and shores. Why, recently, I have returned to my Mexican origins. But that's another story.)

Wheatley is acknowledged by Johnson to have sustained the "bootstrap operation of passivity." She, "the abjected mother of African American poetry," led a stealth operation against tyranny, that, dependent upon subtle linguistic raids and equipped by only a handful of rhetorical maneuvers, was often taken for its opposite. Her minority reports spun on minoritized traces that could not be rallied into some sort of recognizable power politics or acts of resistance. In a certain sense, she tai chi'd it: letting the master codes collapse on their own energies, she'd step aside after a slight push on language and watch the whole house crumble and tumble under its own oppressive weight. Phillis Wheatley, largely forgotten and repressed, sweeter on peaceful means than any pacifist, a shattered sister, opened "a whole tradition of protest through excessive compliance."[13] She went into writing unarmed.

Passive to a point of discursive inertia, Wheatley passes for not very much more than a recycling bin of the master narrative. Still, her position is metaphysically on target, feminized in terms of codified allowances, and replicating a power imprint of phallic inscription. But it is precisely by holding this pose of nearly militant self-constraint that Wheatley insinuates a practice that consists in disabling the lash and laceration of oppressive inscription. She turns the freedom narrative into an enslaving narrative, holding up the contradictory assertions that mirror the warps and densities of bad faith. The freedom narrative meshes into the slave narrative, throwing off any secure borders between the two urgent appeals. Her method is to quiet down, get real still, so that the freedom song can hear itself think. It falls flat on its own background noise, breaking over the cracks in a logic intolerant to the hypocrisy of intention. "By simply repeating the ideology of freedom, Wheatley exposes the contradiction at the heart of the American Revolution. . . . Under Wheatley's pen, the lessons she has learned so well self-deconstruct."[14] She holds the mirror to liberal hubris, becoming Echo to malignant narcissism and subverts, pianissimo, the ethical presumption of continued racist entrenchment.

It is fitting that one of the prime and primal daughters of deconstruction introduce the possibility of self-deconstructing acts—or precisely, not acts, but part of a deliberate bet placed on tactical withholding and emphatic passivities (which in themselves, as we know, are not indissociable from acts, but I'll stop here before I self-deconstruct). Johnson shows how Wheatley manages her miniscule incursions and micro-revolutions by means such as forced rhyme in her poetry, where she creates a coercive match, for instance, between "Christ" and "priced":

My conversion came high-priced;
I belong to Jesus Christ,
Preacher of humility;
Heathen gods are naught to me. (original emphasis)[15]

The misspent conversion, piping on the scrunch of incompatible sounds, tells its own story, according to Johnson, condensed behind the impoverished rhyme. "Why should a conversion brought about by enslavement produce a *good* rhyme? The seemingly innocuous forcing of the rhyme euphemistically marks the barbarity of the historical process."[16] The poem, refusing to surrender to the smooth solicitude of "rhyme and reason," says "no" to its historical embeddedness by laying over itself another story that comes at too high a price and cannot comply with leading fictions of harmony. The Christianization of Africans, part of a costly and debilitating narrative that continues to fray many happy endings to this day, culminates in another, perhaps related type of enslavement that follows upon the renunciation of familiar archetypes and gods: "I belong to Jesus Christ."

What is high and no doubt also mighty, pinned to an escalating notion of transcendence, is not Christ but the price paid for having converted one's spirit into the soul of Christianity.[17] In her poem "On Being Brought from Africa to America," the constrained pilgrim writes: "Once I redemption neither sought nor knew."[18] All of these terms run on a losing economy in which one can only win by losing, by redeeming a new set of coercive imperatives, trading in gods and familiarity for all sorts of distant savings, booking flight with the god of the master, the master allied to and as envoy of Gd. Yet Christianity itself double-crosses any sure existential bet since day one, even before converting into its own higher price and rolling over into a redemptive account: aside from its abuses, it places a premium on suffering and destitution, on nailing its holy emissary to a masochistic pose. By surrendering to Jesus Christ, Wheatley also surrenders to surrender, cleared to explore the upside of abandon. Well, maybe it's not fair to Wheatley to have her join hands with a type of purposefully illicit thinking: she does not appear to sign up for a type of writing that instigates a gleeful brand of mysticism without mysticism; she hardly means to protect a way of savoring abandonment and its obscene upside. It might really be too high a price to convert her currency into what doubles for the obsessions of Georges Bataille. Moreover, Phillis Wheatley tiptoed past the demons of hounding oppression.

One of the qualities that draws Johnson to Wheatley is her reluctance to participate in what readers dipped in Heidegger call (and are called by) the *SCHREIben* attitude—somewhat less poignantly rendered in English as the inscribing/cry. This means, among other things, that, when faced with the muffled cry of Phillis Wheatley, we are no longer in the sway of grandiose or nihilistic or horizon-opening expectations but are constrained by the smallest of mutations in what used to be called being or thinking, shifted by the nuanced cuts of the plaint. If her utterance does not give in to grandiose temptation, it is not simple, or simply surrendered, either. "No agonizing cry, perhaps, but controlled and devastating irony."[19] It is not so much the case that Wheatley backs herself into a corner. Instead, she shines the light on the corner, blinking at the ferocious cornering that she has endured: her language sinks into the drab if telling "defective cornerstone" that Derrida, in his *Mémoires* and elsewhere, has shown deconstruction repeatedly to tap.

For Barbara Johnson—and here she deviates from her teachers—irony can be put under control, even as it devastates and glacializes the spirited terrain onto which it spills. In fact, irony appears to ensure control, underwriting a certain stance of sovereignty. One can understand the strategic benefits of putting a primal mother, abjected and largely dropped from memory, in control of her utterance. Phillis Wheatley hardly deserves to be resurrected in order to be thrown to the lionesses of *écriture féminine*, where language laughingly pitches against itself, encouraged to collide and slide all over the signifying space, rolled onto permanent displacement and laboring under the persistent anxiety of reference. Who would want to resurrect an out of control and sliding signifier? Phillis Wheatley is not Valerie Solanas. There is not a psychoticizing bone in her body.[20] Even so, extreme compliance cannot always be far from the hysteric's bind; nor can the exhausted step simply shirk any and all sorts of complicity with pre-schizoid constraints, the frozen hold of unreachable resolve. Sometimes historical paralysis takes refuge in somatic hideouts and displaced pain centers. But somatic complaisance is not where I'm intending to go, nor where Johnson leads us.

Still, when compliance turns into control, there must be another level or lever of control at stake. If this be irony, then let the dice roll, I say, somewhat irresponsibly—but no more irresponsibly than the thrownness of being or the outrageous feints of linguistic positing. There is no way that Johnson can give Wheatley a "mad woman in the attic" byline if she is meant to face down the unreason of reason—often masking the conspiracy of white ideologies and their highly indulged master narratives. There is still, however, room for Wheatley's micro-maneuvers within the slamming hits of irony. According to de Man's interpretations of Friedrich Schlegel and Charles Baudelaire, the "ironic mind" shares the same "dialectic of self-destruction and self-invention," which is "an endless process that leads to no synthesis."[21] Irony, in de Man, constitutes neither a figure of knowledge nor a figure of subjective consciousness; holding an awareness of nonconsciousness to the severe light of nonknowledge, irony is a repetition of interruption—Schlegel calls this "permanent parabasis"—that disarticulates the hope for synthesis. For de Man, as opposed to, say, Wayne Booth, irony, powered by destructive throttles, can hardly slam on the brakes in time for a save or swerve. But could it be that irony in the corpus of Wheatley registers the birthmark of destroyed being? That, like Benjamin's allegory, it leaves the scene empty-handed, diced by melancholia, and only as a trade name for loss? Irony donates nothing, yet holds a place open for the yields of unaccountability, the undoing of being.

I don't know Barbara Johnson as well as I would like to think I do, I say to myself. I remember once having had dinner with her at the Derridas' in the late 1980s. It was summer. She had come to France to go on a walking tour. I remember thinking how brave and Zen that was, and scary. At dinner she spoke about her dog, Nietzschie. I vaguely remember Jacques telling me later in the summer that she had gotten blisters on the trek, was encumbered by its level of hardship. I'm not sure if in the end she considered the trip to have been a good idea or not. Another time, maybe earlier, at an Irvine or UCLA conference, I can't remember which, I had dinner with her and Fred Jameson and Denis Hollier. She was worried about making the move from Yale to Harvard. I was worried about being unable to land a job and, at that time, about my friend Werner Hamacher, who was in a similar situation in Berlin. We both considered career alternatives as cabdrivers. Maybe "alternatives" is the wrong word. It's not like we had a choice or were asked to decide between different possibilities. Life was hard as I was heading toward my own well-documented abysses. Then there's a blur, a huge blank in the tape until she and Judith Butler

The Right Not to Complain

and I are sitting on a panel, giving ethics-of-something lectures at NYU. I did a thing on Nietzsche, folding into the scene my Cordelia complex. Afterward, Barbara Johnson and I exchanged a few words—she was extremely gracious, I thought, forthcoming and enthusiastic. Another time she was sitting in my office, resting, waiting for Derrida's seminar to begin. We talked; later I accompanied her to the car waiting for her outside. During the seminar she had raised her hand and engaged Derrida on Shakespeare and mercy. Very trusting, very friendly, I thought. She held her own, was scholarly and self-possessed, undeterred when making her point. Jacques was glad to have seen her so many years after the intricate triangulations and implicit dispute around "The Purloined Letter" series.

So I've more or less come clean. Barbara Johnson, object of fascination for me, held me at a distance, and why not? Even though we come from the same family, springing in a certain kind of way from a determinable matrix of deconstruction, we evolved from a world of difference. I guess that if I feel held at all, it's usually at a distance, so maybe Barbara held me after all. This is fully irrelevant, a voice stomps inside my headspace. Who cares about your holding patterns? Can you stay on point and please tender the desired tribute to Barbara Johnson? Stay on point, eyes on the prize, early to bed and early to rise. Isn't slipping off point kind of feminist, another voice weakly retorts? Still another voice, the closer and compromise broker offers, let's just say for the moment that we are performing irony's collapsing control tower of Babel. We all grudgingly take the compromise formation, knowing full well that we're just tabling the catastrophe for another time, having parked "loss of control" in the spaces reserved for allegorical control and mastered performance. Even though Derrida had made it a selling point, it was Barbara Johnson in her early works who taught me how to renounce mastery. Her works were formative for a whole generation of readers, setting limits and establishing often startling conjunctions of improbables such as plaintive drops and arresting insight.

Making Good. Another "issue" comes up in this morning's meditation. I don't know where to locate Johnson in "Euphemism, Understatement, and the Passive Voice," and I am not certain that this quandary raises a legitimate concern. We've received rigorously mixed signals from what I tend to consider the clashing schools of Nietzsche and Lacoue-Labarthe, one saying that everything bears a biographical trace, the other insisting that nothing, not even the explicit autobiographical endeavor, can stabilize the "I" or render it a reappropriable entity. I'm split between these conflicting possibilities, as perhaps we are meant to be. Nonetheless, no one can deny that Barbara Johnson performs a hallucinatory spiral of identificatory peekaboo in this text. We cannot simply say that euphemism, understatement, and the passive voice identify her prime tools or heuristic markers, though a study of the syntax and tendential initiatives of her language might corroborate such a hypothesis. All I can say is that when Barbara Johnson ascribes controlling qualities to the (maybe) trope of irony, she establishes herself in an ironic pose, yielding to the surrender of ironic free fall—which represents the only freedom for which the unreliability of irony makes allowances. The ironic withholding for which the text appears to stand as it falls would be related to the disseminated signature that the essay carries out and over into its stated concerns.

Maybe nothing meaty can be gained from traversing the mirroring layers that the text sets up, no substantial sense of the autobiographical cry, and yet there is a restitutional fervor for which Johnson makes herself responsible, an ethical appeal to which she responds. Maybe it has nothing to do with the girl who sat across from me at table or whose nervous laughter enchanted me from the start. Maybe it's closer to the dismissive grunts of the dimwit, my chair at Berkeley, who belched out, "You mean that black woman." Or, on an incomparably brighter note, in the gym, Phil Harper told me that Skip Gates was told by Ishmael Reed on a flight to somewhere that Barbara Johnson, whom he had never met, was probably one of his preferred Black critical minds.

The anecdote returns in meditation, I try to coax it away so that I can empty my mind. I can't put this in the desired commentary, it has no place in a chapter of a serious book, does it, I say to myself? What are we to do with this morsel of gossip that I retrieved between reps at the gym one day? Does it belong to the genre of autobiography? Have I crossed the line? Will Phil kill me and the others censure me, or just shrug their shoulders at the appearance of idle chatter that I airily invite into these reflections, scouring the gutter of *Gerede* for which Heidegger, that big mouth, shows so much scorn? But these sniper shots that come from nowhere, or from the gym, during yoga or cardio, in conversation with Hent at MLA, on the phone with Diane, when walking with Emily, seeking counsel from Judith, a reunion with Moten, analyzing an insult with Elissa, or trading memories with Bernhard, transpierce an oeuvre, sign on to its destinal dispatch. *Does Barbara Johnson know that she's an African American critic?* Maybe so; necessarily so, I say to myself. But she also knows, or her corpus knows, that she has no fusional pass regardless of the constructions around her name's double-duty fate. She may have to work both sides of the inherited divide, and I have the sense that the logic of diverted inheritance occupies much of her thought. Here I find myself in blinding identificatory sympathy, not always a good thing, and not as dire as Arendt's compassion, but in a crunch sudden annexation puts propellers on you, and boosters, even as you knowingly head only for trouble and psychological gridlock.

The Right Not to Complain

Her name. I repeat it as if it were in Sanskrit, litcrit, skrit, script, crypt, scrypt. Today's mantra, the address of a prayer and the energy I still send to her, in her beyond. After a gratitude pose and downing some triphala, I return to the encrypted complaint. It's as if the name of Barbara Johnson were calling the shots and forcing her to direct the flow of incalculable reparations. She has become historically indebted to what repeats and replicates her own name, split off from herself or from any concept of agency or subjective volition. Another way of stating this thought is that her name (its alias and iteration) has become the creditor of Barbara Johnson, pressing her toward infinite arbitration, the work of political translation and ethical accommodation—applying the ceaseless pressure of adjustment for which justice calls when it, or she, comes calling. (My name does other things to me, so I don't know what I was thinking when I said above that I was in identification with the way she had to answer to the pressure of *her* name. Oh, yes. I was thinking of the restitutional drivenness that has utterly vanquished me, prescribing my thematic exercises and theoretical habits, my OCD "method" of research. Listen, there is method to my methodical research. I froze in front of the screen when I caught those aggressive air quotes carpet bombing my method in a recklessly self-undermining manner. Now, let me dust myself off. The name carries one along, creates its own pathways to which we cannot be sure to have the key. Name happens. Johnson's name must have pushed her in certain directions. All in all, my name disseminates according to different rules and regs, often pushing me to examine, when Latinizing its reach, for example, metaphysical *fatigue*, failures of vitality. My first idea for this tribute was to write about exhaustion and the marks of chronic fatigue that scarify Johnson's text. In principal, that could be a way to join our names to the extent that, when read catachrestically, through Latin lenses, my name could indicate a privative drainage, a loss of vitality. [Another mailing route that my name has taken is driven by *irony*—iRony or I-RONy—disclosed in the second chapter as a naming that Hamacher delivered to me as game-changing bestowal.]) But then I was drawn in her texts to the way her name is disseminated through nearly hidden folds of her argument, nestled neither in the grammatical nor strictly rhetorical and gendered zones of registration.

We've already seen the word *barbarity* occur in an essay under consideration. What a difficult, if unconscious, burden for a sensitive and alert writer to carry. When I saw the way it rose up in a crucial passage, I thought that this one occurrence would not in itself suffice to confirm my hunches concerning the occult propulsion of a signature. How and where does she sign in this work— a properly Derridean question? Another way of putting it is, What kinds of obstacles need to be removed and disabled in order for Barbara Johnson to sign? Does she owe reparations to her name, and what kind of tax burden does she carry? These questions may seem a bit sci-fi if one hasn't kept up with the writings of Derrida on the remarkable itineraries of the name and signature. Even if one hasn't tracked the fate of the patronym or signature policies in the highly invested reflections offered by Derrida, one has been shackled to one's name—or, precisely, cut away from one's name, made non-identitical with it, left behind by its structural power of survival and the uses to which it can be put. In any case, and closer to home (though Derrida is home to me, the house of being and all that), no one who has inherited the name of a slaveholder or has had to change names along borders or at Ellis Island would be insensitive to the covert moves that a name makes on you, even if you haven't had to reassign or change names but have only seen your name abbreviated, nationalized or modified, conscripted by an unbearable history. I do not say that Barbara Johnson bore her name with pathos or difficulty. That would be absurd. Yet her texts, at least those under scrutiny here, also tell the drama of another yet "identical" patronym that makes its fateful mark, *making* a name for itself, while effacing another name, pressing the double trigger, rolling over and ruling out a name in order to sign. That name, in this essay, is "Johnson."

And so, with Johnson taking Johnson to historical account, we enter what I have been seeing as an area of critical disturbance, a drama of restitution. Johnson will restore to Wheatley what Johnson has taken. Dispossessed, deprived, historically edged off the page, Wheatley is enrolled by Johnson for reparations. Not at this point from the slaveholder, whose name she inherited, but from yet another persecutor in the series, the one who has suppressed her work in a critical anthology of "Negro Poetry."

In 1921, at the start of the Harlem Renaissance, "Johnson edited what he hoped would be a major anthology of African-American poetry."[22] I guess if I were filming this I would now quote the final shot of Stanley Kubrick's *The Shining* and, shifting the frame of reference only slightly from that of Stephen King, show an image of Barbara Johnson seated as James Weldon Johnson, her/his double and original, the paterno-maternal instigation of a reparative procedure.

Johnson writes, "Again." Alright, maybe this doesn't qualify as an argument. I'm trying to demonstrate that the repetition of the name is marked as repetition, beginning with "again." Let me restart that sentence. I want to get it right. Here goes. Johnson writes, "Again, Johnson." Ahem. Well, still not enough material evidence, much less a depot of supplies for immaterial intuition. I'll reapproach. Johnson writes: "Again, Johnson uses the passive voice as a cover for unspecified (here, all-conquering) agency: 'As for Ragtime, I go straight to the statement that it is the one artistic production by which America is known the world over. It has been all-conquering. Everywhere it is hailed as "American music."'" A multiplication of vampiric bite marks, the quotes are holding up their limit of alien incorporation. Circuited through Johnson, Johnson gets to say something about herself, as if she were allocuting, passing into the third person, passing into the passivity of the other for whom she advocates and who has left her with an outstanding debt to cover: "Johnson uses the passive voice as a cover." The logic gets vertiginous, it's spiraling and can be transmuted to "Johnson uses Johnson to use the passive voice for a cover covering Johnson," and so on. Page limits block my pass here, because I would very much like to go on and fan out to Levinas, Ponge, Emily Dickinson, and so many others whose more direct negotiation still strike a chord as they continue to consult with voices so passive that they cannot be deemed mere voices. But I have to phallicize myself and get to the or even *a* point. It's going to happen, I promise. "Through his use of ellipsis, understatement, unspecified agency, and non-binarity, Johnson is thus attempting to bring about a change in the 'national mental attitude' without explicitly acknowledging or processing blindness and dispossession." So far the Johnsons are keeping apace, traveling parallel universes or, depending on your particular neighborhood, sharing the sidewalk and historical custody of a repressed heritage. Now comes the split, announcing the pathway the name must take in order to repair textual injury and referential insult, the drama of Wheatley's exclusion: "Johnson wishes to combat the injustice of her exclusion, yet cannot quite bring himself to place her first." This is where Johnson comes in, to combat the injustice of her exclusion. The acts of doubling become halved, as Johnson multiplies the incidents of "half." And so the Johnsons split over the mother, to whom reparation is owed, for "Johnson, too, does not grant Phillis Wheatley her rightful place at the head of the list, but rather confines her to the space of his preference, the place of prehistory. She is the ancestor half acknowledged, half obscured, the abjected mother of African-American poetry."[23]

"What Johnson holds against Wheatley is her avoidance of passionate oppositional utterance: 'One looks in vain for some outburst or even some complaint against the bondage of her people, for some agonizing cry about her native land.'" The grievance against Wheatley is that she has *failed* to complain, disrupting the historically mandated expectation that she put her protest in play, lash out against the lacerators. This fathomed failure justifies her brutal marginalization by the prior Johnson from the table of contents—made more or less to disappear into prehistory, left off as another abjected mother whose unreadable moans discount her, overlook her concealed linguistic weapons that pick off the otherwise routed and muted complaint. Having split off from Johnson, Johnson now returns to perfect an associative climb: "In other words, what Johnson holds against Wheatley is precisely the stylistic avoidance of conflict and outcry that characterizes his own writing."[24]

Here we have a signature moment, with Johnson identifying in Johnson the avoidance of the very withholding to which Johnson objects or which Johnson, dissociating, expels as an alien fragment. Reading these reciprocal intrusions into each other's texts, owing to the operation of effacement, the "half obscuring" of a maternal facilitator, encourages one to ride the signifier as it moves in and out of its countersignature, trading gender, time and places. Johnson picks up the relay from Johnson, who has shunned the origin, averted his gaze from the very source of his historical project. To be honest, it would give me too much pleasure to pursue the logic and direction of the routes, or roots, they take, the subtle deviations effected, the sense of original crime deflected. I see a pacing of passivities, a sublime quarrel over the negative mother who induces blockage, paralysis, while withholding the breakthrough energy that allows for the frank cry of justice. I would want to reach down into the mother's well, to the breakoff moment of a splintering between a poisoned source and the recovered, decontaminated and proficient force that Johnson reclaims. Yet there's a law coming down on me, telling me to stop, to breathe, to get back in my body. And that the quest after a decontaminated origin would be ill-advised, strictly irretrievable.

In order to end, to achieve some sort of closure (the narcissistic stunt that helps us get on, according to psychoanalysis), I need first to open a dossier that will help us read the score that I have been following. Here I can only indicate one of the futures that Johnson's work holds for us—something I would call, along with Mark Sanders, the psychopolitics of reparations.[25] Now that I think of it, she was often trying to clean up after a stated or displaced grievance. To a certain degree, Barbara, too, set up her writing desk as a Bureau of Complaints, taking all sorts of incoming calls and aggrieved reports. She may have wanted the repair to take hold and, so, found herself enmeshed in a few compromise formations, some sticky, some successful in her sense of that word and endeavor—what it means to succeed, to offer a wrap, calm a complainant, create a credible alliance. Her commitment to reparations may have begun when she sought to restore some balance to the strife between Derrida and Lacan; it may have settled in her account of the Frankenstein monster; it may have helped shape the contours of the departments she held together at Harvard, or on any other occasion when Barbara Johnson uniquely set to work on the incoming plaints of literary, political, and other poetic or referential networks. Maybe I should book a return trip to this site of vexed repair, its necessity and the impossibly bloated horizons of expectation, even *need*, that it sets. There are cases where the complainer might find solace, if only momentarily, but without a wholesale recuperation of the lethal oversights, aggression, and distress that beset her. Returning to the irreparable with which we live and struggle to survive, one looks to those whose earnest efforts have involved sifting and sorting through stockpiles of complaints, some bogus, some irrelevant, yet so many bearing dead earnest objections, barely pronounceable, to the "what is" of a cruelly dispatched history.

Perhaps, in this context, we can momentarily reestablish the line of thought begun by another bad news mother, whom Lacan scorns and with whose timelines Freud himself had quickly grown impatient: with Melanie Klein, namely, who clocked aggression ahead of the Freudian schedule, and kept us in depressive mode on good days (when we're not thrown into paranoid-schizoid terror from day one until doomsday). Known in psychoanalytic circles as "Mrs. Klein," Melanie develops reparation to comb original guilt fields, showing how the human infant makes good, stilling the little one's panicked rounds with aggrieved encounters of early life. Working with Baby's relation to the injured object, she locates violence at the root of ethical agency.[26] In "Freud and the Scene of Writing," Derrida considers the thought on reparations—Klein tracks how the damaged object is made good in retrospect—to be her brand of the *Genealogy of Morals*. According to Klein there are different modalities of reparation, including manic reparation, where violence persists, and mock reparations, where the restitutional urge is merely simulated. Be that as it may, there is an impulse to locate reparation at the root of responsibility. At the same time, we are faced with the aporia of reparations: one must make reparation, one can't make reparation—no economy can possibly guarantee returns on an incalculably painful history of injury.[27] Yet, making reparations would be the penchant of one who has been able to introject a good object.

Even on the good side of the maternal breast, trouble was announced, reparation bills were being formulated and postdated, frustration building, complaints were marinating. Mother's feeding time wasn't always a matter of a gift that was being gently proffered. Sometimes it looked like a breast was coming after you, an assault weapon meant to silence the helpless child for good, the fleshed emblem of a persecutory object rather than the purveyor of any fable of beatitude. The much acclaimed bliss of breast feeding was nowhere to be found or felt. You were "fed up" from the start.[28] So, where am I going with this? I am still contemplating the plaint of the "hand that feeds you" in Barbara Johnson's self-presentation and the figure of chewing it off, which it seems to me comprises a classically Kleinian scene of aggression, devouring and polluting a metonymy of alma mater's breast, chomping down on the institutional hand. But, still within Klein's scale of aggression, why would this be a scene in Johnson's writing that called out to me, even as I retreated and meditated, formed an intention to engage a peaceful alternative to carnophal-logocentric practices and policies?

In retreat I eat mindfully, honor vegan constraints, practice nonharming, center and meditate, tend to my subtle and energetic bodies, and yet I appear to be taking a bite out of a purportedly good object, be this in some ways a metonymy and morsel of Barbara, or, more overtly, I bite into part of my own institutional bonds and history, those of others, some aspects of which were not entirely polluted. Melanie: "It is my hypothesis that one of the deepest sources of guilt is always linked with the envy of the feeding breast, and with the feeling of having spoilt its goodness by envious attacks."[29] Is she talking to me? Is she talking to Barbara? Maybe to our separate but equally ambivalent relations to the institutional incubators that in my case, spit me out, threw me up, and then was forced to tolerate the unmovable squatter? When Lacan tries to give us a readout on racism, he, too, indicates that something like envy is at work: we project plenitude on the Other, we feed on fantasies of a certain overcapacitation that we ourselves lack, and then try to destroy the carrier of imaginary abundance.[30] This is not the place (though I am sorely tempted) to open a dossier on the secret histories of Black nannies and related figurations of maternal safety zones attached to the outdated yet still trafficked imago of Mammy.

Scoring the difference among complications of jealousy, greed ,and envy, Melanie Klein, citing a passage from Othello, writes: "One is reminded of the saying 'to bite the hand which feeds one,' which is almost synonymous with biting, destroying, and spoiling the breast." She explains that envy "contributes to the infant's difficulties in building up his good object, for he feels that the gratification of which he was deprived has been kept for itself by the breast that frustrated." Envy, viewed as a very important factor in projective identification and arises from oral-, urethral-, as well as anal-sadistic sources, is "connected with the desire to spoil the mother's possessions, in particular the father's penis which in the infant's phantasy she contains."[31] Institution stores the penis, destination of spoilage, inflamed, bruising rage. I . . .

. . . Wait. Just as I was going to consider how envy, my envy, as oral-sadistic expression of destructive impulses, operative from earliest life, and, as signaled by Melanie Klein and Karl Abraham, secured by a constitutional basis—I mean, just as I was going to explore my own primitive envy, going overtime into anal-sadistic bouts of fury, revived in the transference situation with Barbara Johnson's work (as a part conduit to my work but, for the greater part, in its own right)—in view of the way Melanie Klein addresses "envious criticism" and "destructive criticism" that come from split-off parts, building up defense, and how I, for my part, was not given the good breast when I most craved it, as recently as this morning, "and therefore when it is offered, he does not want it anymore. He turns away from it and sucks his fingers instead. . . . SOME INFANTS OBVIOUSLY HAVE GREAT DIFFICULTY IN OVERCOMING SUCH GRIEVANCES. With others these feelings, even though based on actual frustrations, are soon overcome; the breast is taken and the feed is fully enjoyed" (emphasis added).[32] Purr, purr. Ha!

Well, even though I was fully prepared to take responsibility for some of my *Lebensneid* (life envy), even *Penisneid* (penis envy) in relation to Barbara (though I must say that my engines of aggression have died down, and I no longer go after others with unsparing ferocity or turn against myself as in the past), I note my time is up, my space is gone, the complainer's registry closed, I have to let go of these envy-and-gratitude exercises, return to the mat, practice nonharm, to conclude in the same way I send off each of my sessions, by curling into the yogic gratitude pose: seated, stretching my arms out on the floor, bowing before the one addressed, breaking, to the extent possible, the narcissistic circuit, softening my positions.

Thank you, Barbara.

Planning Ahead. So. Let me rewind, pull this together, bring it to a place where no one wanted to go. As I approached the finish line of this work, the problem and culture of complaint blew up in the face of a stunned citizenry. Carrier of a lethal strain of narcissistically charged complaint, the "whiner-in-chief" secured his entry into the body politic. Chronically aggrieved, he regularly signs off on tweets, saturated with malice, "It's sad." Sadness, however, knows no mockery and cannot be traced back to the hyperbolic flex of disdain; it will not serve as the disruption of carefully accommodated claims for social justice. Sadness, a way of leaning into the emptiness of being, a melancholic sway in the winds of finite capacity, would study the lassitude of letting be. Part of the complex and mature avowal that sadness gives up reaches still another level of being-in the-world, when it signs a *resolve*, orienting us toward mending, a repair work. Here sadness aims to disclose a disposition toward acceptance, even a healing, in some ways mustering a cohesive face open to the destitution of world. Part of a political vocabulary, sadness or—to stick with Arendt's version of Lessing—*joy* binds us where we are unbound, radically unhinged. These modalities of relatedness, which may or may not bear unique facets of social affect, interiority, or lead to satisfactory understanding, send out a life line that primes political action. Both sadness and joy, part of the same polarity, yoke concepts ("political," "action") that need carefully to be rechecked, readied with utmost concern and ethical probity. This involves

CHAPTER 6

hard work, calling upon all of us, straining patience, undermining for the most part all practices of hopeful petition, prayer, and protest. *Ach!* A woman's job is never done, especially when she and her allies are historically sidelined, slammed by insult and dismissive grammars of power.

So. Where were we?, asks the scholar. One cannot underestimate the traumatic whacks coming from institutional forms of hatred, the storm of grievances revealing the downside of blustering complaint—the complaint of privilege. In terms of the backslides we are forced to witness and, in far too many cases, made to endure, I can say little more than that I am stupid with grief. Enfeebled by so much injury, I am stupefied, at least for now, yet possibly for my time as a life-form. How did it come to this? Is the wave of regressive malice new, or very old, too old for memory? Let us not fail to note a package deal at play of "traditional values" and their mutation in an overflow of familial tropologies. The traumatic Trump intrusion projects a family, a clan, a towering mass of vulgar certitudes, a collapsed and whimpering phallus of the defunct Father-function supported by a colluding daughter. *Ach, ach!*

I'm not done yet. Scanning the wreckage of nihilistic disclosure, I find a buildup of negative bequeathals. Trump & Co., incapable of the production of value, stand merely as symptoms of an overdrawn account, featuring the victory lap of predatory narcissism, part of the accumulation of nullifying discharge: reckless governance, stupefying stupidity, sci-fi villainy, shabby morphs of Enlightenment prediction. However radically exposed, the weakness of the figure of man and what we think we need in terms of leadership precedes the current sham manifestation of the assumption of power and roll call of agency. Not everything disclosed at this time is entirely new to us. For one finds so much inherited and brought forward by ancient habits of metaphysical positing, the particular resilience of exclusionary operations, which meet their most decadent outlet in the configurations that have allowed for a Donald Trump investiture and sustain his bumbling vulgarity. Somehow, we must find nurturance in social grief, the way legendary tribes in times of drought drew water from hidden roots.

I tell myself that such destructions cannot lay us low, not definitively. This thought, more a petition than a declaration, is not anchored in certainty. I'm scheduled to come out of the grief I have swiped in, ready to rumble, unsticking from a uniformly frozen pose of Medusoid petrification. I've gone in and out of inert states and their frenetic counterpart in hopped-up mobility, locked and loaded. Whatever. In the past many months I have been a certifiable mess. Or rather, I am and remain a reflector of a mess, transmitting in a desert of despair. And so we're still reeling from the U.S. elections of November 2016, which threw some of us an existential curveball. How resolutely we lost—yet, to whom, *to what,* one continues to wonder!? The scope of the loss that must be borne—massive, embarrassing, harbinger of body harm—pitches one into a catatonic stall whose shelf life and stealth articulations, somatic jostles, disturbed sleep patterns, lost trust, rage outbreaks, unconscious scrapes, decisive breakups, social suspicion, cannot be fully predicted. Under such circumstances, it is not clear how to maintain the protest engine set in gear, how to keep it viable and sustainable, something "we can believe in." The quasi-election of a team supercharged by masculinist pathologies jolted us as a protest in its own right—in terms of Nietzschean evaluation, as the bad and decadent side of the very notion of protest. Trump is the mark of a protest gone bad, very bad, tremendously bad. Folks, it's very, very bad. I can't believe I am imitating his disintegrating language usage, that of a foundering father who has replaced, for reasons still to be explored, the founding fathers—also to be further explored. This man can barely read, yet he has talked and acted, poked fun at and tries to legislate against the vulnerable; he occasionally hits a note, strangely contradictory, then collapses into the lowest rumble of complaining culture. Grievance cuts across different territories, allowing the worst tendencies and ethical destructions to emerge as blindingly hurtful complaint and ballistic address.

The presidential charge, laced with destructive *jouissance,* holds steady on first chakra intensities that boost familial, tribal, nation-hugging idioms—for the most part false appropriations, strong but pitched very low, very, very low. *When they went low, we were nearly KO'd.* As for me, I await instructions daily from the community of warrior-agitators and other highly articulate activists on the ground in order to see how to move up against the impossible.

Unattended by musical lament, my head fills with static bombs. I'd like to change that and invite music back into my life. A long trek of mourning has switched off the music. Maybe I should listen to Beethoven's "Complaining Song," I say to myself, the one cued up for me by Ann Smock. She indicated his next-to-last piano sonata, No. 31, op. 110, when I wrote on Werner. Listen to the last movement, feel your way back in, I heard her intone. *Moderato cantabile molto espressivo.* Bring back the music. Sometimes, I tell myself, it is alright and even necessary to l'anguish, to stay with a language prior to any protection. This does not mean that we are not constantly at the ready. For the time being, I sit in anticipatory bereavement of the next years, trying to rouse, looking for energy surges and the stores of public language that let me fuse for a spell with other citizens of rage—the righteous indignant, the defeated and sublime whimperers, the ones awakening to another logic of complaint, another daybreak. . . *Ach!*

A girl can dream.

CHAPTER 6

Notes

Introduction: Taking a Knee

1. See in particular Derrida's discussion of friendship's turnovers in the *Nicomachean Ethics* and *Eudemian Ethics*, in addition to reflections on the intensification of friendship offered by its flip side in Blake: "Be my enemy for friendship's sake," in *Politics of Friendship*, transl. George R. Collins (London: Verso, 1997).

2. Philip Roth, *Portnoy's Complaint* (New York: Vintage Books, 1967), 77–78.

3. Ibid., 94.

1. Raising the Visor: The Complaint of Modernity

1. Jérôme Lebre, *La justice sans condition* (Paris: Baryard, 2014), 66.

2. Jacques Derrida, *Specters of Marx* (New York: Routledge, 1994), 22; "comment distinguer entre deux désajustements, entre las disjointure de l'injustice et celle qui ouvre la dissymétrie infinie du rapport à l'autre, c'est-à-dire le lieu pour la justice?" *Spectres de Marx* (Paris: Éditions Galilée, 1993), 48.

3. I have decided to leave intact a possible trip-up—something that may or may not amount to a lapsus. The last time I jammed on the quote "It speaks!" was in seminar. In The Poets Take Philosophy class at NYU in 2015, we took a time-out to consider Celan's "Meridian" and the exclamation "It speaks!" Derrida gave serious thought to the exclamation mark, which I realize now resembles a ghostly figure, perhaps Hamlet's father hovering over the globe, or Shakespere's (a spelling that accrues to this name) Globe Theatre. Perhaps I should have left the more recognizable quote on the page, namely, "Speak to it, Horatio!" The way that poetic language speaks or communicates infrastructurally, without the anchor of strict chronicity or historical buildup, can open new dossiers. I am not the only one to note that Hamlet mysteriously calls to the "murder done in Vienna" when he plunges a sword into the membrane hiding Polonius, one of his victims. Who would be so small-minded as to deny the evidence showing that Hamlet was already telepathizing with Freud? "It speaks!" *Ça parle!*

4. See Rebecca Comay on the awkward downgrade that Horatio marks in the passing down and out of Hamlet the Dane's heritage. "Paradoxes of Lament: Ben-

jamin and Hamlet," in *Lament in Jewish Thought,* ed. Ilit Ferber and Paula Schweber (Berlin: De Gruyter, 2014).

5. Derrida, *Specters of Marx,* xix.

6. For more good times—hollow times, bad timing, the empty interval, dead zones—see my *Finitude's Score: Essays for the End of the Millennium* (Lincoln: University of Nebraska Press, 1994), 5ff.

7. See Rebecca Comay, "Paradoxes of Lament," for the step-by-step demo of Hamlet's stammering death drive and short-lived election campaign.

8. Derrida, *Specters of Marx,* 21.

9. Avital Ronell, *Loser Sons: Politics and Authority* (Urbana: University of Illinois Press, 2012), 176.

10. Ibid., 177.

11. Jean-François Lyotard, "Emma: Between Philosophy and Psychoanalysis," in *Lyotard: Philosophy, Politics, and the Sublime,* ed. Hugh Silverman, transl. Michael Sanders, Richard Brons, and Norah Martin (New York: Routledge, 2002), 42.

12. Ronell, *Loser Sons,* 175.

13. Ibid., 177.

14. Ibid., 177ff.

15. Ibid., 176.

16. The motif of the call moves through all my writing, but the ambivalent necessity of *refusing* a call is formalized in *The Telephone Book: Technology, Schizophrenia, Electric Speech* (Lincoln: University of Nebraska Press, 1989).

17. Lyotard, "Emma," 37, 25.

18. I take this up and pursue the implications of teen excitability for politics in *Loser Sons;* see especially chapter 7, *"Was war Aufklärung?* / What Was Enlightenment?"

19. Laurence Rickels, stellar scholar of adolescence and teen passion, together with Donald Winnicott, K. R. Eissler, Stanley Cavell, and others, renders a political theory of uncontained adolescence. Consider these strong statements that arise from a reflection on juvenile delinquency and politics on the loose: "The secular era (or Teen Age) that begins with Hamlet schedules the origin of its subject according to the first suicidal ideation and the first identification with the ghost." Moreover, when analyzing what it means, according to Winnicott, for the teen "to skip the relationship to the death of the parents . . . and proceed directly to a position of authority," Rickels reminds us, at the end of this section: "There was, by [Winnicott's] reckoning one instance in the recent past of this alternative stabilization of the Teen Age by positioning it society-wide as ego ideal and that was Nazi Germany." In "The Other Coast of Terrorism: On Sue de Berr's *Hans & Grete,*" in *Terror and the Roots of Poetics,* ed. Jeffrey Champlin (New York: Atropos Press, 2013), 22 and 25. See also D. W. Winnicott, "Creativity and Its Origins," in *Playing and Reality* (New York: Routledge, 1996 [1971]), 65–85, and "Aggression in Relation to Emotional Development," in *Through Paediatrics to Psycho-Analysis: Collected Papers* (New York: Brunner-Routledge, 1992 [1950]), 204–18; and Stanley Cavell, "Hamlet's Burden of Proof," in *Disowning Knowledge in Seven Plays of Shakespeare* (Cambridge: Cambridge University Press, 2003 [1987]).

2. *Ach!* The History of a Complaint

1. See Eduardo Cadava, *Emerson and the Climates of History* (Stanford, CA: Stanford University Press, 1997).

2. Jacques Derrida, *Politics of Friendship*, transl. George Collins (New York: Verso, 1997).

3. In Anders Kølle, *Beyond Reflection* (New York: Atropos Press, 2013), 60.

4. Peter Fenves, ed., "Transformative Critique" by Jacques Derrida, in *Raising the Tone of Philosophy: Late Essays by Immanuel Kant*, (Baltimore, MD: Johns Hopkins University Press, 1998).

5. According to Michael Levine, there was yet another option, differently totemized: Rainer Nägele, on whose team I did in fact play in the heyday of my Germanistik affiliation. He kept some essential doors open for the French fringe. David Wellbery represented another type of leadership that also shuttled between Friedrich Kittler and Werner Hamacher. Benjamin Bennett flagged still a separate district of exegetical intensity that discretely attached to these proper names.

Both Hamacher and Kittler exceed the field to which I provisionally link them here. Most recently, Hamacher figures significantly in Mangalika de Silva's "No Longer a 'Whore,' Not Yet a 'Terrorist,' Never a Citizen: Majoritarian Right and the Rabble" (*Social Text* 117 [Winter 2013]) for his notion of a promissory subject of rights as a never fully constituted actuality in "Wild Promises on the Language 'Leviathan'" (*New Centennial Review* 4, no. 3 [2004]: 215–45).

6. Susan Bernstein, "The *Philia* of Philology," in "Give the Word: Responses to Werner Hamacher's *95 Theses on Philology*," ed. Gerhard Richter and Ann Smock (Lincoln: University of Nebraska Press, forthcoming).

7. I have explored these points in "The Right Not to Complain: A Philology of Kinship" in "Give the Word." In the same volume, Hamacher responds to my essay, focusing on my analysis of "l'anguish," which he sees as putting into question Heidegger's famous statement "Die Sprache spricht" (language languages/speaks). Structurally bound up in *l'anguish*, complaint, which I make a matter of intolerable existence, is prior to any recourse to rights, thus marking our abandonment by a discourse of rights.

8. Walter Benjamin, *Lettres françaises* (Région Basse-Normandie: Nous, 2013), 101. "Rivalry" and "parricide" were terms introduced by Professor Kevin McLaughlin in his Walter Benjamin seminar at Brown University, where I was invited to present some of these ideas on October 28, 2016. The seminar's focus was on "the civil war in Germanistik" waged over the stakes and meaning of German literature. Benjamin played a key role in drawing up sides, aiming to pull the field of German away from traditionalists.

9. Walter Benjamin, *The Correspondence of Walter Benjamin, 1910–1940*, ed. Gershom Sholem and Theodor W. Adorno, transl. Manfred R. Jacobson and Evelyn M. Jacobson (Chicago: University of Chicago Press, 1994), 359.

10. Ibid., 359–60.

11. Both the Derrida and Kittler texts are parked in *Glyph* 7, ed. Samuel Weber (Baltimore, MD: Johns Hopkins University Press, 1980).

12. "Die deutsche Dichtung hebt an mit einem Seufzer" is the opening sentence and salvo of Kittler's *Aufschreibesysteme: 1800/1900* (München: Wilhelm Fink Verlag, 2003), 11; *Discourse Networks 1800/1900*, transl. Michael Metteer (Stanford, CA: Stanford University Press, 1990), 3. The first chapter, given the heading that riffs off Goethe, "The Scholar's Tragedy: Prelude in the Theater," starts with this exhale: "German Poetry begins with a sigh."

13. Werner Hamacher, Jan Ritsema, and Gerhard Gamm, "Klage, Anspruch und Fürsprache," in Werner Hamacher, *Philosophische Salons: Frankfurter Dialoge IV*, ed. Elisabeth Schweeger (Frankfurt am Main: Belleville, 2007), 13–33.

14. Friedrich Nietzsche, *Daybreak: Thoughts on the Prejudices of Morality*, ed. Brian Leiter, transl. R. J. Hollingdale (Cambridge: Cambridge University Press, 2007), 5.

15. Werner Hamacher and Catharine Diehl, "95 Theses on Philology," *diacritics* 39, no. 1 (2009), 11.

16. Sometimes it hurts when people play with your name, especially if it's a weird one to start off with, like mine. While Derrida threw light on the ultrafeminine "elle" in Ronell(e), Hamacher tied me, with epiphanic verve, I thought, to iRony. Friends rename you or name you according to different unconscious assessments that can become determining. They have acquired the right to *nick*name, to nick and name you.

17. Ibid., on the *Klage* (lament).

18. Reading the event of appropriation as in itself an event of expropriation, Reiner Schürmann reminds us in a magisterial work dedicated "To the memory of Hannah Arendt": "The play of appropriation . . . conveys something *aletheia* cannot say," in *Heidegger: On Being and Acting: From Principles to Anarchy* (Bloomington: Indiana University Press, 1990), 218.

19. Johann Wolfgang von Goethe, *The Sufferings of Young Werther*, transl. Stanley Corngold (New York: W. W. Norton, 2012), 21–22; final phrase added for clarity and approved by Goethe.

20. I have explored Goethe's latency in Freud in *Dictations: On Haunted Writing* (Bloomington: Indiana University Press, 1986).

21. I offer an analysis of the figure of the noble traitor in *The Test Drive* (Urbana: University of Illinois Press, 2005), 310–16.

22. The Caribbean writer and philosopher Eduard Glissant argues in his work for the right to opacity, as do the Schlegel brothers, and a number of brothers and sisters of German romanticism.

23. "Des Tours de Babel," in *Difference in Translation*, ed. Joseph F. Graham (Ithaca, NY: Cornell University Press), 165–248.

24. Babel gets even more complicated, twisted. The prohibition that it lands goes into overtime, enticing a sustained double bind. Peter Connor explains that Gd's intervention at Babel—where he confounded the "one language" spoken by "the whole earth"—places translation, from its inception, in a double bind, enjoining it to a task that, for Derrida, is at once "necessary and impossible" (196): "necessary," because of the mutual incomprehension introduced by the *confusio linguarum*, but

Notes to Chapter 2

"impossible," because "Babel," the inaugurating word of a radically new regime, being both a common noun (meaning, in the unique tongue of the builders, "confusion") and a proper name (Voltaire points out that "Ba" signifies "father" and "Bel" signifies "God": "Babel" is thus the name of Gd the father), it must remain, like all proper names, "forever untranslatable" (197). Or rather, the impossible conjunction of the common and the proper renders the word "translatable-untranslatable" (199): God *at the same time imposes and forbids translation* (196), in "Beckett, Derrida, Babel: Some Remarks on Translation," unpublished manuscript, Barnard College.

25. I have been working through motifs investing *work, labor force, service* and their supposed opposites, including the invention of sloth, in *Stupidity* (Urbana: University of Illinois Press, 2002) and *Loser Sons: Politics and Authority* (Urbana: University of Illinois Press, 2012).

26. Johann Wolfgang von Goethe, *Wilhelm Meister's Apprenticeship*, vol. 9 of *The Collected Works*, ed. and transl. Eric A. Blackall with Victor Lange (Princeton, NJ: Princeton University Press, 1989), 17.

27. See in particular Jeffrey Champlin's astute analysis of violent economies in "Reading Terrorism in Kleist: The Violence and Mandates of *Michael Kohlhaas*," *German Quarterly* 85, no. 4 (November 2012): 439–54.

28. François Roustang, *La Fin de la plainte* (Paris: Éditions Odile Jacob, 2000), 19, 29.

29. Ibid., 29.

30. Ibid.

31. Ibid., 10.

32. Ibid., 11.

33. Ibid., 39.

34. Ibid., 170.

35. Ibid., 169.

36. I have addressed the movement from narcissism to identification, reading Nancy and Lacoue-Labarthe's work on political panic in *Loser Sons*.

37. Roustang, *La Fin de la plainte*, 175, 183, 19.

3. The Trouble with Deconstruction

1. Jacques Derrida, *Post Card: From Socrates to Freud and Beyond*, transl. Alan Bass (Chicago: University of Chicago Press, 1987); originally published as *La carte postale. De Socrate à Freud et au-delà* (Paris: Flammarion, 1980). Avital Ronell, *The Telephone Book: Technology—Schizophrenia—Electric Speech* (Lincoln: University of Nebraska Press, 1989).

2. In *Dictations: On Haunted Writing* (Urbana: University of Illinois Press, 1986, 2006).

3. Jacques Derrida, *Politics of Friendship*, transl. George Collins (London: Verso, 1997), 24.

4. Ibid.

5. Ibid.

6. Ibid.

7. In my *Loser Sons: Politics and Authority* (Urbana: University of Illinois Press, 2012).

8. Jacques Derrida, *Aporias*, transl. Thomas Dutoit (Stanford, CA: Stanford University Press, 1993), 4.

9. Derrida, *Aporias*, 15.

10. The subject of uncontrolled voice modulations motivates Robert Musil's obsession with the plight of male adolescents who are reduced to a "lautlose Klage," a level of muteness when it comes to sounding off in *Stimmbruch*, the voice in breakage. "(E)ine **wortlose Klage** flutete durch Törleß' Seele, wie das Heulen eines Hundes, das über die weiten, nächtlichen Felder zittert" (A wordless lament flooded Törless's soul like a dog's howl that trembles thought the wide nocturnal fields). Robert Musil, *Die Verwirrungen des Zöglings Törleß* (Hamburg: Rowohlt, 2006), 123. Dominik Zechner first brought this passage to my attention.

11. Derrida addresses the problem of *-isms* of all kinds in *The States of Theory*, ed. David Carroll (New York: Columbia University Press, 1989).

12. See in particular Ruth HaCohen, *The Music Libel against the Jews* (New Haven, CT: Yale University Press, 2011).

13. Jacques Derrida, "Edmond Jabès and the Question of the Book," in *Writing and Difference*, transl. Alan Bass (Chicago: University of Chicago Press, 1978), 73.

4. A Pass of Friendship

1. I discuss the avian conversations of Goethe and Eckermann at length in *Dictations: On Haunted Writing* (Lincoln: University of Nebraska Press, 1986), 161ff.

2. In my *Finitude's Score: Essays for the End of the Millennium* (Lincoln: University of Nebraska Press, 1994), 105–29.

3. Phillippe Lacoue-Labarthe, *Phrase* (Paris: Éditions Christian Bourgois, 2000), 36.

4. Phillippe Lacoue-Labarthe, "La Philosophie Fantôme," in *La Réponse d'Ulysse et autres Textes sur l'Occident* (Paris: Archives de la pensée critique, 2012), 23. His articulation is careful and precise: in fact, Lacoue does not say he knows humiliation but has felt it: "L'humiliation colonial, je l'ai ressentie, je crois, autant qu'un Européen pouvait la ressentir." Here he identifies himself as European.

5. Christopher Fynsk, *Philippe Lacoue-Labarthe's "Phrase": Infancy, Survival* (Albany: State University of New York Press, 2017).

6. "The address, pure and empty"; "prayer and discourse." Lacoue-Labarthe, *Phrase*, 16, 15.

7. Lacoue-Labarthe, *Phrase*, 105, 72.

8. Ibid., 67, 20, 20.

9. Ibid., 12.

10. Ibid., 11.

11. Ibid., 46.

12. Ibid., 12.

13. Ibid., 69.

14. Ibid., 27.

15. Ibid., 20–21.

16. Jean-Luc Nancy, *L'intrus* [The Intruder], transl. Susan Hanson, *New Centennial Review* 2, no. 3 (Fall 2002): 1–14.

17. Lacoue-Labarthe, *Phrase*, 20.

18. Ibid., 107, 20.

19. Ibid., 107.

20. Ibid., 32.

21. Ibid., 37.

22. Ibid., 29.

23. Ibid., 30.

24. Ibid., 31.

25. Ibid.

26. Parmenides, fragment 6.

27. Lacoue-Labarthe, *Phrase*, 60–61.

28. Ibid., 60.

29. Ibid., 32.

30. Ibid., 31.

31. Ibid., 107.

32. Ibid.

33. Ibid.

34. Lacoue-Labarthe, *Le Chant des Muses* (Paris: Bayard, coll. "Les petites Conférences," 2005), 23.

35. "Consider Jean-François Lyotard's thinking of the tortured child and the fantasy of emancipatory politics, which I analyze in "On the Unrelenting Creepiness of Childhood: Lyotard, Kid-Tested," in *The ÜberReader: Selected Works of Avital Ronell*, ed. Diane Davis (Urbana: University of Illinois Press, 2008).

36. For more on the Death Mother and polluted forms of being, see the works of psychoanalyst Marion Woodman, which I discuss in the final chapter of this work.

37. Lacoue-Labarthe, *Phrase*, 108.

38. Ibid., 109.

39. Ibid., 110.

40. The atopos of the maternal in Lacoue-Labarthe and Nancy is something I address in *Loser Sons: Politics and Authority* (Urbana: University of Illinois Press, 2012).

41. Lacoue-Labarthe, *Phrase*, 110.

42. Ibid., 111.

43. Jean-Christophe Bailly, *La fin de l'hymne* (Paris: Titre, 2015), 10.

44. Lacoue-Labarthe, *Poetry as Experience*, transl. Andrea Tarnowski (Stanford, CA: Stanford University Press, 1999), 68.

45. I explore Goethe's paralyzing effects on Freud in *Dictations*.

46. Lacoue-Labarthe, *Poetry as Experience*, 67.

47. Ibid.

48. Ibid., 119.

49. Ibid., 126.

50. Alain Badiou, "A la recherché de la prose perdue, *Europe: Revue littéraire mensuelle* (Paris: 2010), 165, Special Issue on Philippe Lacoue-Labarthe. Badiou remarks by paraphrase that the maternal curse condemns Lacoue to alcoholic dissolution; he says that Mother announces that "notre Lacoue. . . s'effondrera dans l'alcool" (our Lacoue. . .will dissipate in alcohol, 167). On one level the announcement signals an implicit consequence of the curse, to drown him in alcohol. I see the circumlocution to which Lacoue avails himself as his way of inviting a *reading* rather than something of an unfalsifiable doctor's report. While his alcoholism as an "ism" does not seem to be stated as part of the content of Mom's amped-up complaint of "pure meanness" and Badiou has added the straight-up spirits to the mean-spirited condemnation, Lacoue dilutes the utterance by saying she predicted his downfall by means of Apollinaire's title. I understand that Badiou would take a shortcut to Philippe's addiction here. One can safely suppose that the passage refers to the work *Alcools*, and not *The Breasts of Tiresias* or *Calligrams*. Still, this averted statement in *Phrase* goes through literary types of poetic dousing that open a different dossier. Lacoue's mediated indications of addictive struggle lead us to reintegrate another semantic level to our reading of the work and explore how poetry and phrasing flood ecstatic channels, drugged dissociation, visionary and blind intoxication. This register includes, in German philosophy, a thinking of *Rausch*, rush. Kittler links *Rausch* to noise and static, which would also provide a detour to the thinking of the buzz of prose and the poetic word in this work. I am not trying to make light of Lacoue's history with alcohol, with which I tried to confront him in Berkeley and had a tug-of-war of denial/avowal for several years. Friendship and intervention, knowing where your nose does and does not belong has haunted my most intense friendships. I, who do not believe in drug-free zones, try to concern myself with the health cleanses and vitaminizations of my friends. Now, that's a laugh, especially in face of Nietzsche's nearly prescribed *Untergänge*, the breakdowns and free falls. *What kind of vain rescue missions have I permitted myself? Ach!—*.

51. Lacoue-Labarthe, *Poetry as Experience*, 89.

52. Ibid., 113.

53. Ibid., 114.

54. Ibid., 113.

55. Ibid.

56. Jean-Luc Nancy and Phillippe Lacoue-Labarthe, *Scène* (Paris: Christian Bourgois, 2013).

57. Lacoue-Labarthe, *Poetry as Experience*, 113.

58. Ibid., 114.

59. Ibid., 115.

60. Alain Badiou, "À la recherche de la prose perdue," *Cahier d'Europe* 88, no. 973 (May 2010): 167.

61. Ibid., 167.

Notes to Chapter 4

62. Ibid.

63. Ibid.

64. Ibid., 168.

65. Ibid., 169.

66. Ibid.

67. Ibid., 176–77.

68. Ibid., 177.

69. Ibid., 173.

70. Phillippe Lacoue-Labarthe, *La Fiction du politique. Heidegger, l'art et la politique* (Paris: Christian Bourgois, 1987), 19.

71. Badiou, "À la recherche de la prose perdue," 173.

72. Lacoue-Labarthe, *La Fiction du politique*, 18.

73. Badiou, "À la recherche de la prose perdue," 174.

74. Ibid., 174–75.

75. Ibid., 175.

76. Ibid., 176.

77. Lacoue-Labarthe, *Phrase*, 119–20.

78. Badiou, "À la recherche de la prose perdue," 176.

79. Lacoue-Labarthe, *Phrase*, 115.

80. Phillippe Lacoue-Labarthe, "*Katharsis* et *Mathèsis*," *Cahier d'Europe* 88, 973 (May 2010): 81.

5. Hannah Arendt Swallows the Lessing Prize

1. Hannah Arendt, "On Humanity in Dark Times: Thoughts about Lessing" (address on accepting the Lessing Prize of the Free City of Hamburg), in *Men in Dark Times* (San Diego, CA: Harcourt, Brace, 1995), 15. Originally published as "Gedanken zu Lessing: Von der Menschlichkeit in finsteren Zeiten" (1959), in *Menschen in finsteren Zeiten* (1989) (München: Piper, 2001).

2. Arendt, "On Humanity in Dark Times," 16.

3. Ibid., 25.

4. For more on the travel points of Lessing's imperative "must," see Thomas Schestag, *Der Unbewältige Sprache: Hannah Arendt's Theorie der Dichtung* (Basel: Engeler, 2006).

5. I was tempted to use the title "Hannah Arendt Swallows a Distinction" rather than involving the name of the prize as titular instance. In view of Arendt's own writing, the term *distinction* would create a significant switchboard whose implications one does not want to neglect. In "The Jew as Pariah: A Hidden Tradition," Arendt offers reflections on Kafka's *Castle* as an allegory of the isolation ("completely desolately alone," 116) of a Jew as human rights seeker, living as the only Jew in the whole wide world. Existing "utterly alone" reveals the condition of the assimilationist Jew, one "who really wants no more than his rights as a human being: home, work, family and citizenship" (116) This is not the place to start a graceless brawl about her literary reductions and hair-raising conclusions involving

Kafka's depiction of "groundless fear, baseless feelings of dread," and assertion, concerning K., that "[n]othing more serious happens to him," or that "K. dies a perfectly normal death; he gets exhausted" (120). I would get exhausted engaging these off-the-wall statements in view of the rhetoric and literary snares of Kafka's text. Still, Arendt uses the novel as a springboard for a fascinating discussion of civic abandonment. Let me just state that the pathos and aim of her Kafka section is meant to show how earnestly the assimilated Jew strives to secure the status of an *indistinguishable figure* for his gentile neighbors, demonstrating a committed resolve to maintain an existence without distinctive features or distinction, hiding out. Dealing with the conferral of a distinction must therefore entail another level, endangering and socially problematic, of revealing oneself as a Jew. The modern Jewish fear of distinction is not an explicit motif of the acceptance speech, but explains some rumbles of anxiety that the presentation nonetheless implies and displays. *Jewish Social Studies* 6, no. 2 (April 1944): 99–122.

6. *Mainmise* is a term used by Lyotard to gain leverage on mystifications of emancipatory politics: Jean-François Lyotard and Eberhard Gruber, "Mainmise," in *The Hyphen: Between Judaism and Christianity*, transl. Pascale-Anne Brault and Michael Naas (Atlantic Highlands, NJ: Humanity Books, 1999), and discussed by me at length in *Loser Sons: Politics and Authority* (Urbana: University of Illinois Press, 2012).

7. Arendt, "On Humanity in Dark Times," 16, 13.

8. Ibid., 14.

9. Ibid., 14.

10. Ibid. To the extent that fraternity, sanctioned by decree and law, becomes convention and incorporated as revolutionary injunction, one cannot simply leave intact its "natural" status. Derrida in *Politics of Friendship*, transl. George Collins (New York: Verso Books, 1997), points out that there are no brothers in nature, so that fraternal orders of various stripes, including gang formations, brother- and nationhoods, are from the start an effect of convention, etc. The question, I suppose, is why Arendt needs to keep it natural in order to supersede, hierarchize, manage political affect and its cooling-off periods. In *Papier machine*, Derrida reads the "with" as a mark of distance when considering the "suffering with" from which compassion comes to us, precluding democratic reciprocity or substitutability. *Papier machine. Le ruban de machine à écrire et autres réponses* (Paris: Éditions Galilée, 2001). Jacques Rancière follows this path: "The international extension of the field of democratic action means its extension up to a point where there can be no reciprocity. It is only where reciprocity is impossible that we can find true otherness, an otherness that obliges us absolutely." "Ethics and Politics in Derrida," in *Derrida and the Time of the Political*, ed. Pheng Cheah and Suzanne Guerlac (Durham, NC: Duke University Press, 2009), 281.

11. Arendt, "On Humanity in Dark Times," 14.

12. Ibid.

13. Ibid., 15.

14. Ibid.

15. Ibid., 16.

16. Jacques Derrida, "Otobiographies: The Teaching of Nietzsche and the Politics of the Proper Name," transl. A. Ronell, in *The Ear of the Other: Otobiography, Transference, Translation* (New York: Schocken Books, 1985).

17. Arendt, "On Humanity in Dark Times," 17.

18. Ibid.

19. Ibid., 17, 18, 18.

20. Ibid., 24.

21. I leave aside the fine points involving acts of self-gathering that should not be confused with giving up on the world. Schiller saw Rousseau's retreat as surrender, but in his writings Paul de Man called out Schiller on Rousseau's supposed passivity, revalorizing the political implications of withdrawal.

22. Arendt, "On Humanity in Dark Times," 25.

23. Ibid., 25. The democratic-revolutionary stamp of fraternity, a Christian notion (Arendt does not go there), returns us to paternity (ditto) and governing structures that stem from a patriarchal groundwork of tropologies I have tracked in *Loser Sons*. On the implications of friendship and fraternity, see Derrida, *Politics of Friendship*, and Jean-Luc Nancy, *La Possibilité d'un Monde* (Poitiers: Les Dialogues des petits Platons, 2015).

24. Arendt, "On Humanity in Dark Times," 5–6.

25. Ibid., 21.

26. Ibid.

27. Friedrich Hölderlin, "Andenken" (1803), in *Sämtliche Werke und Briefe*, Erster Band, Gedichte, Hrsg. Günter Mieth (Berlin: Aufbau-Verlag, 1995), 491.

28. Arendt, *Men in Dark Times*, vii.

29. Arendt, "On Humanity in Dark Times," 21.

30. Ibid., 21, 20.

31. Ibid., 21.

32. I addressed theatrical foreplay in Goethe in my "Taking It Philosophically: *Torquato Tasso*'s Women as Theorists," in *Finitude's Score* (Lincoln: University of Nebraska Press, 1994).

33. Johann Wolfgang von Goethe, *Faust*, ed. R.-M.S. Heffner (Madison: University of Wisconsin Press, 1975), 167.

34. Arendt, "On Humanity in Dark Times," 20.

35. Hans-Harder Biermann-Ratjen, Hamburg's secretary of culture, makes a pitch for Arendt's capacity to bridge prewar and postwar German intellectual spheres. Introducing the acceptance speech, he sets up a hope, revealing, "we would like to reclaim you as one of us, and it would be a great and moving honor for us, if you would permit us to do so." Cited in Liliane Weissberg, "Humanity and Its Limits: Hannah Arendt Reads Lessing," in *Practicing Progress: The Promise and Limitations of Enlightenment*, festschrift for John A. McCarthy, ed. Richard E. Schade and Dieter Sevin (New York: Editions Rodopi, 2007), 195.

36. Arendt, "Gedanken zu Lessing: Von der Menschlichkeit in finsteren Zeiten," 5–7.

37. Ibid., 16.

6. The Right Not to Complain: On Johnson's Reparative Process

This chapter is a heavily revised version of "Surrender and the Ethically Binding Signature: On Johnson's Reparative Process," *differences: A Journal of Feminist Cultural Studies* 17, 5 (2006).

1. I consider the fate of *spliterature* in "Kathy Goes to Hell: On the Irresolvable Stupidity of Acker's Demise," in *Lust for Life: On the Writings of Kathy Acker*, ed. Amy Scholder, Carla Harryman, Avital Ronell (New York: Verso, 2006), 12–35. Barbara Johnson and I have split the spoils of many formations, if not always retrievable, some unconscious ones—such as students we share or who have traveled from one of us to the other in a way that typically allows in academia for shared custody and genealogical movement in the transferential grid.

2. Barbara Johnson, "Gender Theory and the Yale School," in *Rhetoric and Form: Deconstruction at Yale*, ed. Robert Con Davis and Ronald Schleifer (Norman: University of Oklahoma Press, 1985), 112.

3. Pierre Alféri, *Brefs. Discours* (Paris: POL, 2016).

4. Johnson, "Gender Theory and the Yale School," 101.

5. Ibid., 103.

6. William Wordsworth, "To Dora."

7. Johnson, "Gender Theory and the Yale School," 110.

8. Ibid., 111–12.

9. Barbara Johnson, "Gender and Poetry: Charles Baudelaire and Marceline Desbordes-Valmore," in *The Feminist Difference: Literature, Psychoanalysis, Race, and Gender* (Cambridge, MA: Harvard University Press, 1998), 115.

10. Barbara Johnson, "Euphemism, Understatement, and the Passive Voice: A Genealogy of African-American Poetry," in *Feminist Difference*, 100.

11. Phillis Wheatley quoted in ibid., 99.

12. Johnson, "Euphemism, Understatement, and the Passive Voice," 100.

13. Ibid., 94, 95, 97.

14. Ibid., 99.

15. Phillis Wheatley quoted in ibid., 97.

16. Johnson, "Euphemism, Understatement, and the Passive Voice."

17. On the distinction between spirit and soul, see Jacques Derrida, *Specters of Marx* (New York: Routledge, 1994).

18. Johnson, "Euphemism, Understatement, and the Passive Voice," 98.

19. Ibid., 100.

20. See Valerie Solanas, *The Scum Manifesto* (New York: Verso, 2004).

21. Paul de Man, "The Rhetoric of Temporality," in *Blindness and Insight: Essays on the Rhetoric of Contemporary Criticism* (Minneapolis: University of Minnesota Press, 1983), 216. See the remarkable discussions of Werner Hamacher, Peter Fenves, and

Susan Bernstein. I have tried to address some of these concerns and the importance of fading cognition in Barbara Johnson's reading of Melville in *Stupidity* (Urbana: University of Illinois Press, 2002).

22. Johnson, "Euphemism, Understatement, and the Passive Voice."

23. Ibid, 93, 94, 94.

24. Ibid., 94. The curbing of complaint returns as a motif of disappointed social judgment in the film "Brief Interviews with Hideous Men" (dir. John Krasinski, 2009). Two Black men are in conversation, one commenting on the contested dignity of an impeccable bathroom attendant, compliant and polite: "Never a word of complaint."

25. Mark Sanders, part of a paper presented at New York University, "Trauma and Remembrance," Research in Trauma & Violence Project, January 27, 2006, and developed in *Learning Zulu: A Secret History of Language in South Africa (Translation/ Transnation)* (Princeton, NJ: Princeton University Press, 2016).

26. See Melanie Klein, "Mourning and Its Relation to Manic-Depressive States" (1940), in *Love, Guilt, and Reparation and Later Works 1921–1945*, ed. Hanna Segal (London: Vintage, 1998).

27. Mark Sanders introduces the aporia of reparation in his work on South Africa. Material on manic reparation is further developed in *Ambiguities of Witnessing: Law and Literature in the Time of a Truth Commission* (Stanford, CA: Stanford University Press, 2007).

28. In conversation during a 1990s study group, Maria Torok told me that the English term and senses linked to being "fed up" served as conceptual grist for her work on cryptonomy and phantom agitation in Freud.

29. Melanie Klein, "Envy and Gratitude," in *Love, Guilt, and Reparation*, 195.

30. I have analyzed this in "TraumaTV" when exploring the brutal policing of Black bodies and the ongoing beating of Rodney King, in *Finitude's Score: Essays for the End of the Millennium* (Lincoln: University of Nebraska Press, 1994), 305–27.

31. Ronell, *Finitude's Score*, 182, 180, 180–81.

32. Ibid., 185.

Index

Abbau, 99
Abraham, Karl, 221
Abraham, Nicolas, 107
Acker, Kathy, 66, 204
adikia, 16
Adorno, Theodor, 36, 38, 42, 122, 126
Agamben, Giorgio, 88
Alexander the Great, 6
Alféri, Pierre, 128, 130, 206
Ali, Muhammad, 31, 63
Allen, Woody, *Deconstructing Harry*, 102
Anaximander, 16
Anklage, 5, 42, 71, 102, 105, 151, 198
Anne, Saint, 205
Antigone, 2, 9, 96
Apollinaire, 232n50
Apter, Emily, 215
Arendt, Hannah, 4, 7, 27, 42, 108, 127, 175–98, 215, 222; "The Aftermath of Nazi Rule," 175
Aristotle, 7, 28–29, 54, 93, 131, 156, 174
Arnim, Bettina von, 31, 43
Atemwende, 156

Babel, 228n24
Bacchus, 148
Bachmann, Ingeborg, 9; mentioned, 39
Bacon, Francis (painter), 103
Badiou, Alain Georges, 6, 160, 162, 164–74; *Manifeste pour la philosophie*, 169
Baer, Uli, 188
Bailly, Jean-Christophe, 128, 150, 153

Baldwin, James, 66
Banki, Peter, 36
Barthes, Roland, 112
Bataille, Georges, 24, 30–32, 135, 174, 212
Baudelaire, Charles, 37, 70, 167, 208, 213
Beethoven, Ludwig van, *Opus 110*, 224
Behrmann, Nicola, 36
Benjamin, Walter, 39–42, 92, 169, 188, 213; and Babel, 61–62; and Derrida, 88, 89, 104; and Goethe, 192; and Heinrich Heine, 74; heirs of, 38; on Karl Kraus, 5, 54, 75; "Kritik der Gewalt" ["Critique of Violence"], 86; and phantom body of the police, 98; and poetry, 141; and "rights of nerves," 64, 85, 107; and vengeance, 23; and *Zerstörung*, 109
Bennington, Geoffrey, 117
Bernhard, Thomas, 163, 195
Bernstein, Susan, 36, 227n6, 237n21
Beschwerde, 49, 56, 106, 188
Bible, 4, 51, 62, 73
Biermann-Ratjen, Hans-Harder, 235n35
Blake, William, 225n1
Blanchot, Maurice, 39, 142, 199; and books, 116; and friendship, 28, 186; and Goethe, 192; and Hölderlin, 119; and masters/teachers, 115; and television, 98
Booth, Wayne, 213
Boyer, Frédéric, 37
Brando, Marlon, 127
Brecht, Bertolt, 38
Breton, André, 169

Brinkman und Bose (publisher), 37
Brod, Max, 34
Butler, Judith, 37, 200, 215

Cadava, Eduardo, 227n1
Cavell, Stanley, 226n19
Celan, Giselle, 91, 101
Celan, Paul, 37; Derrida's *Schibboleth*, 99; and doors as laws, 48, 101; and Heidegger, 35, 142; and lament, 141–42; "Meridian," 154, 188, 225n3; *Nachlass*, 91; *Niemandsrose*, 142, 157–58; and poetry, 154; and prizes, 188; "Totnauberg," 142; and the *unWo*, 90, 141, 198; mentioned, 6, 39
Champlin, Jeffrey, 36, 226n19
Christ, 50
Cicero, *Tusculanae Disputationes*, 182
Cixous, Hélène, 37
Comay, Rebecca, 225n4
Connor, Peter, 47, 78
Cooper, Dennis, 66
Cope, Stephen, 202
Cordelia complex, 214
Cranfield and Slade, *10 Riot Songs*, 62

Davis, Diane, 215, 231n35
de Man, Paul, 36, 37, 38, 40, 90–92, 204, 235n21
de Stael, Madame Anna Louise Germain, 40
Deleuze, Gilles, 88, 111, 114
Derrida, Jacques, 39, 58, 59, 66, 78, 84–117, 124, 142, 184, 192, 203–4, 212; and Badiou, 169, 171; on beyond, 67; dinner with, 213; and disjointure, 15; on doors as laws, 48; on forgiveness, 147; and Foucault, 74; on friendship, 8, 9, 28–29; and the functioning of man, 17; and justice, 158; and *Hamlet*, 20; and Heidegger, 53; and Barbara Johnson, 207, 214, 216–17, 219; and Lacan, 169, 203, 219; and Lacoue-Labarthe, 162; on mourning, v; and tone/register, 35; and Samuel Weber, 36; and translators, 40; University of Nebraska Press publishing, 199; on what is not there, 19; on "without," 22
Derrida, Jacques, works by: *Aporias*, 95,

99; *La Carte postale* [*The Post Card*], 85, 91, 116, 133, 205; *Dissemination*, 204; "Exordium," 84; "Freud and the Scene of Writing," 220; "Jabès and the Question of the Book," 116; "Law of Genre/Gender," 43; *Of Grammatology*, 116; "Otobiographies," 235n16; *Papier machine*, 234n10; "Plato's Pharmacy," 121; *Politics of Friendship*, 234n10; *Psyché: Inventions de l'autre*, 99; "Rams," 99; *Schibboleth pour Paul Celan*, 99; *The Sovereign and the Beast*, 114; *Specters of Marx*, 16, 23; "Tours de Babel," 61–62
Derrida, Marguerite, 94, 95
Desbordes-Valmore, Marceline, 208
Dickinson, Emily, 126, 202, 203, 218
Diotima, 96, 173
Dis-tanz, 10, 29, 31, 150
Doppelt, Suzanne, 37
Dostoevsky, Fyodor, 50, 157
Dufourmantelle, Anne, v, 37, 76
Dylan, Bob, 60, 126

Echo, 93–94, 105
Eckart, Meister, 78
Eckermann, Johann Peter, 67, 92–94, 115
écriture, 17
Éditions Galilée, 113
Einstein, Albert, 63, 112
Eissler, K. R., 26, 226n19
ekplèxis, 174
Eliot, George, 93
Eliot, T. S., 163
Emerson, Ralph Waldo, 28, 30
Entsagung, 128
Erasmus, Desiderius, *Complaint of Peace*, 21
Euripides, 156
European Graduate School, 113

Faulkner, William, 189, 193
Fenves, Peter, 35, 227n4, 236n21
Fink Verlag, 37
Flaubert, Gustave, 135; *Madame Bovary*, 31, 70, 95
Förster-Nietzsche, Elisabeth, 152
Foucault, Michel, 74, 88, 124

Frankfurt School, 38
freedom, 4, 51
Freud, Sigmund, 88, 105, 117, 121–22, 201–2; "American" approaches to, 121, 125; *Civilization and Its Discontents*, 34–35; and Einstein, 63; and Goethe, 57, 67, 155, 192; and the Goethe-prize, 188; *Interpretation of Dreams*, 155; and Jung, 87, 201–2, 2013; and Melanie Klein, 220; and Nietzsche, 61; and the Rat Man, 85, 115, 121–22, 155; mentioned, 39
Freudian ideas and theory, 44, 59, 81, 122, 220; on anger, 145; on hatred born of love, 152; on laughter, 24; on narcissism, 82, 94; on paranoid excess, 75; on pleasure principle, 67; on puberty, 25
Fynsk, Christopher, 36, 128

Gadamer, Hans-Georg, 37, 99
Gasché, Rodolphe, 48
Gates, Henry Louis, Jr. (Skip), 215
Gd, 7, 50, 61, 154, 211; and Babel, 62; and forgiveness, 110; and infractions, 133; and Job, 50, 66; Barbara Johnson and, 206; and master, 211; and misery, 154; and Niemandsrose, 157
Gerede, 215
Gesprächspartner, 30
Geworfenheit, 102, 153
Glissant, Edouard, 66
Glover, Edward, 122
Godfrey, Sima, 205
Goethe, Johann Wolfgang von, 53, 64, 67–69, 93–94, 141, 155, 168, 188–91, 194; *East-Westerly Divan*, 24; *Elective Affinities*, 67; *Faust*, 43–44, 71, 189; and Freud, 57, 67, 155, 192; and German studies, 38; and mother, 165; and puberty, 23–24; and renunciation / *Entsagung*, 128; *Sorrows of Young Werther*, 44, 56–59, 67–69, 106, 168, 188; *Wilhelm Meisters Lehrjahre*, 70–72
Grundstruktur, 30

Habermas, Jürgen, 38, 84
Hamacher, Ursula (Ursel), 48
Hamacher, Werner, 35, 36, 38, 46, 58, 69, 216, 224; and Derrida's "Law of Genre /

Gender," 43; as friend, v, 213; and lament, 51–52; and language, 48Haraway, Donna, 37
Harper, Phillip B., 215
Harvard University, 204, 213, 219
Hawthorne, Nathaniel, 45
Hegel, Georg Wilhelm Friedrich, 8, 9, 68, 105, 137, 138, 173
Heidegger, Martin, 66, 114, 153, 161; and *Abbau*, 99; and the Alexander fragment, 16; and Being, 21, 126, 137–38; and Benjamin, 41; on colon, 132; and *Destruktion*, 109; and Freud, 81; and *Gerede*, 215; and *Gewissensruf*, 85; and greeting, 47, 108; and Hölderlin, 140, 191–92; *Holzweg*, 101; and impoverishment, 133; and Kittler, 38; lecture on, 121; and poetry, 141, 191–92; and proximity, 101; and serenification, 173; silence of, on Shoah, 142; and *Sorge*, 202; and technology, 15, 49–50; and thinking, criticism, and questioning, 52–53, 58, 104; and time, 20–21; and Wagner, 167, 203–4; *Was heißt Denken?* [*What Is Called Thinking?*], 34–35, 49; and withdrawal, 90; mentioned, 23, 39, 65, 212
Heine, Heinrich, 74, 110
Hitchcock, Alfred, 93; *Rope*, 102; *The Trouble with Harry*, 100, 102
Hitler, Adolf, 185
Hofmann, E. T. A., mentioned, 39
Hölderlin, Friedrich, 135; "Andenken," 8, 47, 108; and Arendt, 191; "Dichtermut," 163; and *Gespräch*, 198; and greeting, 108; and Hegel, 138; and Heidegger, 140, 191–92; and Lacoue-Labarthe, 119, 133, 137, 142, 151, 157, 163, 168; and mourning, v, 8; *Patmos*, 136; and *poiesis*, 141
Hollier, Denis, 124, 201, 213
Holocaust, 51
Homer, 168
Huet, Marie-Hélène, 124
Hughes, Ted, 202
Husserl, Edmund, 61, 66

Indiana University Press, 37
Isaac, 99
Ismene, 96

Jabès, Edmond, 116
Jael, 205–6
Jameson, Fredric, 213
Jeremiah, 4, 50, 66
Jesus of Nazareth, 50, 211–12
Job, 4, 66
Johnson, Barbara, 37, 199–224; *The Critical Difference*, 207; "Euphemism, Under-statement, and the Passive Voice," 214; *Persons and Things*, 201
Johnson, James Weldon, 217
Jung, Carl, 201–02

Kafka, Franz, 48, 54, 64, 68, 85, 113, 115, 125, 135; *The Castle*, 233n5; "Country Doctor," 160; *Judgment*, 70, 151; "Letter to Father," 90, 151; *The Metamorphosis*, 5; "My Neighbor," 11
Kant, Immanuel, 2, 4, 27, 64, 112, 114, 176; and enthusiasm, 175; and Goethe's *Faust*, 44; and immaturity, 24–25, 84; *Perpetual Peace*, 63, 173; and tone / register, 35; mentioned, 55
Kierkegaard, Søren, 57
King, Rodney, 98
King, Stephen, *The Shining*, 217
Kittler, Friedrich, 35, 36, 38, 43, 46, 100, 102, 124, 232n50
Klage, 5, 188–92, 194–95; and *Anklage*, 5, 42, 102, 105, 151; 198; and *Beschwerde*, 106; as graceless, 49; Lessing and, 176; overcoming, 69; and structure of complaint, 56
Klagekultur, Jewish culture as, 50
Klein, Melanie, 182–83, 195, 220–22
Kleist, Heinrich von, 9, 72; *Marquise von O . . .* , 44–45; *Prinz von Homburg*, 208
Kofman, Sarah, 39
Kølle, Anders, 227n3
Krasinski, John, 237n24
Kraus, Karl, 5, 54, 64, 75
Kubrik, Stanley, *The Shining*, 217

Lacan, Jacques, 39, 114, 122, 125, 145, 169, 203, 219, 220; "The Ethics of Psycho-analysis," 96
Lacoue-Labarthe, Madame, 151

Lacoue-Labarthe, Philippe, 6, 27, 36, 39, 88, 94, 95, 118–74, 214; *La Fiction du politique*, 169; *Musica Ficta*, 167; *Phrase*, 118–74; *Poetry as Experience*, 154; *Typography*, 122
Leonardo da Vinci, 204
Lenz, Jacob Michael Rheinhold, 160
Lessing, Gotthold Ephraim, 176–79, 181, 184, 186–87, 189–96, 222; *Laocöon*, 194; *Nathan der Weise (Nathan the Wise)*, 185, 194, 196–97
Lessing-Preis (Lessing Prize), 7, 175–98
Levinas, Emmanuel, 21, 98, 100, 112, 159, 218
Levine, Michael, 227n5
Lévy, Bernard-Henri, 170
Lewis, Jerry, 126
Liriope, 82
Lot, 110
Luhmann, Niklas, 38
Luther, Martin, 78
Lyotard, Jean-François, 24, 25–27, 39, 124, 128, 175

mainmise, 179, 231n35, 234n6
Manet, Édouard, 32
Marder, Elissa, 215
Marx, Karl, 20, 105
McLaughlin, Kevin, 36
Milton, John, 206–7
Mnemosyne, 136
Moeller-Schoell, Nikolaus, 36
Montaigne, Michel de, 28, 124
Monteverdi, Claudio, 143
Moten, Fred, 215
Mozart, Wolfgang Amadeus, 103; *Don Giovanni*, 197; "Der Hölle Rache," 103, 150; *The Magic Flute*, 150
Musil, Robert, 112, 230n10

Nägele, Rainer, 48, 91, 227n5
Nancy, Claire, 127, 134, 159, 161
Nancy, Jean-Luc, 36, 39, 50, 66, 112; and the unavowable, 142; and blurbs, 120; and Derrida, 88; and *L'intrus*, 134; and laugh-ter, 24; and love, 159; and narcissism, 94
Napoleon, 56
Narcissus, 76–78, 82, 93

Nazi Germany, 68–69, 119, 121
New York Times, 95–96
New York University, 204, 205, 214, 225n3
Nietzsche, Friedrich Wilhelm, 43, 59–61, 75, 101, 105, 109, 151, 152, 153–54, 160, 162, 163, 167, 173, 177, 184, 214, 232n50; and the Crucifixion, 50; and death/ending, 116, 135; and *Dis-tanz*, 31; and enthusiasm, 175; and experimental disposition, 104; as faultfinder, 66; and friendship, 29, 30, 33, 186; and Goethe, 23–24, 67, 189, 192; and Heidegger, 34–35; and justice, 22, 23; and the *Nicht*, 55; and "noble traitor," 59, 142, 143, 203; and pity, 181; and *ressentiment*, 3, 55, 192; and Russian fatalism, 157; and thinking and thanking, 34, 50; and transvaluation, 15; and Wagner, 87, 203–4; mentioned, 1, 10, 28, 36, 39, 88, 141
Nietzsche, Friedrich Wilhelm, works by: *Daybreak*, 48; *Genealogy of Morals*, 220; *Untimely Meditations*, 80
Noudelmann, François, 37

Obama, Barack, 63
Ossian, 68, 168
Ovid, *Metamorphoses*, 82

Panofsky, Erwin, 42
Parmenides, 138
Parsifal, 167
Penis-neid, 10
Pepper, Thomas, 36
Pesci, Joe, 127
Plath, Sylvia, 9, 202
Plato, 205
Poe, Edgar Allan, 126
Ponge, Francis, 218
Princeton University, 32, 122
Pynchon, Thomas, 112, 126

Rancière, Jacques, 234n10
Rat Man, 85, 115, 120, 122, 155
Reed, Ishmael, 215
Regier, Willis Goth (Bill), vi, 37, 95, 120, 199–200
ressentiment, 3

Richter, Gerhard, 36
Rickels, Laurence (Larry), 36, 166, 199, 203, 226n19
Rilke, Rainer Marie, 7
Rimbaud, Arthur, 168, 172–73
Robespierre, Maximilien, 181
Ronell, Avital: "Beckett, Derrida, Babel," 229n24; *Dictations*, 230n1; *Finitude's Score*, 230n2; *Loser Sons*, 23–24, 229n25, 234n6; "The Sujet Suppositaire," 121; *Stupidity*, 114, 229n25; *The Telephone Book*, 85, 226n16; "Trouble in Parricide," 100; *The ÜberReader*, 231n35
Ronell, Avital, nicknames of: "Abyssale," 149; "Diotima," 173; "Echo," 93; "Miss Prision," 31–32
Roth, Philip, *Portnoy's Complaint*, 11–12, 49
Rousseau, Jean-Jacques, 74, 96, 147, 181, 186–87, 206, 235n21; *Rêveries*, 135–36
Roustang, François, *La Fin de la plainte*, 76–82

sacrifice, 66, 73
Sade, Marquis de, 53
Sanders, Bernie, 63
Sanders, Mark, 219
Sartre, Jean-Paul, 170
Schäfer, Martin, 36
Schelling, Friedrich Wilhelm Joseph, 137
Schiller, Friedrich, 235n21
Schirmacher, Wolfgang, 113
Schlegel, August, 141
Schlegel, Friedrich, 42, 68, 71, 141, 213
Schmitt, Carl, mentioned, 39
Scholem, Gershom, 39–42
Schreber, Daniel Paul, 160
Schreiben/Schrei, 34, 48, 53, 212
Schürmann, Reiner, 42
Selbstbehauptung, 24, 55, 74
Seneca the Younger, 95
Seoane, Mariano López, 79
Seufzer, 43
Shakespeare, William, 7, 10, 42, 58, 125–26, 214; *Hamlet*, 15–27, 34, 58, 100, 103, 122, 125, 139, 161, 164, 225n3; *Othello*, 221; *Richard II*, 33, 44

Shelley, Mary, *Frankenstein*, 58, 125
Siegler, Bernhard, 215
Sisera, 205
Sisyphus, 166
Smith, Bessie, 126
Smock, Ann, 36, 124, 199, 224
Solanas, Valerie, 9, 66, 212
Solomon, 158
Sorge, 2, 50, 197, 202
Stewart, Jimmy, 102
Stimmung, 101
Szondi, Peter, 36, 38, 42

Talking Heads, "Burning Down the House," 48
Tao, 81
Taubes, Jacob, 37
Torok, Maria, 107
Trakl, Georg, 192
Trump, Donald, 223–24

Unfug, 19
University of California, Berkeley, 64–65, 209, 215; mentioned, 15, 120, 121, 124, 137, 161, 201, 232n50
University of California, Riverside, 65
University of Nebraska Press, 199
University of Virginia, 37, 65, 97

Verdi, Giuseppe, 155
Verdrängung, 31
Verfwerfung, 31
Verneinung, 31
Visman, Cornelia, 36

Wagner, Richard, 30, 60, 87, 154, 167, 204, 208, 213
Walser, Robert, 64, 68
Weber, Samuel, 36, 38, 73–75
Weed, Elizabeth, 37
Weissberg, Liliane, 235n35
Wellbery, David, 48, 227n5
Wheatley, John, 209
Wheatley, Phillis, 55, 208–13, 217–19
Wheatley, Susanna, 209
Winnicott, Donald, 226n19
Woodman, Marion, 202, 204
Woolf, Leonard, 34
Wordsworth, William, 206–07

Yale School, 207
Yale University, 204, 205, 207
yoga, 200, 201, 215

Zechner, Dominik, 230n10
Zen, 78, 213
Žižek, Slavoj, 166, 203

AVITAL RONELL is University Professor of the Humanities at New York University, where she is Professor of German, Comparative Literature, and English. She holds the Jacques Derrida Chair of Media and Philosophy at the European Graduate School. Her books include *The Telephone Book*, *Stupidity*, *The Test Drive*, and *Fighting Theory* (with Anne Dufourmantelle).